'I have never y̶e̶t̶ ̶m̶e̶t̶ ... ̶ ̶u̶n̶d̶e̶r̶-
standing of the ̶r̶e̶a̶l̶i̶t̶ ... ̶ ̶h̶a̶t̶ ̶w̶a̶r̶'

André Bach

The paths of glory lead but to the grave

THOMAS GRAY 1716–71

Elegy Written in a Country Churchyard

Anthony Clayton was Senior Lecturer at the Royal Military Academy, Sandhurst from 1965 to 1994. One of Britain's leading military historians, he was made a Chevalier dans l'Ordre des Palmes Académiques in 1988 in recognition of his expertise in French military history. He is the author of *The British Empire as Superpower* (1986), *France, Soldiers and Africa* (1988), *Three Marshals of France* (1992), *Forearmed: The History of the Intelligence Corps* (1993) and *The Wars of French Decolonisation* (1994).

PATHS GLORY

of

The French Army 1914–18

ANTHONY CLAYTON

CASSELL

Cassell Military Paperbacks

Cassell
Wellington House, 125 Strand
London WC2R 0BB

1 3 5 7 9 10 8 6 4 2

First published in 2003
by Cassell
This Cassell Military Paperbacks edition 2005

Distributed in the USA by
Sterling Publishing Co Inc.,
387 Park Avenue South,
New York NY 10016-8810

British Library Cataloguing-in-Publication Data.
A catalogue record for this book is available
from the British Library.

ISBN 0 304 36652 8

Printed and bound in Great Britain by
Cox & Wyman Ltd, Reading, Berkshire

www.orionbooks.co.uk

'... that sorely tried, glorious Army upon whose sacrifices the liberties of Europe had through three fearful campaigns mainly depended.'

WINSTON CHURCHILL,

The World Crisis 1916–18 Royal Military College Sandhurst edition, 1933, p.364

On 29 October 1914, Captain Jolivet, a pharmacist
from Châteaudun serving with the 268th Infantry
Regiment near Zillebeke, saved the life of a British
Royal Artillery forward observation officer.
Badly wounded, the British officer had managed to
crawl back to the French lines after being struck down.
The British officer was my father.

Contents

List of maps

Foreword

This book investigates the campaigns and the hardships facing the French army and its soldiers in the 'Great War' 1914–18. It pays particular attention to morale. For the French army, often faced with numerical inferiority, frequent disadvantage over terrain on the field of battle, the war being fought in their own homeland, and with the dread memory of 1870–1 behind them, the psychological dimension of the combat was of especial significance. The work also records the equipments and the conditions of service of the French army and the patterns of the major campaigns; it is less concerned with the detail of differences of opinion between Allied commanders, covered more than sufficiently in other works. In recounting the hardship and suffering that the French soldier had to endure it is obviously necessary to emphasise that soldiers in other armies, especially the British, had comparable experience. However, the French *poilu* was, generally, worse fed, worse equipped, worse clothed and lodged in trenches or shellholes worse than those of the British, making his war experience fully deserving of Churchill's tribute: 'sorely tried and glorious'. A British historian in a recent work argued that men went on fighting on the Western Front because they did not mind the war. Whatever may be applicable to other armies, it is far from the truth in the case of the French army.

The British have tended to view the France of 1914–18 through the prism of 1940. The service rendered to the free world by the French army from August 1914 to November 1918 is thereby diminished. With the close co-operation and mutual respect that currently exists between the French and British armies, it is now timely for a reminder of that debt and the experiences shared in those years.

As the bibliographical essay in the appendix indicates, this work has necessarily drawn extensively on several major French texts, most notably William Serman's and Jean Paul Bertrand's magisterial *Nouvelle Histoire Militaire de la France,* Jules Maurin's *Armée-Guerre-Societé Soldats Languedociens,* (1889–1919), Guy Pedroncini's *Pétain, le soldat et la Gloire* and *Les Mutineries de 1917,* together with Jean Nicot's *Les Poilus ont la Parole: Lettres du Front 1917–1918.*

It is a pleasure both to acknowledge this debt and to express admiration for the research and scholarship contained in these works.

I owe two other especial debts of gratitude, one to General André Bach for his comments on different sections of this work, which I have valued enormously. The other is to the Librarian, Andrew Orgill, and staff of that quietly remarkable institution, the Library of the Royal Military Academy Sandhurst. Generous facilities, the obtaining of books from other libraries and, certainly not least, the welcome always offered on my research days will long remain in my memory.

I also have thanks for comments, advice or encouragement to Michael Broadway, Paul Franceschi, Frédéric Guelton, Ralph Goldsmith, Alec Halliley, Paul Harris, Charles-Armand Klein, Paul Latawski, Angus MacKinnon, André Martin-Siegfried, Michael Orr, Darrol Stinton and Ned Willmott. Without such friends and colleagues history writing would be dull days' work.

In the production of this work, in particular in respect of maps and illustrations my sincere thanks go to Ian Drury, of Weidenfeld & Nicolson and the Cassell imprint, and all who have worked with him.

Finally, this work would never have appeared without the patient deciphering and typing of my manuscript by Monica Alexander to whom also goes my warmest appreciation and gratitude, and also my appreciation of the professional work of Amazon Systems in transferring the typescript to disk.

CHAPTER 1

1914

Manoeuvre War, The French Frontier Offensives

Altkirch is a small picturesque town lying a few kilometres from the Rhine amid the woods and hills of southern Alsace. In August 1914 Alsace formed part of the German Empire, ceded by France after the war of 1870–1. The town was to be the scene of the first significant clash between French and German soldiers in the First World War, a small-scale prelude to the vast struggle to follow for four long years.

On the extreme right of the Franco-German border the Rhine flowed less than 45 kilometres from the post-1870 frontier, presenting a temptation and challenge for France, recovery of the territory lost in the Franco-Prussian War being a national priority in any war with Germany.

The French Army Command's strategic plan, Plan XVII, was essentially a plan for mobilisation. It was based on the assessment that, to avoid the fortification system constructed on the post-1870 frontier, the main German thrust would be launched from the Metz area of Lorraine. If indications of a German attack through Belgium were correct they represented only a supporting flank move limited to eastern Belgium. To the last moment the French remained uncertain whether the Germans would breach Belgian neutrality and their fortification system was not extended along the Belgian frontier. Imbued with a doctrine of attack, the French Commander-in-

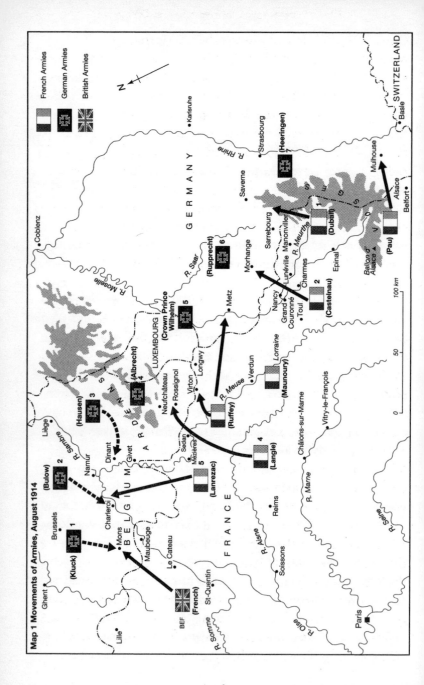

Map 1 Movements of Armies, August 1914

Chief, General Joseph Joffre, believed that any German onslaught could best be spoiled by a series of tactical offensives. The first was to be into northern Alsace, the Saar and German-occupied Lorraine, threatening the left flank of the German attack. This would compel the Germans to mount their attack through a gap in their lines of forts in the hills to the south-east of Nancy between Toul and Epinal known as the Trouée de Charmes, the Charmes Gap. They had left this almost unfortified as a bait, but with its flanks well protected. A little later, following the success the French confidently expected, a second and more important offensive would be launched to the north of Metz. If the Germans invaded neutral territory, the French would strike through the eastern Ardennes, threatening both the flanks of the German main thrust. Together the four armies concerned in these attacks, supported by a fifth on the left flank of the French front, could destroy the German centre, isolate the German right flank if it did enter eastern Belgium, and liberate the territories lost in 1870. Invasion into the German heartland was not envisaged, despite the 'À Berlin' signs chalked on troop trains.

These plans would provide France, numerically weaker than Germany, with a chance to strike in areas where the high command believed they possessed a local superiority. Mobilisation had been ordered on 1 August, twenty-seven year classes being recalled for service. Deployment followed meticulously prepared railway timetabling, largely the work of Joffre. Some 4,300 trains steamed across France transporting 1,500,000 men to their appointed rail-heads, all the men for the five front armies by 10 August, for the reserve divisions by the 13th and for the units tasked for the defence of Paris by the 15th. After reaching the rail-heads there followed marches, 25–30 kilometres per day, apparently never-ending, with nights, fine or wet, spent in cornfields or small woods – in Winston Churchill's words, 'the measured silent-drawing together of gigantic forces' in preparation for the high drama to come. Germany issued a declaration of war against France on the 3rd, justifying the action by spurious claims of French air attacks on Karlsrühe and Nuremberg. Joffre established his own headquarters, the Grand Quartier Général, in school buildings at Vitry-le-François.

Alsace and Lorraine

As a curtain-raiser for his large-scale offensive operations, which could only be undertaken when mobilisation was complete, Joffre directed the commander of the French 1st Army, General Dubail, on the extreme right flank of the French front, to order one corps, supported by the 8th Cavalry Division, to advance into southern Alsace. Bonneau's VII Corps was to occupy the city of Mulhouse, partly to raise the population in revolt against their German occupiers, and partly to secure a foothold on the left bank of the Rhine. He was also told to destroy the bridges, both for and to provide a springboard for a march down the Rhine to Colmar and Strasbourg. On the basis of aerial reconnaissance reports, General Joffre believed the area was undefended. An assault might oblige the Germans to direct forces away from any planned incursion into the western Vosges.

Bonneau was an irresolute force commander. He had received reports via Switzerland of the arrival of an Austrian army corps in the area, possibly disinformation circulated by German agents. On 7 August he crossed the frontier and moved into lower Alsace in two columns, approaching Mulhouse from the south-west via Altkirch and the north-west after a crossing of the southern Vosges. Recruited from the Besançon area, his soldiers made a glorious sight in their brilliant nineteenth-century uniforms, the infantry in blue tunics, red trousers and képi running at the double behind their officers with white gloves and swords, the cavalry in dark

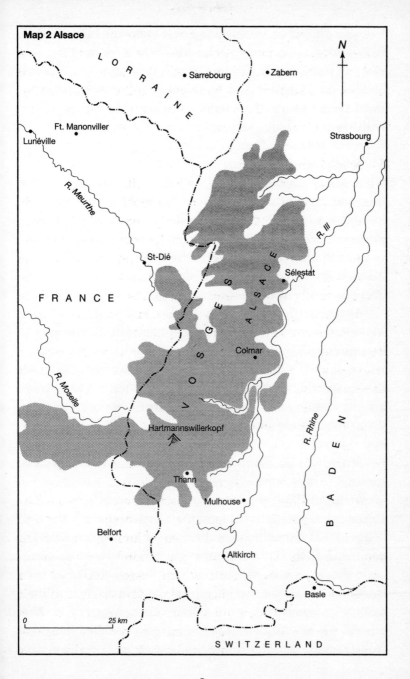

Map 2 Alsace

LORRAINE

Sarrebourg

Zabern

Ft. Manonviller

Lunéville

Strasbourg

R. Meurthe

R. Ill

St-Dié

Sélestat

FRANCE

VOSGES

ALSACE

Colmar

R. Moselle

Hartmannswillerkopf

R. Rhine

BADEN

Thann

Mulhouse

Belfort

Altkirch

Basle

0   25 km

SWITZERLAND

N

5

blue jackets, red breeches with a blue seam and brass helmets with a long black plume down the back. They met the first German resistance at Altkirch, which they overcame at a cost of a hundred killed in a six-hour battle culminating in a spirited bayonet charge. Further small-scale resistance was dealt with by the column advancing from the north-west which took the town of Thann. Bonneau sent a telegram to the Minister of War in Paris claiming a victory in a covering operation. Joffre was displeased at both the direct message and the misunderstanding of the objective. Worse, he was now uncomfortably aware that the Germans were assembling sizeable forces in the nearby forests. French intelligence staff had failed to grasp that the German army would commit its reserve formations straight into battle. Other far more serious consequences of this misjudgement were soon to follow.

Although Bonneau pushed cautiously on, occupying Mulhouse without further fighting on the 8th, he was ejected from the city by German counter-attacks launched by General von Heeringen's 7th Army the next day, German Alsatians having revealed the small size of Bonneau's force. The German attacks threatened to cut him off, Dubail's reinforcement of a division being obviously inadequate and too late. After some stiff fighting he withdrew on the 10th towards the fortress of Belfort, where he claimed that further attacks had not been possible as his troops were exhausted.

At Belfort both Bonneau and Aubier, the cavalry division commander, were relieved from their commands by Joffre who believed that the failure was more one of lack of fitness in the commanders than in the troops. The whole operation, small-scale though it was, showed up both the ferocity of German firepower and all the weaknesses in the French 1914 military system – incompetent, often elderly commanders, regimental officers too few in number for effective command and with inadequate maps, combat intelligence unreliable or incorrectly evaluated, cavalry steeped in a doctrine of sabre charges rather than reconnaissance, and infantry of reckless bravery but low tactical competence. Other losers were those many citizens of Mulhouse and southern Alsace who had rejoiced at the French arrival, but after Bonneau's withdrawal were left to face German reprisals.

Joffre was not to be diverted from the next stage of his pre-emptive tactical offensives and discounted the significance of the increasing number of reports of German action in Belgium. He maintained his view that the main German thrust would be launched into western Lorraine by the regular army corps positioned against his centre. The French attack in Alsace and eastern Lorraine to thwart such a German move seemed to him all the more important. Joffre's thinking was also based on the incorrect intelligence assessments of the German use of reserve formations; he was convinced that only six German corps stood in the planned line of advance whereas in fact there were eight, and their plans could provide for offence rather than defence.

For this full-scale attack a new 'Army of Alsace' including VII Corps, one regular and three reserve divisions, was formed and its command given to a one-armed hero of the 1870 war recalled from retirement, General Pau. It was to form the right flank of the attack with Dubail's 1st Army in the centre and General de Castelnau's 2nd Army on the left. After four days of preparation the offensive began on 14 August; French formations crossed the frontier with bands playing on the 15th, the 1st Army advancing through a corridor in the hills leading towards Sarrebourg and then on into the Vosges and down into the Rhine valley, the 2nd moving from the hills surrounding Nancy along a valley ending at Morhange. They gained four days of advance, dislodging groups of German infantry but taking heavy casualties from German artillery. Accurately ranged by means of pre-selected aiming points, the French columns were severely harassed. The Germans, mostly Bavarians, sacked towns and villages as they withdrew. Although successful in taking or masking heights on the flanks of their advance and in places reaching as far as 30 kilometres into Germany, the French advance was hindered by the terrain. Rivers, canals and roads all ran parallel to their axis of advance, forcing the French either to keep to conspicuous roads or to move more slowly across country, rolling hills and woods.

The overall plan of the German army under its Chief-of-Staff, General von Moltke, was based on better intelligence. The Germans were aware of the broad outline of Plan XVII, if not all the details, and understood Joffre's deployments. For Lorraine and Alsace their aim was to secure the commitment of the maximum number of the best French formations away from the main German thrust, to be through central Belgium. Withdrawal for a few days and the appearance of a French tactical success was a price worth paying. Execution of this strategy fell to the German 6th and 7th Armies commanded respectively by Crown Prince Rupprecht of Bavaria and General von Heeringen, the Bavarian Prince having a co-ordinating authority.

By the 17th Castelnau's XX Corps – men from the Nancy area and commanded by General Ferdinand Foch – was approaching Morhange. On the 18th Dubail's VIII Corps – men from the Alps – captured Sarrebourg, both successes despite German resistance which inflicted severe casualties. Dubail's advance into the Vosges was then halted. Pau, more easily, recaptured Mulhouse on the 19th, though in the operations a general, Pelissier, was killed, the first of many senior commanders to lose his life in battle. At first sight it seemed that the French strategy was succeeding. A captured German regimental colour was sent in triumph to Joffre. However, the poor road network forced commanders to follow valleys not properly on their line of advance, and there were grave signals problems. On the 18th Joffre directed that the 2nd Army should face north rather than north-east. The paths of the leading columns in consequence diverged, and the 1st and 2nd Armies lost touch with each other. Dubail proposed to restore contact by an attack on the night of the 19th/20th which he hoped would also enable the Cavalry Corps, commanded by General Conneau, to penetrate deep into the German rear. But the Germans were no longer prepared to conform to the French plan.

The local German command had only accepted the withdrawal reluctantly. Rupprecht and his Chief-of-Staff, General Krafft von Dellmensingen, had pressed Moltke for permission to counter-attack, claiming that attack would lead to greater French involvement to the advantage of the Germans attacking in Belgium. Argument raged for three days while Moltke hesitated, undecided as to whether the French attack might weaken the French ability to resist his attack through Belgium or present a threat to the flank of this onslaught. There was also the dazzling possibility of a vast pincer movement by simultaneous right and left flank attacks. Eventually Rupprecht was permitted to attack, so committing troops that could have been made available to reinforce the German right wing.

The first French reverse was the repulse of Dubail. Much worse was to follow on the 20th when the eight German corps of the combined 6th and 7th Armies mounted well co-ordinated general attacks on the weary and weakened two centre corps of the 2nd Army, exposed by Foch's over-extended advance (not authorised by Castelnau) and on Dubail's VII Corps at Sarrebourg. German heavy artillery annihilated that of the French 2nd Army. Infantry attacks followed in vast columns, wave upon wave, and two 2nd Army corps – the XV and XVI – composed mainly of Provençal men from Marseille and Toulon, gave way. They retreated in headlong confusion, in the words of one officer in one village, 'a sublime chaos, infantrymen, gunners with their clumsy wagons, combat supplies, regimental stores, brilliant motor cars of our brilliant staffs all meeting, criss-crossing, not knowing what to do or where to go'. To add to his difficulties Castelnau had been ordered by Joffre to accept the transfer of one of his corps and part of another to Belgium; he received only three reserve divisions as replacement. To escape a potentially fatal envelopment by German forces now obviously numerically superior, Castlenau, furious with Foch, was obliged to withdraw back to the 14 August start line, the River Meurthe and the Grand Couronné de Nancy on the 23rd.

Dubail fared no better. He tried to support the 16th Division fighting for the Saar bridges beyond Sarrebourg, by ordering his 15th Division to mount a dawn attack after a long night march. But attacks by the Bavarian I Corps pushed his divisions back. In Sarrebourg itself, after violent street fighting, the use of barricades and house-to-house engagements, the 16th Division were forced to withdraw from the town. Its commander, the Comte de Maud'huy, saluted the survivors as they withdrew with their band playing the 'Marche Lorraine'. Despite the reverse, French enthusiasm was undismayed. The fifty-nine-year-old Comte de Pelleport, who had come back from retirement to rejoin his regiment, was the first to lead a French attack and one of the first to be wounded. Before he died he wrote to his wife: 'I have behaved as a Pelleport. Morale is perfect.' But Dubail was in peril, his flank uncovered as a result of the 2nd Army's withdrawal. Joffre ordered a 1st Army withdrawal, to the anger of Dubail who disliked Castlenau and saw no reason to yield further ground that his army had won at so much cost. A retreat that could have turned into a rout, involving the loss of Nancy and perhaps a major German breakthrough, was saved from disaster by the covering action of Foch and his XX Corps, which had been strengthened by some of the best troops in the French army, long-service regulars of the white Troupes Coloniales infantry and artillery. Foch had been unable to take Morhange but his corps had held firm despite the very heavy firepower of successive Bavarian attacks. In the words of one soldier as the form of the battle increased: 'Rage took us over, we fired, we fired, we yelled, the smell of powder intoxicated us.' Withdrawal was inevitable, and after a night-long forced march Foch was able to start preparations for defensive positions on the high ground of the Grand Couronné, the key to the defence of the Meurthe line and the city of Nancy which Joffre had ordered to be defended at all costs.

Foch refused to accept the gloomy view of Castelnau, who had just lost a son in battle, that Nancy might have to be abandoned. His resolution was fortified by the slowness of the German pursuit which gave the French three vital days to recuperate and prepare to defend the Meurthe river line. Foch's defensive preparations were accomplished after a very quick and efficient reorganisation on a line from Gerbévillier across the Meurthe west of Lunéville and on and beyond Amance. The physical rest was as important, 'Uniforms brushed were no longer covered in mire, these few hours of repose returned lost serenity to men's faces,' commented one soldier.

The combined 6th and 7th Armies under Rupprecht then launched a series of attacks, supported by heavy artillery bombardments, on the French Lorraine front. 'Shells keep falling all around but there are so many that one takes no notice of them,' remarked a lieutenant. The German attacks gained initial success but on the 25th a vigorous counter-attack by Foch's XX Corps on the left and an equally spirited attack by the *chasseurs alpins* of General Maud'huy's division in Dubail's army on the right threw the Germans back. Nevertheless German attacks had enabled them to enter

Lunéville on the 23rd and then Saint-Dié and the fortress of Manonviller, built to dominate the Paris–Strasbourg railway. Manonviller was struck by over 1,500 shells, the fumes from the bursts rendering the fort untenable. On 27 August, Mulhouse, too, was evacuated on the orders of Joffre, to the fury of Pau who correctly foresaw a further set of German reprisals on French loyalists. All that was left to the French in Alsace was a small area of the south, covered by the fortress guns of Belfort. Nevertheless, the Germans' inability to move round the French right flank in the Vosges meant that when events elsewhere became critical, the French were able to draw on units and formations from the area.

The Ardennes

Still adhering to his plans while the Sarrebourg and Morhange fighting was at its height, Joffre issued orders on the 20th for the final stage of his plans, the Ardennes mission for the 3rd and 4th Armies, commanded by General Ruffey at Verdun and General de Langle de Cary at St Dizier respectively. These two armies fielded three regular cavalry and twenty regular infantry divisions (three of the latter being Coloniale) together with two reserve divisions – over 350,000 men. However, the German drive through Belgium, including the occupation of Brussels on the 20th, obliged Joffre to order the transfer of General Lanrezac's 5th Army, the left flank formation on the Franco-German border, north-west to the River Sambre, an operation examined in a following chapter as being the first major French response to the German war of movement. Lanrezac's move, however, exposed the left flank of the 4th Army. There was also a considerable distance between the left flank of the 2nd Army and the right flank of the 3rd. To act as a reserve and fill the gaps Joffre created an 'Army of Lorraine' at Verdun under General Maunoury, sixty-seven years old but indefatigable, to prevent any German crossing of the Meuse, using three divisions taken from Ruffey. Although Joffre knew that the withdrawal of the 2nd Army was under way he nevertheless issued the order for the advance of the 3rd and 4th to begin on the 22nd. He believed the Ardennes was either unoccupied or held only by a cavalry screen, and his original strategy of an eventual linking between all four armies in a pincer movement remained feasible. In defence of Joffre, the Cavalry Corps of General Sordet, its attached infantry *groupe* riding in buses, had traversed the Ardennes with great energy (the horses' backs were worn bare) between the 6th and 15th August but they had not ridden sufficiently far to the west to encounter the advancing Germans. Nor had aerial reconnaissance revealed any enemy presence.

The 4th Army was given the town of Neufchâteau as its objective, the 3rd was tasked to push the Germans back towards Metz. General Lanrezac and his 5th Army were told to attack what was described as 'the northern group'. The use of this term appeared to accept that there might be some German northern threat but in fact only illustrates the depth of Joffre's delusion as to its size. Joffre added that Lanrezac should not expect either Belgian or British support. Joffre believed these moves would frustrate any German attack in the centre of the front. Despite Lanrezac's warnings of the threat developing in eastern Belgium, he persisted in believing the centre still to be the main danger. As he saw it, an enveloping attack on the German centre would cut off their right flank and open the way to the Rhine; the more Germans in Belgium, the more could be cut off.

The original German war plans had not provided for an attack in this area; it was to be held as a pivot for the main drive through eastern Belgium, moving forward only slowly. Both the commanders of the two German armies opposite Ruffey and de Langle, on the right the 4th Army under Albrecht, Duke of Württemberg, and on his left the 5th Army under Crown Prince Wilhelm of Prussia, expected a French attack. They advanced slowly, entrenching themselves as they went. The Crown Prince personally wished to take the important iron industry area of Longwy. The two armies, eight corps, were about the same size as the French force. German knowledge of the terrain and the provision of better maps gave them a useful advantage, particularly as Joffre forbade preliminary reconnaissance by the French to avoid revealing axes of advance. The hills and woods did not favour a French advance and to make matters worse, a fog blinded their advance cavalry patrols, composed of irresolute reservists, the regular units having been transferred to the Cavalry Corps. As a result they found themselves often taken by surprise, their 75mm guns an immediate target for German artillery when the fog lifted. The fighting that resulted developed in scale from small encounters between the opposing forward units to major battles as, in successive echelons, bodies of men came upon one another, often in rain and poor visibility or fading light at the end of a day. The Germans, whose advance guards were always stronger than the French, would immediately entrench themselves, while the French attacked with the utmost valour. Wave after wave of French infantrymen rushed forward regardless and with no thought of envelopment on their flanks, only to be cut down by German machine-gunners in the absence of any French artillery support to protect them. German artillery intelligence was extremely efficient, the French wrongly blaming their accuracy on spies. The overall confusion was made worse by poor communications within formations and with flanking formations. Increasing fatigue also played its part. While the regular soldiers could endure the endless marching and counter-marching, recalled reservists were less fit and either fell out or marched in increasing pain and difficulty. On the 3rd Army front V Corps in the centre suffered severely, stumbling headlong in a fog into German units advancing as for attack and well supported by artillery; it withdrew in panic. In consequence, despite fierce fighting, General Sarrail's VI Corps on the right was also forced to retreat, and General Boelle's IV Corps on the left was halted. Sarrail, however, managed to achieve virtually the only success of the whole offensive when his artillery smashed into the flank of a German formation at Virton, a success which Ruffey was later to claim could have been exploited had he not lost his three divisions to Maunoury. But in turn the check to Boelle had made any advance by the right flank corps of de Langle's 4th Army hazardous, while on de Langle's left flank, despite epic fighting, a disaster befell the French. The left flank corps was the elite Coloniale under the command of General Lefèvre, mostly soldiers with recent experience of hard fighting in Morocco. Undeterred by German ambushes, two Coloniale columns advanced in marching order of four along the narrow roads and pathways towards their objective, the town of Neufchâteau. But both columns were stopped by an unexpectedly massive volume of artillery, machine-gun and infantry fire. The 2nd Coloniale Artillery Regiment, for example endured twelve hours of bombardment, its own guns firing until the ammunition was exhausted, the horses disembowelled and half of its men killed or wounded. One gunner wrote: 'The men fought with unequalled bravery. Not a man stumbled or flinched even when they knew all was lost. They served their guns as if on manoeuvres.' Bayonet charges of fanatical courage led by officers wearing white shakos and gloves simply served to increase the totals of the dead, and at the village of Rossignol one brigade became cut off, its only line of retreat across a bridge being under constant German shrapnel bombardment.

By the night of the 23rd the 3rd Colonial Division, at the outset 16,000 strong, had suffered 11,000 killed, missing or wounded, the divisional commander, General Raffenel, and one brigade commander, General Rondoney, among the dead, with another, General Montignault, a prisoner. De Langle's XVII Corps suffered as severely and was pushed into a disorderly withdrawal. Despite this carnage Joffre, still unaware of the strength of the two German armies, gave orders to de Langle to make a further effort, but neither he nor Ruffey's 3rd Army could make any dent in the German lines. On the 25th the 4th Army, covered in a fighting withdrawal by the 2nd Colonial Division, fell back to the south bank of the Meuse; a little later Ruffey and Maunoury abandoned their attacks and also turned to defence. The withdrawal was one of exhausted and emaciated men in uniforms now ragged and dirty, through villages still blazing or shattered by shellfire with dead men by the roadside, roads jammed with panic-stricken refugees and military transport, the wounded in hasty, blood-soaked and muddy field dressings, some carried in rough farm carts, flanked by dying or dead horses in ditches. German artillery fire was incessant, directed by flares from spotting Albatros aircraft pouring *une pluie de schrapnel* on troops scampering for any cover available. It was all far removed from the glorious attacks that the French soldier had been led to expect.

The Paris press carried reports of refusal to fight among the Marseille and Toulon soldiers of the XV Corps. The 3rd Army moved to cover the Verdun area and the 4th Sedan, the majority of Maunoury's units, were moved to Amiens to be included in a new 6th Army. A heroic stand by the garrison of Longwy under Colonel d'Arche delayed the Germans for two days, but on the 27th the Crown Prince triumphantly occupied the area. Lorraine's iron and coal now passed into the hands of the Germans who were to make good use of it. But the stiffness of the French resistance had obliged Hausen's 3rd Army to deflect eastwards to help Albrecht's 4th Army, thus in some measure weakening the German right flank drive. In sum, however, the failure of these French frontier offensives, costing casualties of some 200,000 including over 4,700 officers, was not only one of the operations themselves but also one of the Plan XVII strategy and the whole national concept of war. Acres of northern France were strewn with the blue and red uniforms of French infantry and the brass helmets and cuirasses of the cavalry. Afterwards Charles de Gaulle was to write: 'Tactically the realisation of the German firepower made nonsense of the current military doctrines. Morally, all the people's illusions, with which they had steeled themselves went up in smoke ... Between 20 and 23 August a perfect sense of security was turned into a frantic feeling of danger.'

CHAPTER 2

1914

Republic, Strategy and Army

Plan XVII, with its rigidity of thinking on mobilisation and deployment, represented a major failure in what later in the twentieth century would be called 'strategic intelligence'. That the Germans might attack through Belgium in order to deploy sufficient force to secure a quick victory had been seen as a possibility by the Deuxième Bureau, the intelligence branch of the General Staff, for at least eight years. Agents, among them the French military attachés in Berlin and Brussels, supplied a mass of strategic intelligence, sufficient to create confusion. Material that appeared to suggest a German move limited to eastern Belgium, with the main German thrust in the centre, was selected for attention as it fitted in with the preconceived deployment of Plan XVII. Signs of the real danger – reports from 1909–10 onward – suggested that a German invasion would not be limited to eastern Belgium and that German manoeuvres and tactical exercises would be built around flanking movements. Early hints, followed early in 1914 by corroboration from intercepted German mobilisation plans, that the Germans might throw reserve formations straight into battle, and warnings of the massive development of German heavy artillery, were not given the attention that they deserved by the operations branch of the Staff. Reserve units, it was believed, would be used only as garrisons in occupied territory. Nor were the lessons of the 1904–5 Russo-Japanese war heeded – the defence of dug-in defences protected by wire, the importance of machine-guns and of artillery capable of firing at invisible targets, the tactical value of envelopment and the dangers of massive frontal attacks. Such reports presented challenges to the orthodoxy of Plan XVII to which Joffre, being in large measure the author, was inescapably committed. The crippling casualties sustained by officers and regiments that were the cream of the French army at Morhange, Neufchâteau and Rossignol were the first of the heavy prices to be paid for failure to adhere to the basic principles of military intelligence – targeting of key indicator areas, prejudice-free evaluation of material collected, and effective presentation by a well- trained and respected intelligence staff.

The Tactical Offensive Strategy

Rigid adherence to this general deployment plan and a neglect of intelligence that warned of its dangers resulted in an army, already inferior in size to its likely opponent, being in addition wrongly equipped. At soldier level, the metropolitan infantryman's 1914 heavy blue and red uniform offered no camouflage protection, his burnished metal cantine or cooking pot on top of his 54 pounds of backpack equipment would give his position away whenever it caught the sun. His 8mm Lebel rifle was an obsolete weapon and in most infantry regiments machine-guns were limited to a section of two guns in each of the battalions of the regiment. Machine-guns, heavy and difficult to man-handle, were seen as defensive and not an essential part of an attack. Subordinate formation and unit commanders were allowed little or no freedom of action, control was tightly centralised. Although in the 1904 and 1914 infantry tactics manuals mention was made of the use of ground cover when under fire, the essential element remained, in the words of the 1914 manual, 'the will to eliminate the enemy with the bayonet in close combat'. In this spirit infantrymen in the Ardennes attacks would throw away their digging tools, and regiments advance to their officers' shouts of *'En avant à la baionette'*, with little or no concern for an immediate tactical reserve. Infantry assaults would be launched too far from the objective and without co-ordinated artillery support; little thought was given to consolidation when the assaults achieved a temporary success. German advance guard tactics, digging in after a forward bound, were far superior. At a more mundane level, German units were provided with mobile field cookers; the French infantryman had to cook his own food over his own fire – whatever the weather or battle conditions. The bright colours of the uniforms of the cavalry regiments – dark blue and red for cuirassiers, dragoons and chasseurs, light blue and red for hussars, with burnished brass helmets with plumes for cuirassiers and dragons and a gleaming front and back cuirass for the cuirassiers – were all again nineteenth rather than twentieth century, pre-industrial rather than modern. For the individual soldier the uniforms were to prove exceedingly uncomfortable in a sweltering August, glamorous but dangerous when opposed by a defence with machine-guns. The lance was seen by some theorists as contributing to cavalry *élan*, but proved an encumbrance on long rides.

Perhaps the artillery was the arm which suffered most from the attack philosophy which saw artillery primarily as close support, paying scant attention to the role of preliminary bombardment in preparation for an attack. Little need was seen for heavy artillery, except in fortresses. In April 1914 there were in France only fifty-eight batteries in contrast to sixty-two field artillery regiments of 618 field and thirty horse artillery batteries, with a further seventeen in North Africa. All batteries were of four guns, the heavy batteries either

155mm, 120mm or 105mm guns, the horse batteries 3-inch guns, and the field, the vast majority, equipped with the renowned 75mm gun with a 16lb shell, one of the classic artillery pieces of all time. The four-gun battery organisation in respect of heavy guns was shown to be a handicap in August–September 1914, when the heavy artillery achieved little. Some 1,500 horses were needed to move each of the major units and their movements blocked roads. For the 75mm gun, however, the four-gun battery was highly successful, providing very effective fire with rapid mobility. The 75mm gun designed by Commandant de Port of the Ateliers de Puteaux in the 1890s, was accurate, sturdy and reliable with an impressive rate of fire, six rounds a minute in normal conditions but up to fifteen or more in an emergency. This was achieved by a long recoil cylinder which absorbed the recoil and returned the gun without disturbing the carriage, so removing an otherwise time-consuming need to re-lay the gun. It was a superb close-support weapon in attack and defence that could be brought into action at a quick trot, and fire from the open or light concealment. Indirect fire, however, was more difficult, there being insufficient telephone line for direction available in the first months of the war. A *groupe* of three batteries – twelve guns – could strike twelve hectares of ground with 100 shells in under a minute. The shells were also better quality than those of German field artillery, of 15.95 and 11.25 pounds shrapnel and high explosive respectively. On occasion German soldiers died from a stun effect, leading to German allegations of barbarity. The guns' crews were protected by a bullet-proof shield. But the gun, designed for a war of movement, suffered from some limitations in the later static defensive operations – a flat trajectory that unless dug in (so losing mobility) could not strike targets behind a hill, a range limited to 9 kilometres, and a shell too small to impact effectively on entrenched defences. French artillerymen

21

were trained mathematically, and their close-support fire plans were scientifically prepared. But the doctrine of the time did not provide for fire at ranges above 5,000 metres, so denying a counter-bombardment capability. The gun's very efficiency, however, led French officers to overestimate its overall value in conditions other than attack and neglect the need for proper co-ordinated artillery infantry fire plans. Joffre's requests in the last months before the war for more modern equipment, in particular for a 105mm howitzer and greatly increased ammunition supplies, had not been granted. The lack of effective heavy artillery in infantry divisions to prepare for French advances and cover withdrawals in the Ardennes was the first of many hard lessons that French commanders were to learn.

France's strategic dilemma lay in the worsening population imbalance, forty million against the sixty million of Germany. To counter this, and despite the widest political and ideological differences, France had allied herself with Russia, so providing a massive superiority over Germany and her ally, the Dual Monarchy of the Austrian-Hungarian Empire. However, the vast distances over which Russian soldiers would have to travel on mobilisation, together with the inadequate railway network of Russia, meant that Russia might not be able to field a powerful army for some considerable time after mobilisation was ordered. It was in that time, correctly appreciated by the French government and military staffs, that Germany would launch an attack, seeking a quick and total destruction of French military power before the full weight of Russia's millions could invade eastern Germany. Fears of Germany's capacity to mobilise quickly were well founded. The French plans, in reply, provided for the first echelons of the active regular divisions to be on the frontier by the fifth day after mobilisation, the remainder by the ninth day, with reserve divisions to be available between the eleventh and thirteenth day.

It was expected that even from the start of war Russian forces would be of sufficient strength to menace East Prussia, so reducing the German forces available for an attack on France. The Russians for long refused to provide any firm commitment. However, with an increasing awareness that a quick German victory over the French would be disastrous for them and perhaps some appreciation of the weaknesses in the Austria–Hungary armies, a commitment was made. By the July 1912 France–Russian Military Protocol, Russia undertook to attack Germany with a force of 700,000–800,000 men fifteen days after mobilisation. It was also hoped, with both growing anxiety and increasing optimism in the six years prior to 1914, that if the Germans attacked through Belgium the British would provide an adequate force for the French left flank.

In these conditions the French army might have been best advised to adopt a defensive strategy. Indeed, this had been the thinking behind Plan XVII's predecessor, Plan XVI, the work of Vice-President of the Conseil Supérieur de la Guerre, the Commander-in-Chief designate in 1911, General Michel. Michel argued that the Germans would not be able to gain the instant victory they needed in Lorraine or east of the Meuse, but that they would attack, using their reserves, through the whole of Belgium. His plan provided for reinforcing the left flank of the French army to the coast, using reserves, and a pre-emptive entry into Belgium. Eminently sensible, the plan was nevertheless rejected by the Minister of War, Messimy, and senior generals.

The military reasons for this and the preference for offensive rather than defensive action had long historical roots. French armies, under the Bourbon monarchy, in the Revolutionary Wars, and under Napoleon, had all achieved glory in the attack. Offensive action was believed to match the impulsive French 'Latin' character. Plan XVII was thought to provide an opportunity for France to use this national aptitude in a manoeuvre war strategy, forcing the Germans to fight on ground of French choosing and so avoiding any German surprise direction of attack. In this way the lost territories would be regained and the Germans would learn that France could not again be subdued in the manner of 1870. The objectives were limited and local, deep advance into Germany was not planned.

Military writers, notably a Colonel Ardant du Picq, argued that defeat followed 'passivity', allowing the enemy to choose the course of events. 'He who is determined to advance will win,' he wrote. Du Picq was killed in the 1870 war but his writings, published posthumously, were seen to offer the correct lessons. It was further thought that an offensive strategy would at least impress, and perhaps actually help, the Russians. French generals held reserves in disdain, and saw Michel's fears as groundless. Believing the Germans would take the same view of reserves, it was thought that early French attacks would strike the Germans before their reserves could be deployed. More rationally it was argued that Michel's plan would take the army away from the area, Lorraine, where the French wished to fight, and it would not be possible to return quickly enough if the Germans were to break through there. Finally, within an officer corps that had been sharply divided by political events, an attack doctrine served as a rallying call to which all good men and true should respond, with unbelievers defeatist or weak in character.

There were also crucial political reasons for the change in strategy. Michel was a 'republican' general. Messimy, a minister in the coalition government that came to power in 1911 and himself a former officer, shared the conservative views of the majority of generals concerning reserves, believing that they could not be mobilised and deployed in time, that they would be poorly trained, and – most dangerously – that they might be an embryonic citizen force, politically undesirable and likely to dilute the vigour and enthusiasm of the standing army. Accordingly Michel was relieved of his command-designate and Joffre, who was seen to combine a loyalty to the republic with politically acceptable military thinking, appointed in his stead. Joffre, an engineer officer and Ecole Polytechnique graduate, came from a poor family. He had earned a reputation for steadiness and shrewdness of character in campaigns in Indochina, West Africa and Madagascar but was otherwise little known. He had had only brief experience as a division and corps commander.

At the same time, among the military, an extremist cult of the offensive had been developing, its leading figure being Lieutenant-Colonel Loyzeau de Grandmaison, in 1911 the head of the General Staff's 3rd Bureau, Operations. Grandmaison had first expounded his theories in 1906; in 1911 he developed his argument in two lectures, that notwithstanding the power of artillery and other defensive weapons, the surest route to success was the irresistible offensive. Tactics, he asserted, were of no importance compared with the psychological factor of soldiers with battle enthusiasm. Properly inspired soldiers would fear no risks, individual stress would be overcome by training, shoulder to shoulder small-group cohesion and the will to win. The army would destroy its opponents by the sheer audacity and violence of attacks pushed to the limit, regardless of casualties. All that was needed was knowledge of the enemy positions, clear orders for an attack, and local superiority in numbers. Rigid unquestioning obedience to orders was heavily emphasised. Any other form of operational art was contrary to the true nature of warfare.

A series of tactical and infantry manuals were drafted to set out the practice of these theories. Defence and fortresses were only acceptable in areas from which troops had been thinned out so as to provide more men for the attack; intelligence concerning the enemy need not be a priority, infantry should advance man to man side by side, one firing, on divisional fronts of between 1,500 and 2,500 metres – in the event to prove too broad. The role of artillery was simply support, not preparation, for an attack, and cavalry should charge with side arms and not dismount to fight on foot. If any ground was lost it had to be regained by an immediate counter-attack. Battle was reduced to guts (*cran*) and the bayonet (*La Rosalie*), a twenty-second charge over 50 metres designed to hit the enemy before he had time to take aim. Junior officers and NCOs were not trained to think any further than the charge, and sergeants were to knock out any soldier behaving in a cowardly fashion This doctrine began to take on the mystique characteristics of a cult. Its followers drew further inspiration from the philosopher Henri Bergson who argued that the vital energy force of life would always master the material world, and an all-conquering will would provide an *élan vital* that carried men on to superhuman successes. On the battlefield it was claimed this success could even be gained against superior numbers and result in a short, victorious war.

The cult may be viewed as an irrational consequence of the defeats of 1870, the need to rebuild national self-confidence to counter a numerically stronger adversary and as a remedy for the army's weakness resulting from the hostility of a succession of political ministers. It was supported also by the political left who saw in it a revolutionary fervour that could replace the need for a long professional training. Its most articulate advocates included Castelnau and Foch, who lectured at the Ecole de Guerre and became its commandant. He published two books, historical studies from which he developed the theory of absolute war and *offensive à l'outrance*; these works became required reading for French officers. The strategy's few critics included Colonel Philippe Pétain and General

Lanrezac who wrote: 'If every subordinate corps commander has the right to ram home an attack on the first opponent he sees, the commander in chief is incapable of exercising any form of direction.' This perceptive comment reveals the extent to which tactical offensive doctrine was progressively confusing the priority of strategic defence. Another with reservations was General Ruffey, who argued for heavy artillery.

The long-running argument over the colourful uniforms of the army well illustrates the hold taken by the cult. Some officers, particularly those with African experience and notably General Galliéni, did advocate a less conspicuous uniform that could provide personal camouflage and save lives. Against this practical view it was first argued that pale grey or beige uniforms would be confused with those of the German or Italian armies. But the real objection was based on the assertion that red trousers contributed to the *élan* of true French soldiers and were an essential emblem. 'Red trousers are France,' declared Eugène Etienne, the Minister for War in 1913. Dull grey or khaki uniforms, it was alleged, were all part of a left-wing plot to change the army into a Boer-style citizens' militia which could never muster the necessary *élan vital*.

The Army and Politics

The offensive strategy also accorded well with French public opinion in 1914, though only after several changes in attitude since the defeat of 1870. Public debate and controversy over what a French army should be had originated in the early years of the Revolution, such arguments reappearing in only slightly varying form until the 1930s.

In 1791 all had agreed that the army should be a citizen force and no longer the personal executive projection of the monarchy; but differing views were put forward about its composition and role. These views reflected the divisions in

French society created by the Revolution. What form should the political regime take? Related to this, should the army be a professional army, *une armée de métier* or a revolutionary *levée en masse*? Should military effectiveness or political reliability be the priority? The political left feared a professional army would be used against them, the right feared a conscript army as an instrument of revolution. The immediate post-1870 years saw the army as popular, military revival as a national must. Legislation in the period 1871–5 saw the beginning of a consensus view (excluding the extreme left), that the army should be professional, well-trained and equipped. As such it was able to attract a large percentage of its officers from traditional sources, the aristocracy, gentry *(petite noblesse)* and bourgeoisie who felt able to serve a republican army no matter what their own views might be. This popularity lasted until the late 1880s despite the furore aroused by the ignominious fate of General Boulanger. The media of the time had built the general up as a second Napoleon I, set to take power in a coup. But the general's nerve collapsed and his life ended in a shabby suicide. By 1888–9, however, the pendulum had swung to an anti-military public opinion, resentful of the costs and long periods of conscription demanded by the army. Worse was to follow in the next two decades with events that divided the officer corps and for a while turned public opinion very sharply against the military.

The first and most serious of these events was *l'Affaire,* the well-known case of Captain Alfred Dreyfus. In 1894 a docket of artillery secrets was found to be on its way to the German military attaché. It was alleged by the staff to have been written by Dreyfus, a convenient scapegoat as he was a Jew. Dreyfus denied the charges, but he was court-martialled, convicted on worthless circumstantial evidence but with documents doctored to show his guilt. He was ceremonially disgraced and despatched for life to the infamous penal settlement of Devil's Island, all to general public approval at the time. It was then discovered that another officer of a disreputable personal character, Major Esterhazy, was the real culprit. However, the officers in the Ministry of War endeavoured to conceal this discovery even to the extent of further forging of documents to secure the acquittal of Esterhazy and maintain the fiction of Dreyfus's guilt. The army's honour and reputation for justice was argued by most (but not all) senior officers to be at stake – a reason of state that was an ideal none should dare to question. As the shabby details emerged, largely via an officer, Colonel Picquart, who would not be a party to the injustice, a public outcry gathered steam and the acrimony between Dreyfusards and anti-Dreyfusards verged upon hysteria. In the Dreyfusard camp were radical and socialist political leaders, together with a number of liberals, progressives and intellectuals. Ranged against them in the anti-Dreyfusard camp were the political right, monarchists, anti-semites, clericals and nationalists claiming to be the true defenders of nation and army. Bitter controversy in the press, the courts and the legislature tore the country apart until eventually in 1906 Dreyfus was recognised as innocent, reinstated and later awarded the Legion of Honour.

During this national hysteria Dreyfusards could present themselves as honest men representing decency and justice, while the conservative and Catholic senior officers of the army, hitherto accepted as willing to serve the republic, were now revealed as anti-semitic, prepared to forge documents and to keep an innocent man in prison in order to preserve the face and prestige of the General Staff. The well-known writer Emile Zola was forced to flee the country after being tried and found guilty on a charge of treason, following his newspaper accusation that the Ministry of War had committed a crime. In nine years of fevered controversy the army became decoupled from the political stage, its leaders widely – if wrongly –

suspected of planning a *coup d'état*. Once again questions were asked about the nature of the army and the choice of its officers.

It was in part a consequence of the passions aroused that the 1902 French elections returned a radical legislature which from 1903, under a small-minded Prime Minister, Combes, set out in a crude manner to separate Church from State and ensure that only true republicans would control the civil service and the army. The latter, to the disgust and horror of many of its officers, was directed to participate in the forcible expropriation of a number of religious institutions. Within the War Ministry a republican general, André, had earlier, in 1900, been appointed as minister. André saw his duty as that of 'republicanising' the officer corps, officers were to help teach republican values and democracy, disassociating themselves from any Catholic upbringing and schooling. He immediately singled out certain officers of known Republican and Dreyfusard views for fast-track promotion but also to organise a system of files *(fiches)*, in which officers spied upon one another. Many known regular churchgoers in the infantry and cavalry, among them Foch, were passed over for promotion, while officers of the logistic services, where a higher proportion were republican, were advanced – to the detriment of combat efficiency. Being seen to eat fish on a Friday could blight an officer's career. This so-called *affaire des fiches* led to the fall of the government and André in 1904 but military morale slumped in the climate of suspicion and the overt political correctness displayed by ambitious officers. In the highly anti-military political climate of the time the length of compulsory service was in 1905 reduced from three years to two, so cutting the size of the standing army by over 100,000.

To discredit the army still further, troops were used to put down industrial disquiet in 1906 and 1907, so straining discipline. A regiment recruited from a Languedoc wine-growing area, one scene of unrest, actually mutinied and conscripts from other areas were openly restive. By 1910 the French army was in very poor shape, with large numbers of desertions among soldiers and reservists failing to report for training. Officers were badly paid, with poor promotion prospects and inadequate pensions. Recruitment suffered, with many units short of officers. At the top, the retiring ages, sixty for a colonel, sixty-five for a general, left too many elderly officers in commands, men brave enough but simply past their peak when faced with the physical and nervous fatigue of battle.

The Nation Unites

Increasing German militarism, however, in particular the visit in 1911 of a German warship to Agadir in Morocco, considered a French preserve, began slowly to reawaken national awareness. The mood now changed again, the army returning to popular favour. A compromise was reached. In 1913, faced with the harsh reality of the worsening population imbalance between France and Germany, together with Germany's formidable industrialisation, the length of conscript service was extended to three years; the first year was to be devoted to basic training, the second to appropriate specialist training and in the third to training the best conscripts as NCOs. By 1914, therefore, the army was provided with an additional 200,000 men.

Two further factors were to prove of great benefit and support to the French army in the ordeal to come. The first was the living in the field and combat experience gained by many French officers and soldiers, among them Joffre, in colonial wars. This experience and the development of the North African army and La Coloniale, with its sponsored African tirailleurs, was to provide France with vast additional manpower resources in the war. Moreover, active colonial service developed powers of initiative among officers whose normal careers would otherwise have been the garrison monotony of conscript training, and the campaigns themselves tested equipments and provided opportunities for new ideas – aerial reconnaissance, for example, was first used by the French army in Morocco in 1913. Secondly, the educational reforms of Jules Ferry when Minister for Public Instruction in the 1880s came to bear rich fruit. These reforms provided the cultural formation for the ordinary conscript soldiers, still mainly countrymen from small towns and villages. By 1914 conscripts, as schoolboys, had all received a free, compulsory, secular primary education in which the leitmotif was patriotism, pro-military and egalitarian – a redefinition, almost a reinvention, of France. The nation was presented as suffering, mutilated by the amputation of Alsace and Lorraine. Two examples indicate the process at work. In a Basse-Alpes village school there were three lessons each week devoted to patriotic and military themes, daily singing of patriotic songs, and talks about the Crimean and Franco-Prussian wars. The future General Humbert, in 1913 serving with the 140th Infantry at Grenoble, noted how parents and teachers had brought up their young with the memory of the 1870 war, and that pacifists and anti-militarists were presented simply as eccentric and insignificant. The patriotic cult was furthered in the field of art by military painters, in particular Edouard Détaille, with works portraying heroism in the 1870 fighting.

The army, through its system of military regions and subdistricts that arranged the draft of conscripts into regiments linked to particular departments, maintained a much higher profile in pre-1914 France than in Britain. The military supported local shooting and gymnastic societies for teenage boys as a preparation for the draft. Military service was seen as the norm, part of the pattern of everyday life. Even amid the peasant culture of Languedoc, where poverty had created a rural radicalism, the duty of military service was, with some resignation, accepted. Everywhere the high point of the annual Bastille Day celebrations was the local military parade.

In service the flame of patriotism was fanned as recruits were instructed in the traditions of their regiments and came to take pride in them. Humbert accepted that there were on occasion *de torpeur et d'inertie* ... and a *fonctionnaire* spirit among conscripts, but added that in conversation with soldiers he found an acceptance of the needs and sacrifices of warfare, the compulsion to do one's duty, together with confidence in their commanders, the offensive strategy and eventual victory at the point of the bayonet.

The years between 1911 and the outbreak of war saw some drawing together of nation and army. Within the army, although correct political views still counted, Joffre selected Castelnau, an aristocrat and member of a distinguished military family but known as *le Capucin botté* for his deep Catholic convictions, as Chief-of-Staff, in recognition of his abilities. In politics, the 1914 elections saw a victory of the anti-military left, but the determination of the President, Poincaré, a man from Lorraine, ensured the preservation of the three-year conscription law in a political trade-off permitting income tax legislation. The enormously popular and influential socialist leader, Jaurès, wrote and spoke out in favour of preparation for war in the form of an army of the people in face of the German threat – until his assassination by a nationalist fanatic on 31 July 1914. At the outbreak of war Poincaré called for a *union sacrée*, a call that met with universal acceptance, extremes of right and left and all social classes rallying to the defence of *la patrie*. Viviani, the Prime Minister, broadened his government to reflect all political groups, Millerand, a Socialist, replacing Messimy as War Minister.

In this national mood of patriotism, mobilisation proceeded with very little difficulty. The actual process was by stages, according to the category of reserve. The number of deserters,

1.5 per cent, fell well below the level that had been anticipated. While the street crowds, in the belief that the war was bound to be short, cheered soldiers on their way to the stations, the general mood among the men was more reserved. Almost universally shared was a resolute acceptance of a duty, together with feeling of solidarity and a certain sense of relief that the war, so long expected had finally arrived, *L'heure a sonné*. Many took the opportunity of a farewell binge. Two of the most popular farewells from relatives were '*Sois prudent*' and '*Sois bon soldat*'. On 5 August the government set out arrangements for the payment of an allowance of Fr 1.25 per day together with an extra 0.50 for each child under sixteen for families in need following the mobilisation. The amount was of more use for agricultural labour families than those in the towns and in industry, but was nevertheless welcomed by all. Enthusiasm was displayed during patrol work in the first days of the war. In one brush with the Germans in Lorraine the French army sustained its first casualty, Corporal Peugeot; in another the young Lieutenant de Lattre, a future Marshal of France, serving with the 12th Dragoons, received the first of his several wounds.

The French army, then, entered the war with sound morale, confident that the nation was now behind it, but with serious leadership weaknesses at command, regimental officer and non-commissioned officer levels, together with serious material and training deficiencies, that stemmed from years of political strife or indifference. Tasked for offensive operations and constrained by the general belief in the limited value of reservists, events after the first disastrous three weeks of August were to highlight the exact reverse – a valour, determination and skill in defensive operations in the standing army and reserve units alike.

CHAPTER 3

1914

Manoeuvre War, The German Advance to the Marne

The failure of the great French frontier offensives marked an important stage in a process that had already, slowly and belatedly begun, that of forcing the French army into specific proactive operations in face of the developing German war of movement. The operations overlapped. As already seen, the first French offensives had been checked while the German attacks were under way; throughout, from the start, the Germans had been on the march through Belgium.

The German strategy in 1914, based on the plan of General Count von Schlieffen, Chief of the German General Staff from 1891 to 1906, is well known. France was to be knocked out quickly in four weeks before Russia could fully mobilise; after the defeat of France it was hoped that Russia could be dealt with, or at least contained. The plan was based on a meticulously time-tabled, massive right-wing enveloping movement of some forty divisions through Belgium, so providing space for the full deployment of German numerical advantage including reserves, and avoiding the necessity of attacking the heavily defended and fortified French frontier regions. If Belgian acquiescence was not forthcoming, a drastic military occupation, extending to the shooting of civilians in any areas of opposition, was to be imposed on the civil population, thus reducing the number of reserve units necessary for occupation.

The French army's deployment was well known, and neither the Belgian nor the British armies – if the latter actually arrived in time or at all – were thought to be serious obstacles. Once across the Belgian-French frontier, the right-wing armies, 700,000 men, would turn to encircle Paris and cut off the capital from the French armies on the frontier. To keep these armies where they were, the German left flank was to remain weak, tempting the French to attack. As a strategy it was flawed by its dogmatic inflexibility in day-to-day time-tabling and its serious underestimation of French defensive capabilities – compounded, in execution, with the irresolution of Schlieffen's successor, Moltke, which led the separate elderly and irascible army commanders to pursue their own goals. At formation level the strategy was further flawed by poor communications, and at soldier level by sheer physical exhaustion and shortage of forage for cavalry and horse-drawn artillery.

Joffre's failure to recognise his mortal danger, and his obsession throughout the first three weeks of the war that the more Germans there were, the greater would be their ultimate defeat, played straight into German hands. Joffre's options were further constrained by the Paris government's refusal to allow any French pre-emptive entry into Belgium, its requirement that he withdraw troops 10 kilometres from the frontier to avoid any clash that the Germans might claim as a provocation, and finally by the general belief that the great Belgian fortresses of Liège and Namur would check any German advance west of the Meuse.

As early as 5 August, however, combat intelligence reaching Joffre supplemented the strategic intelligence already available, and was, again, to be largely ignored. From the 8th to the 14th, while the Germans were inexorably gaining control of the Liège area, Joffre's intelligence staff were playing down the reports of the numbers of German army corps in

Belgium, including the warnings provided by Lanrezac's staff that at least six German army corps were attacking Liège. Belgian army intelligence warnings were also ignored. On the 12th, French intelligence assessed that there might already be eight German corps and four cavalry divisions in Belgium, but Joffre's only response was to authorise the move of I Corps of Lanrezac's Army to Dinant; the rest of the 5th Army was to be kept available for his planned Ardennes offensive. Joffre still hoped that the Belgian army, with the British, would try to hold eastern Belgium rather than retreat to the coast at Antwerp – as in the event proved its choice. On 14 August, the day that Dubail's 1st and Castelnau's 2nd Armies began their offensive, Joffre had two visitors at his headquarters at Vitry-le-François. Both warned him of their concerns. The first was Lanrezac who pointed out that the known German force in Belgium was equal to his own army and the British Expeditionary Force (BEF) combined. He urged Joffre not to commit Ruffey's 3rd and de Langle's 4th Armies to any offensive. Joffre insisted that the Germans would remain east and south of the Meuse. The second visitor was France's most famous colonial campaign general, Joseph Galliéni, supposedly the successor to Joffre in case of emergency but at Joffre's insistence limited to working in an office in Paris. After only a brief courtesy interview, he was handed over to Joffre's Chief-of-Staff, General Belin, and his deputy, General Berthelot.

On his return to his own headquarters Lanrezac was told that there were eight German corps in Belgium and on the next day, 15 August, Joffre himself was informed that the Germans had crossed the Meuse at Huy and that I Corps, now commanded by General Franchet d'Esperey, had been under heavy attack in the Dinant area on the previous day. Among its one thousand casualties was the wounded Lieutenant Charles de Gaulle, serving with the 33rd Infantry, a regiment he had chosen out of admiration for its colonel, Philippe Pétain.

Sambre and Meuse

In response Joffre ordered Lanrezac to march his army more than 100 kilometres, in August heat, to the angle formed by the Rivers Sambre and Meuse at Namur. By this time Lanrezac's army had already lost XI Corps, men from Brittany, which had joined the 4th Army for the Ardennes attack. In exchange he had received a group of three reserve divisions, elements of XVIII Corps, men from Bordeaux, Gascons, Basques and Béarnais, en route from Castelnau's army, two extra divisions formed from the white population of Algeria, and the exhausted horsemen of Sordet's cavalry returning from an abortive mission to persuade the Belgian army to form a left flank rather than concentrate around Antwerp. Joffre's orders for Lanrezac were still primarily in the context of preparation for an attack, but he did arrange, as a first precaution, that three reserve divisions under General d'Amade be deployed on a line from Maubeuge to the Channel.

On 16 August, the day the last defences of Liège finally fell, Joffre told Field Marshal Sir John French, the apprehensive and cautious commander of the BEF, that he still believed that, apart from troops used to take Liège, the only German forces in Belgium were cavalry. French's visit to Joffre had, for reasons of personality and language, hardly been a meeting of minds, the cavalryman in French viewing Joffre with some squirearchical distaste, but at least agreeing to deploy the BEF by the 20th, three days earlier than he had advised President Poincaré on the previous day. French's meeting with Lanrezac on 17 August was even less cordial, leaving the able but Anglo-phobe Lanrezac with the clear, and correct, impression that French was going to put the wider interests of the British army before any co-ordinated action, and returning to the 24th as the earliest day for any British deployment. Nevertheless, the rumoured whereabouts of the BEF had also caused the Germans some anxiety, leading them to place Kluck's 1st Army, much to his rage, temporarily under Bülow, commander of the centre of the three right-wing armies, as Moltke feared the BEF might appear between them.

On the 18th, the massive German advance in Belgium was proceeding remorselessly, so giving the lie to Joffre's assurances that the force was merely a cavalry screen. King Albert of the Belgians, doubtful as to the arrival of any French help, made his decision to withdraw his army to the Antwerp area. In the event this was later to prove useful as a threat to Kluck's flank, requiring him to detach a reserve corps to secure his lines of communication. Joffre, encouraged by the 1st Army's apparent success at Sarrebourg, issued to the 3rd and 4th Armies in Special Directive No. 13 the clear orders already set out in Chapter One for the Ardennes offensive. Instructions for the 5th Army were far less clear but, despite their dismissive reference to the 'northern group', nevertheless did represent Joffre's first acceptance of some major operational need to react to the German strategy rather than a completely heedless pursuit of his own plans. The 5th Army, already on its way, was given two options. If the German strength in Belgium was established to have increased to thirteen or more corps, of which possibly eight north of the Sambre and Meuse turned south to the Ardennes, then the 5th Army was to leave the Sambre line to the BEF and the Belgians and join the battle, perceived as decisive, in the Ardennes. But if these eight corps remained on the move north of the Sambre–Meuse line, then Lanrezac was to join with the Belgians and the BEF to guard the front's left flank and outflank the Germans, a contingency not previously envisaged in any staff planning.

For Lanrezac, however, this order increased all and resolved none of his problems. He had no certain news of the

BEF, which he distrusted, and both his flanks seemed dangerously exposed, at least until de Langle's 4th Army arrived on
his right. In the absence of any firm guidance from Joffre he
decided to advance to the Sambre, to cross it and hold a line
from Namur to Charleroi. His troops received a great welcome
from the Belgians, and firm discipline was applied, even summary execution on French soldiers who looted. By the 20th,
the day the German army rode and marched through Brussels,
Lanrezac's weary troops were moving into position; Franchet
d'Esperey's I Corps was on the Meuse, a river whose open
country banks favoured defence as an opponent's moves were
easy to observe and counter with artillery. Outpost parties of
III (Normans and Parisians) and XI Corps were across the
Sambre between Charleroi and Namur in the Borinage, an area
of densely populated small towns and villages easy to infiltrate, difficult to hold. On their left was General Defforges's X
Corps, men from Rennes and Brittany. A heavy German
artillery bombardment in the Charleroi area indicated what
was to come. Back at his headquarters, despite the uncertain-
ties in the Sambre–Meuse triangle and the German attacks on
the 1st and 2nd Armies checking their advance, Joffre confirmed his orders for the 3rd and 4th Army attacks, expecting
Lanrezac to do the same.

The next day, the 21st, began to expose the unreality and
dangers of Lanrezac's position. Elements of Bülow's 2nd Army,
which with Kluck's 1st Army temporarily under command
totalled eleven infantry and two cavalry corps, found bridges
unguarded and managed to cross the Sambre on a broad front,
while Hausen's three-corps-strong 3rd Army, the left flank
army of the great German right enveloping attack, moved to
attack along the Meuse. Lanrezac vacillated – and received no
guidance from Joffre – over whether to hold the Sambre on the
north or the south side. Furthermore, he had been asked by the
hard-pressed Belgians for help, in particular artillery, for the

defence of Namur; the best he could afford was an infantry brigade.

The engagements that followed, known as the battle of Charleroi, or the Sambre, were at the outset ragged, neither side having prepared for a full battle. On the morning of the 22nd the three French corps on the Sambre, aiming to regain lost ground, mounted counter-attacks. By this time, however, Lanrezac had decided a massive attack would end in failure and had issued countermanding orders – which never reached their destination. The X Corps bayonet attacks suffered severely at the hands of the machine-guns of the Prussian Guards, the III Corps attack ran into a fierce German assault and was shattered and forced to retreat. Casualties in the three corps totalled over 6,000. Only the timely arrival of XVIII Corps averted a disaster. Further German assaults the next day compelled the French again to retreat. Lanrezac had unwisely ordered I Corps to move to the aid of X Corps, but his replacement for this corps on the Meuse, a single reserve division, was unable to prevent a crossing by Hausen's troops. In haste Franchet d'Esperey returned to his former positions from which he mounted a vigorous counter-attack. This, although successful, failed to check German progress; nor did a small-scale counter-attack directed by General Mangin. Late on the 23rd Lanrezac issued orders to the entire 5th Army to withdraw south to a line Givet–Maubeuge. He had made no effort to co-ordinate his plans with the BEF on his left and – with more reason – was apprehensive about the 4th Army on his right. There was, however, a compensation. The German placement of Kluck's army under Bülow had delayed its advance, giving the BEF time to move to the Condé Canal and prevent a wide outflanking movement. To justify his withdrawal to Joffre, Lanrezac misrepresented this, despite the fact that the BEF, with its well-trained regular troops and their Lee-Enfield rifles (the best in Europe) was actually securing his left flank. This withdrawal, which he did not properly notify to French, left the BEF exposed and also obliged to retire. Lanrezac's retreat, together with those of the 3rd and 4th Armies, forced the French army entirely on to the defensive. The attacks of the German 6th and 7th Armies in Lorraine can only have added to Joffre's worries, although Castelnau's and Foch's success in repelling them, so saving Nancy, was to earn Foch almost immediate promotion. The heavy fortress guns of Toul and Epinal to the east, directed at night by searchlights, in some measure remedied the deficiencies of the French artillery.

The Great Retreat

Joffre now sought to conduct a fighting withdrawal on his left, issuing somewhat vague orders to the 4th and 5th Armies to prepare 'before Amiens ... or behind the Somme' for a resumption of offensive operations along with the BEF and the new, hurriedly assembled 6th Army of General Maunoury, tasked to move around to the left of the BEF and attack the German right wing west to east on its flank. By 1 September, after frenzied railway activity involving some 160 trains, Maunoury's army now included VII Corps from the 1st Army and V Corps from the 3rd Army together with four reserve divisions, mostly men from Lorraine, Auvergne, Brittany and the Charente. Another makeshift force, later to become the 9th Army, was given to Foch and tasked to fill the gap between the 4th and 5th Armies as they withdrew. Foch was also presented with a new and exceptionally able staff officer, Maxime Weygand, so beginning one of the most remarkable military partnerships in history. As Joffre had not clearly set out at the start of this, the Great Retreat, where it was to stop, the BEF and Lanrezac had to travel distances of 95 to 140 kilometres before reaching the Somme. For Lanzerac's army it was an epic withdrawal, made possible by skilful rearguard action and very effective supporting 75mm artillery fire. The roads were clogged with haggard and unshaven men, uniforms covered in dust, in utter exhaustion, often shuffling heads down rather than marching, some collapsing from fatigue or sunstroke; by the roadsides lay fallen men, dead or dying horses and abandoned equipment. No one knew when the retreat would end and many believed the truth was being concealed from them. The writer Céline (Louis Destouches), serving with the 12th Cuirassiers, calculated that his horse had covered 679 kilometres during August. The French fighting withdrawal was nevertheless marked by several small but notable successes, in particular at Le Cateau on 26 August. Here the arrival on the scene of Sordet's Cavalry Corps played an important part in saving the BEF's II Corps from disaster; and General d'Amade's gallant 84th Territorial reserve division on the BEF's left (a division of men long past their prime), prevented the German II Corps of Kluck's army from entering the main battle.

Sir John French, seriously unnerved by the withdrawal and the casualties suffered by the British II Corps, needed French support if he was to retain the BEF in the line. Accordingly Joffre ordered Lanrezac to hold a line linked by the Somme and the Oise, St Quentin–Guise, and then attack. He found a personal visit and very plain words necessary to secure the compliance of the surly 5th Army commander, not altogether inexcusable as the BEF had just withdrawn from St Quentin, exposing his flank. The next day, the 29th, saw a hard-fought battle when the pressure on the severely suffering X and III Corps at St Quentin was eased by an epic attack at Guise by the I Corps of Franchet d'Esperey, the general himself on horseback in the midst of his men, bands playing and regimental colours flying.

More than valour, however, was needed to check the momentum of the German armies' sweeping advance towards the Seine. This advance, now mistakenly ordered by Moltke to be along the entire front rather than Schlieffen's concentration upon the right wing, was slowed down but not checked by the withdrawal of two corps to meet the Russian advance in East Prussia, the need to detach formations to contain the Belgians in Antwerp, the stout resistance of the 48,000 men, mostly Territorial reservists, of General Fournier at Maubeuge from 27 August to 7 September, and counter-attacks by the 3rd and 4th Armies to cover the flank of Foch's 9th Army. On 2 September Kluck's vanguards had reached Senlis, while Bülow and Hausen had crossed the Vesle, and Bülow was soon to cross the Marne. On the evening of the 3rd small detachments of Germans reached and crossed the Seine and were within eight miles of Paris. Reims, whose protective forts were unmanned, fell to the Germans on the following day.

By the end of the month French casualties – dead, wounded, prisoners or missing – totalled 200,000; units had been reduced to remnants, many officers traumatised. Disaster seemed inescapable. The Germans menaced not only Paris but vital railway lines to the armies of the centre and right, supply depots and factories producing essential war materials. The French government and the Bank of France left Paris for Bordeaux. Joffre himself was forced to move his headquarters twice, on 1 September to Bar-sur-Aube and again on the 5th to Châtillon-sur-Seine.

The desperate situation called for desperate measures. First Joffre reminded all officers and NCOs that they had the right to use force against deserters. On 1 September he obtained permission from the government that except in special cases, court-martial death sentences were to be carried out within twenty-four hours; on the 6th the system of court-martials was extended to unit level, three members of the regiment forming the judges. Desertion or disobedience in face of the enemy was punishable by execution. Firing squads of twelve carried out the sentences after a formal ceremony of degradation in which the buttons were ripped off the victim's tunic. On 3 September Joffre dismissed Lanrezac, a personal friend. Lanrezac's open criticism of him had reached his ears and it was clear that despite his ability as a general the 5th Army commander's rebarbative personality could never work with the BEF. Also progressively removed were Ruffey, ten corps commanders, thirty-three of the seventy-two infantry division generals, five of the ten cavalry division generals and a number of brigade commanders. The term *limogé*, posted to Limoges far from the front, entered French military vocabulary. The spirited Franchet d'Esperey was given the 5th Army, more questionably Sarrail was given the 3rd. Colonels who were seen to have fought well, among them Pétain and Nivelle, were given brigades. Firm control restored cohesion and discipline to the army.

The woefully weak Paris garrison of five Territorial divisions was hurriedly reinforced by General Drude's 45th Division, Zouaves and Tirailleurs Algériens from Algeria, together with a brigade of *fusiliers marins*, mostly recalled Breton reservist sailors under Rear Admiral Ronarc'h. The capital's fortifications were obsolescent and poorly maintained. The garrison's unpreparedness was a major cause in the departure from office of Messimy, and his replacement by Millerand as Minister of War. Although in indifferent health, Galliéni was appointed military governor on 26 August, and Maunoury's 6th Army together with 5,000 newly arrived Moroccans were placed under his command as the 'Armies of Paris'. With volcanic energy Galliéni set about organising the capital's defence, civilian *paniquards* were encouraged to leave, woods, trees and buildings that impeded the fields of fire of the city's 370, 120 and 125mm guns were ruthlessly cleared away, bridges were mined, the Eiffel Tower prepared for demolition and the *fusiliers marins* set to work as reconnaissance patrols. For Joffre, however, what mattered was not Paris but the impending battle.

On 3 September Galliéni received reports from aircraft reconnaissance that Kluck had suddenly decided to change his 1st Army's line of advance, now wheeling it to the south-east and leaving Paris on the right, initially to destroy the 5th Army and then to form the right arm of a pincer cutting off all the French armies. This move was to prove a fatal operational error. Kluck apparently made it in the belief that the BEF had all but been destroyed. Galliéni passed the reports on to Joffre who had received similar intelligence. Both generals saw the opportunity for a large-scale enveloping counter-attack against the weary and overstretched Germans. On 4 September, Joffre, at Galliéni's insistence, issued orders directing the 6th Army, which had completed its move to the left of the BEF and regained control of two divisions that had lost their way, to mount an attack eastward, on Kluck's flank, together with the BEF attacking north-eastward; the 5th was to strike north, the 9th was to cover Sézanne and the Saint Gond marshlands. On his right the 4th Army was to contain the Germans while the 3rd, on the extreme right, was to attack the German flank from the east. French, at Joffre's special pleading, reluctantly concurred the following day, during which two divisions and the Moroccans of Maunoury's army had already begun to attack Kluck's flank. A small incident was to have a wide moral effect on the French army. A lieutenant, Charles de la Cornillière, fatally wounded, rallied his men with his last words: 'Yes, the lieutenant is dead, but keep steady.' At dawn on 6 September, Joffre issued a stirring order of the day proclaiming that the fate of the country was at stake, soldiers must be prepared to die rather than retreat, and no weaknesses would be tolerated; there had been cases of officers having to force men back to the front with revolvers, and of self-inflicted wounds.

So began the series of engagements known collectively as

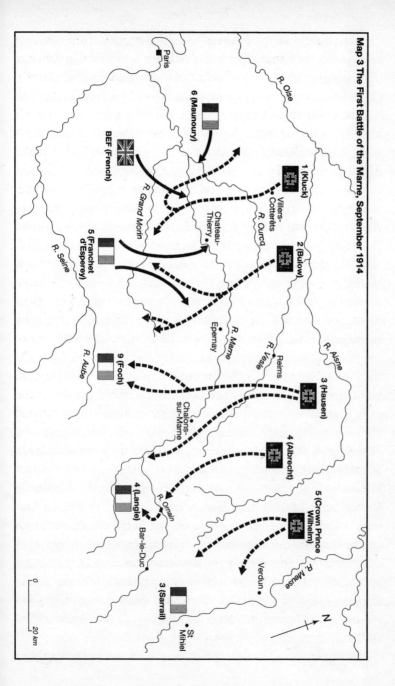

Map 3 The First Battle of the Marne, September 1914

the first battle of the Marne, one of the war's truly decisive encounters, to be fought in the heat of a late summer by men increasingly exhausted by marches and counter-marches. The German attempt to overrun France was to fail, their best chance of victory to be lost. The scale reflected the respective nations' mass mobilisations – 900,000 Germans with 3,300 guns, 100,000 British and 980,000 French soldiers with 3,000 guns of which only 180 were heavy. Although Rupprecht and Heeringen, on the German left, had had to yield formations to the critical Paris basin fronts, both of their armies renewed their attacks on Nancy. Castelnau and Dubail, whose armies had also lost trained regulars, had to fight as tenaciously as those on the Marne itself. Observers described how the French infantry sprang from their trenches as the Germans advanced. Their cold steel turned back the Germans, who were then fired upon by the French 75mm guns – at their most devastating against infantry on open ground – as they withdrew.

The Germans, although surprised by the French attacks, were able to halt them by artillery superiority throughout 6 September. On the 7th Kluck ordered his southernmost corps to face about and march north-west towards the Ourcq River, his intention being to win a spectacular victory by destroying Maunoury's 6th Army, its primary mission – the envelopment of Paris – forgotten. His manoeuvre opened a wide gap, over 35 kilometres, between his left and the right flank of Bülow's Second Army. Bülow, alarmed, began to move his right formations south-west to try to close the gap, requesting Hausen to secure his left. In the next two days the battles developed. In the 'battle of the Ourcq' Maunoury's 6th Army, although stiffened by a further division of de Langle's 4th Army under the command of General Trentinian (mostly rushed in by requisitioned lorries but with five battalions, all organised by Galliéni, arriving by means of 600 Paris Renault taxis each carrying five men), was, nevertheless, reduced to the defence, facing as it did the bulk of Kluck's 1st Army with regiments well dug in and protected by artillery. Massive and furious German attacks by the 3rd, 4th and 5th Armies were contained by the armies of Foch, de Langle and Sarrail in violent fighting. The French 75mm gunners, known to the Germans as the 'black butchers', mowed down the attackers. The tide of the battle began to turn when the BEF, part of Franchet d'Esperey's 5th Army and General Conneau's Cavalry Corps advanced towards the Marne and the Ourcq. They thereby threatened to envelop Kluck's army from the north and cut it off from Bülow, whose army was already in danger of being deflected on its right by the ferocious attacks of the bulk of Franchet d'Esperey's army. The latter, however, had his own problems, which prevented him from following up the BEF success. On his right, Foch, despite Joffre's orders to stand fast, had characteristically met the attacks of the armies of Bülow and Hausen with aggressive but very costly counter-attacks, which the Germans, who had dug in, had thrown back. These counter-attacks may have been seen by Foch as necessary to fill gaps in the French defence, but critics have seen them as rash products of the offensive doctrine. The pressure on him had to be relieved urgently, Franchet d'Esperey, of necessity, providing a corps.

The next day, 9 September, saw the crisis. The BEF and the left formation of the French 5th Army crossed the Marne while the rest of the 5th repulsed Bülow's counter-attacks. The Germans, in particular Moltke, lost their nerve and to the fury of Kluck, still confident of a spectacular victory over Maunoury, ordered Bülow's 2nd Army to withdraw. To avoid isolation Kluck had no option but to follow suit. On the 10th the German 3rd and 4th Armies, and on the 13th also the 5th were all ordered to retreat, Reims was evacuated, and the bulk of Heeringen's 7th Army was hurriedly moved from Alsace to bolster the German right wing. Only the exhaustion of the BEF

– and its commander – prevented a vigorous follow-up and a German disaster. The German weakening of their Alsace Vosges formations was matched by the necessary withdrawal from the line, to regroup, of Castelnau's 2nd Army, leaving Dubail alone on the French right, from where he nevertheless reoccupied Lunéville. But the Germans formed a strong defensive line from the Oise south of Noyon, along the high ground behind the Aisne to the Meuse north of Verdun, and to the south of Saint-Mihiel. The German army, too, had given thought and pre-war training to wire and trench defensive systems, which the French had ignored and were now to pay the price as trench warfare began to replace a war of movement. Acute ammunition shortages – even in the Marne sector guns were rationed to 200–400 rounds per day – prevented the French from harassing the Germans as they dug in. German artillery, on the other hand, included heavy howitzers able to bombard the French whose 75mm guns had lacked the necessary range and trajectory. At German headquarters Moltke was replaced by von Falkenhayn, Hausen by von Einem and a number of other commanders relieved of their commands. On the French side, Galliéni's 'Armies of Paris' was broken up, the 6th Army returning to Joffre's direct command.

Mid-September was to see the first example of the slogging infantry trench warfare to come. Joffre ordered an attack by Maunoury's exhausted 6th Army, the BEF and on the right the 5th Army against the German positions on the steep, scrubby heights north of the Aisne and the Chemin des Dames – the road along the high ridge parallel to the river named, according to legend, after the favourite carriage ride of the daughters of Louis XV. The attack, on 13 September, in wind and heavy rain, was badly co-ordinated. Despite an initial success by General Mangin's 5th Division at Brimont, the attack failed, mainly due to the superiority of the German defence. The French artillery was once again outgunned and severely short of ammunition, and the infantry was mowed down by well-sited German machine-gun positions on the heights. Two battalions surrendered at Brimont and the German counter-attack at Courcy put the French defenders to flight – the first significant warning to French formation commanders of the dangers of pushing men too far. Conneau's Cavalry Corps missed a fine opportunity to strike at German lines of communication; after a successful crossing they halted, horses and men being exhausted and in danger of being cut off. A German counter-attack finally retook the Brimont fort but failed in its objective of reoccupying Reims, although setting the magnificent cathedral ablaze. Heavy fighting continued until 18 September with intermittent fighting further east until the 27th.

Significant for the future, however, had been German operations in the pivotal Verdun area, where an attempt to turn the flank of the 3rd Army was halted by fire from obsolescent forts along the Meuse supported by a few tractor-drawn 120mm guns. One fort, Troyon, ten miles south of Verdun with a garrison of less than 500 under Commandant Toussaint, fought off a five-day bombardment and siege that had begun on 8 September before being overwhelmed. Joffre had accepted a withdrawal from Verdun and its complex of fortresses; the 3rd Army Commander, Sarrail, had wisely decided otherwise. But on 26 September, after a violent artillery bombardment, a second fortress, Camp des Romains between Toul and Verdun, was forced to surrender and a German salient around Saint-Mihiel created. The salient cut one of the main railway lines to Verdun, the other main line fell under the range of German guns following their attack in the Argonne.

In Lorraine, some 300 men under Captain de Colbert, cut off and left behind in August, carried on a guerrilla campaign against German lines of communication until December, by which time all had been caught.

The Race to the Sea

The last attempt, for many years, at a war of movement followed briefly, with the 'race to the sea' in Flanders, each side moving armies northward hoping to outflank the other. Joffre hoped for an envelopment of the Germans in the Bapaume area, a project beyond French strength. His headquarters moved again, on 26 September, to Romilly-sur-Seine. He agreed to the transfer of the BEF to the north where, under Foch as *adjoint au commandant en chef*, were Castelnau's reorganised 2nd Army, a new 10th Army commanded by Maud'huy, d'Amade's four Territorial divisions, now under the command of seventy-four-year-old General Brugère, and the Cavalry Corps of Conneau and de Mitry. Castelnau found himself under the command of his former subordinate. Fighting as desperate as any on the Marne raged until mid-November. An attack designed to threaten Kluck's right flank on 17 September by Maunoury's 6th Army on the Oise was a failure. Castelnau likewise was unable to attack, but from 2 to 7 October he checked first the German 6th and then the 2nd Army in Picardy, while Maud'huy fought with similar grim determination in Artois. Territorial units valiantly held the German cavalry in the Arras area until relieved by regiments of General Legrand-Girarde's elite XXI Corps drawn from the 1st Army; and Mitry's hastily assembled I Cavalry Corps temporarily checked the Germans at Hazebrouck on 10 October, reoccupying the line of the Lys. But after three days of heavy bombardment Lille surrendered on the same day. An offensive launched on 12 October against Rupprecht's 6th Army by the BEF, Maud'huy's 10th Army and the two cavalry corps, ended as a costly failure after three days. On 16 October Albrecht's 4th Army attacked the Belgian army supported by 6,000 of Ronarc'h's *fusiliers marins*, several thousand French

Territorials and a British division along the line of the Yser. The fighting was over mud or water-logged terrain, in harsh weather conditions, and once again with marked German artillery superiority. *The fusiliers marins*, still wearing their sailors' blue berets with red pom-poms, suffered particularly severely but fought well to hold Dixmude; the defenders of the town also included four companies of Tirailleurs Sénégalais. Nevertheless by 22 October, despite brave counter-attacks by General Grossetti's 42nd Infantry Division, the Germans crossed and maintained a bridgehead over the Yser. This advance forced the Belgians to open the Nieuport sluices, thereby progressively flooding the area, leaving German soldiers and horses floundering. The only part of the front left for manoeuvre was around Ypres.

Foch had been unable to help the Belgians as he was preparing to use his only immediately available formation – the corps and divisions of a newly formed 8th Army under General d'Urbal together with the BEF – in an offensive towards Roulers. His plan lacked reality, or more precisely accurate combat intelligence, as the German command was planning an enveloping movement to cut off the BEF and the Belgians, assembling a massive force (its size long underestimated) of two armies with an additional six division reinforcement, to the north-east and south-east of Ypres. Defence of the city, the first battle of Ypres, followed, beginning on 29 October. The hard-pressed divisions of the British army shared the burden of the German assaults, first with Mitry's Cavalry Corps and the 89th and 87th French Territorial Divisions on the British left, and then with General Dubois's IX Corps, hurriedly transferred from the Reims area to relieve the northern part of the sector of General Haig's I Corps. There followed the progressive arrival of five divisions of General Grossetti's XVI Corps and Conneau's II Cavalry Corps on the right, later moved to the centre. All were urged to attack by Foch, whose

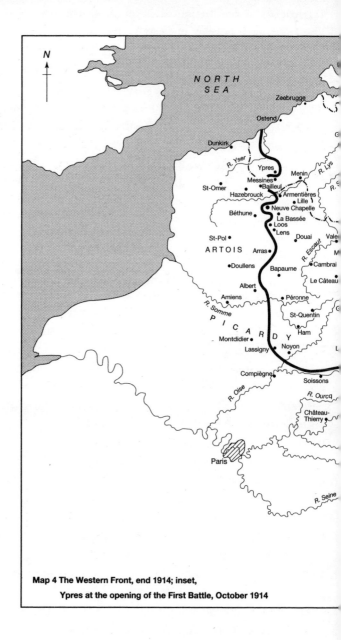

Map 4 The Western Front, end 1914; inset,

Ypres at the opening of the First Battle, October 1914

command throughout was inspirational for both the British and his own commanders and troops. French support for the British, in particular help provided by Dubois, displayed Anglo-French co-operation at its best.

The battle, in effect along the whole 50-kilometre line from Dixmude to the Lys, raged until 5 November, with bitter fighting and complex movements of troops north and south of Ypres. Although on 10 November Dixmude was eventually lost and fighting at a reduced level was to continue until 17 November, the Germans were unable to break through and the battle represented a significant victory for the joint efforts of Foch and the BEF. By late November both sides were exhausted, the Flanders battles having added a further 50,000 to the French casualty list of killed, wounded, prisoners or missing. But it was at Ypres, rather than the Marne, where another of Germany's long-term pre-war strategies unravelled, as the inadequately trained reservists with officers and NCOs recalled from retirement were decimated, suffering over 60,000 casualties in a battle for which they had neither the tactical imagination nor flexibility to handle.

A major factor in the French success was again the ability to move formations westward rapidly by rail and road. At its peak this entailed the use of 200 trains per day and of several hundred vehicles, all organised by two exceptionally able officers, Commandant Gérard and Captain Doumenc, utilising Belgian and captured German rolling stock to replace the heavy French losses of August. Similarly, the French were able to use domestic internal telephone and telegraph systems while German communications were always overextended.

The year 1914 ended with two poorly prepared and abortive major French offensives, one in the Arras area launched on 17 December and the second in Champagne on the 20th. Neither accomplished more than the capture of a first line of German trenches, the army commanders remaining inadequately supplied with heavy artillery and ammunition for their 75mm guns. Subsidiary attacks launched elsewhere along the front, including one at Ypres, and others in the Argonne in October and December, were all unsuccessful, and once again French casualties were heavy.

The 'Western Front' was now established from the Channel to Ypres, Arras, Soissons, Verdun, the Vosges and Alsace, 750 kilometres in length. The immediate threat to the survival of France was over. Joffre moved his headquarters to Chantilly on 28 November and the French government returned to Paris on 8 December. Galliéni and Joffre were, deservedly, the heroes of the hour, although the latter was later to prove ungenerous over Galliéni's substantial contribution. Joffre himself had repeatedly refused to accept unpalatable information and in consequence had made monumental strategic and operational errors. As a result, as many as 300,000 French dead, including many of the best officers, had been incurred in the first four months of the war. Throughout, and for the rest of his life, Joffre retained his belief in the offensive strategy, maintaining that in 1914 all that had happened was a result of mishandling, in particular the failure of artillery properly to prepare for attacks. But supreme command is not entirely a matter of strategy or tactics; it is in some measure also symbolic. Joffre, overweight and stolid, nevertheless possessed to a marked degree that essential quality of generalship described by Lord Wavell in his Lees Knowles lectures at Cambridge in 1936 as 'robustness', the ability to withstand the shocks of war. Almost always calm – a calm based on fixed daily routines of meals and sleep which were not to be disturbed on any account – and backed by an able Chief-of-Staff, General Belin, his deputy, General Berthelot, and a staff major, Maurice Gamelin, Joffre had carried his exhausted armies through a series of traumatic ordeals, retaining the confidence of his soldiers. Despite his personal comfortable life-style, Joffre was a true soldier, concerned for the welfare of his men, although never visiting them in the field. He knew how to get the best from his army and exercised effective control through regular personal conferences with commanders. Both before and at Ypres his resolution proved equally inspirational to Sir John French. Joffre's virtual dictatorship over the Zone des Armeés restrained political interference and enabled him, when he so wished, to withhold information from people and government alike. Such information as was released by his staff served more to reassure public confidence than provide an accurate picture of the battlefront scene. His headquarters, too, soon developed the characteristics of a court, with jealousies and intrigue. Yet when all around was chaos and doom, an army was preserved to fight on, its cohesion kept intact and with a will to win. Joffre was never caught in a German trap, always retaining freedom of manoeuvre. At the Marne he may not have won a spectacular victory, but he assuredly prevented a catastrophic defeat. In fact, the Marne was in those days a turning point, for as Winston Churchill was later to assert, the war was decided in these first twenty days of fighting. Germany's failure to overrun France condemned her to a war on two fronts, suffering attrition and a naval blockade – a war that could not be won.

The laurels of victory, however, ultimately rested on the ordinary French soldier. Morale in these early days of war, despite the retreats, long marches and occasional lapses, remained high, among regulars and reservists alike. Of two reserve divisions ordered to the attack by Joffre on 6 September an eyewitness wrote: 'During the period 1 to 5 September the men had made an all-out effort, some had marched 105 km in forty-eight hours without halt or food. The regimental doctors had advised that the men had reached their extreme physical limit. Despite all the efforts made to bring up food and rations, food supply was precarious, there was no time to cook the food, and one had the impression that the men had reached their absolute limit. Then on the afternoon of 5 September orders arrived for an attack co-ordinated with the 9th Army on the right, the 6th Army and the British on the left. Suddenly the men, forgetting their fatigue, rushed cheerfully forward, exhaustion and privations totally forgotten. In their first contacts with the enemy the men displayed a spirit and offensive vigour beyond anything that one could have imagined after the previous testing days.' In a tribute later paid to the French by one of their chief adversaries, General von Kluck observed: 'That men who have had to retreat for fifteen days, that men having had to sleep on the ground, half dead from fatigue, could at the sound of the bugle pick up their rifles and attack, was something we Germans had never appreciated; this was a possibility that no one had ever considered in our military colleges.'

CHAPTER 4

1915
Position Warfare

As Foch gloomily observed, after the 'race to the sea' and with trench systems established from the Channel to the Alps, there were no flanks to be turned. Manoeuvre warfare appeared to be impossible. It was increasingly evident that the contemporary technology of prepared positional defence – barbed wire, machine-guns, artillery and secure communications – was superior to that of attack where, even after an opening bombardment, men had no option save to advance on foot or on horseback. Nevertheless, Joffre and the British commanders, French and subsequently Haig, continued to believe that formal frontal attack, properly prepared and motivated, must achieve a breakthrough. The story of 1915, then, is one of a series of fruitless attacks by both the French and the British that, at best and at heavy cost, only moved the opposing trench systems forward for short distances. On the German side, Falkenhayn opened an offensive against the British and French at Ypres in April, but was obliged to transfer his reserves and other units to the Eastern Front to support the Austrians. The main effort of the German army for the rest of the year was against Russia, pursuing a generally defensive strategy in France. Falkenhayn himself believed that ultimately the Western Front would be decisive, but he was only able to launch limited-scale attacks on the Western Front. The

1915 offensives, both by Allies and Germans, and all subsequent Western Front battles were aptly described by Winston Churchill as 'desperate and vain appeals against the decision of fate' reached on the Marne.

The Allies and the Central Powers were approximately equally matched in man and fighting power, and both were at the time prepared to fight a war of attrition; despite the heavy casualties, societies at home were sufficiently stable and cohesive to support the burden. Much of 1915 was spent in mass mobilisation, drafting men and forming new formations for the front. The French munitions industry, too, had to expand very rapidly, drawing heavily on skilled manpower. The easing of German pressure on the Western Front gave France time for these preparations, plus the opportunity to withdraw the best trained units from areas where improved defence works, held by older men or units composed of young recruits, were sufficient.

Major Operations

Joffre meanwhile had reorganised his command structure to provide three army groups. By late 1915, the Northern Group of Armies, under Foch, after various troop movements, comprised d'Urbal's 10th and Dubois's 6th Armies, the small French force on the left of the British in the Ypres area, the BEF, expanding by the end of the year to three armies, and the Belgians on the coastal flank. The Central Group, commanded by Joffre himself until July 1915 when the sector was made over to Castelnau and then to Langle de Cary, included Franchet d'Esperey's 5th Army together with the 4th Army, commanded by General Gouraud, and the 3rd Army, commanded by General Humbert. On the French right flank the Eastern Group of Armies, commanded by Dubail, contained General Roques's 1st Army, Maud'huy's 7th Army and the divisions of the Army of Lorraine, commanded by General

Deprez. The Northern Group's sector ran from the Channel to the Soissons area, from where the Central Group sector extended to Saint-Mihiel. Dubail's Eastern Group sector ran from Saint-Mihiel to Alsace and the Alps.

Along this 750-kilometre front three areas presented such geographic problems that fighting was at the time impracticable. On the Flanders coast artillery fire quickly reduced any ground not already flooded to a mire. Artillery destruction among the Argonne hills and woods created almost impassable conditions. The highlands of the Vosges, even less suited to any mass attack, became from mid-1915 an area to which both French and Germans sent lower-grade formations and personnel in need of recuperation, though occasionally *chasseurs alpins* would make small local attacks against a hill feature.

Joffre himself saw the Western Front as being dominated by the great German salient, or bulge, the centre of which, at Compiègne, pointed towards Paris. While awaiting the manpower resources for a major breakthrough offensive (*la percée*), he hoped by attrition attacks (*grignotage*), particularly on the flanks of the bulge in Artois and Champagne where the terrain was suitable, to wear down the Germans' strength, so inflicting heavier casualties upon them than he himself would sustain, and at the same time endangering the vital German north–south and lateral railway communications to and along their fronts. He was convinced that the pattern of German troop-train movements indicated an overall reduction of troops, in particular of the best formations, on the Western Front, although he was to underestimate the worth of their replacements.

The year opened with a continuation of the December 1914 small-scale attacks along the whole front to secure key hilltops or other features needed for artillery observation, among them Notre Dame de Lorette and Vimy in Artois, La

Main de Massiges, Tahure and Souain in Champagne, Vauquois in the Argonne, Linge and 'Le Vieil Armand' (as it was called by its attackers) at Hartmannswillerkopf in Alsace. These attacks were costly; at Eparges, between Verdun and Saint-Mihiel, the French lost 20,000 men, killed or wounded, in eighteen assaults – only partially successful – mounted between 17 February and 9 April. A series of French attacks to recover Hartmannswillerkopf, taken by the Germans in January, were launched in June, July and August. These secured some ground, much of it lost to a German counter-attack in October. A final attempt to take the feature in December failed disastrously. French casualties were heavy, especially among elite *chasseurs alpins* troops.

The first of the larger-scale attrition attacks opened in Champagne on 16 February. After a delay caused by a local German attack and by heavy snow which made ammunition supply difficult, Langle de Cary's 4th Army attempted to break the forward defences of General von Einem's 3rd Army, and in particular cut the German lateral railway line. Opening with a heavy artillery bombardment, French troops made repeated attacks on the German strongpoint system over the bare Champagne hills around Perthes-Les Hurlus for over a month, but by the end of the offensive, on 18 March, the French had only advanced some 3,000 metres at a cost of 40,000 casualties. A supporting attack by the 1st Army in the Saint-Mihiel area met with a similar lack of success and further heavy loss of life.

Joffre had planned for a second attrition attack in the Artois area to open in early March. For this he requested the BEF commander, Sir John French, to help with a British attack on La Bassée, and also for a British formation to relieve the French IV Corps, still in the Ypres area. French, however, refused both requests for his own reasons, preferring to mount a purely British offensive at Neuve-Chapelle which achieved only limited success. Deprived of the support of the British, Joffre postponed his attack until early May.

Before this could be launched, however, Falkenhayn embarked on his one major Western Front offensive of 1915, which led to the second battle of Ypres. The German assault opened on 22 April with the first concerted use of poison gas, 168 tons of chlorine, released from 500 large pre-positioned cylinders and blown towards the Allied lines. The British and the Canadians were to suffer most, but the two French divisions under General Putz on the British left in the Pilckem–Langemarck sector, the 87th Territorial and the 45th, were also affected. Several thousand men fled, terrified, gasping and retching, although the number of soldiers actually killed or disabled proved relatively low. Fatal casualties included white Zouaves of the 45th Division, and men from a unit of the semi-penal African Light Infantry, together with indigenous Algerian Tirailleurs. One of the Tirailleurs battalions broke completely, murdering its officers. The two divisions lost their artillery in their precipitate withdrawal, and while valiantly holding new positions neither they nor the limited French reinforcements that Foch was able to move in haste to the area were capable of giving adequate support to any British counter-attack. The British were forced to consolidate within a smaller and more dangerous Ypres salient, though a local French offensive eventually launched on 15 May did succeed in ejecting the German pocket on the Allied side of the Yser Canal. Fortunately the Germans had failed to follow up the initial advantage gained, and their offensive, after one final attack that began on 8 May and lasted six days, ground to a halt for lack of available reserves to maintain momentum.

On 9 May Joffre's Artois attrition attack was finally opened, after a slow but prolonged six-day artillery bombardment, by Foch's Northern Group of Armies on a 15-kilometre

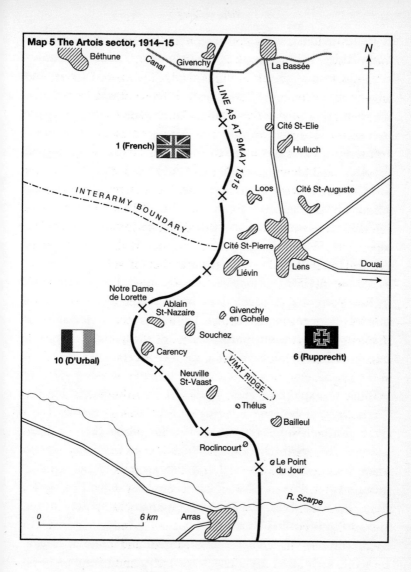

Map 5 The Artois sector, 1914–15

Béthune

Canal   Givenchy   La Bassée

LINE AS AT 9 MAY 1915

1 (French)

Cité St-Elie
Hulluch

INTERARMY BOUNDARY

Loos   Cité St-Auguste

Cité St-Pierre

Liévin   Lens   Douai

Notre Dame
de Lorette

Ablain
St-Nazaire   Givenchy
en Gohelle

Souchez

10 (D'Urbal)   Carency   6 (Rupprecht)

Neuville
St-Vaast   VIMY RIDGE

Thélus

Bailleul

Roclincourt

Le Point
du Jour

R. Scarpe

0   6 km   Arras

N

front between Arras and Lens. Its main mission was to capture Vimy Ridge, while securing the northern and southern flanks, consolidating on the hill spur of Notre Dame de Lorette, and advancing towards the River Scarpe. The area was held by the German 6th Army under Crown Prince Rupprecht, supported in the south by von Below's 2nd Army. The assault was protected by Castelnau's 2nd Army on the right and supported, despite the misgivings of French, by the British 1st Army attack on Festubert on the left. The bitter fighting raged until 18 June. Although Moroccan soldiers from General Pétain's XXXIII Corps succeeded on the first day in taking Vimy Ridge, albeit temporarily, the end result differed little from the great August 1914 offensives – an advance of a mere 4 kilometres at a cost of 300,000 casualties, of whom 100,000 were men killed. Both the February Champagne and the May Artois offensives were handicapped by continuing shortages of artillery ammunition, particularly high explosive, shrapnel failing to destroy German defences. More seriously, the French were unable to move their reserve units forward quickly enough to exploit success. In Artois this delay enabled the Germans still holding the ridges to bring up reserves for a counter-attack unobserved, eventually giving them a local numerical superiority. Some French criticism of the British arose from two pauses in the British attacks, occasioned by ammunition shortages and casualties; these pauses, Joffre held, gave the Germans the opportunities to switch formations to counter French attacks.

In the summer French army expansion and reorganisation brought twelve new divisions to the front, 75mm ammunition supply became adequate, and the steady increase in the size of the BEF freed the French 2nd Army for operations in Champagne. The BEF's sector was now extended from Ypres to Hébuterne 20 kilometres north of the Somme, while the French 10th Army planned once more to take Vimy Ridge, from where artillery fire could sever the German railway lines in the Douai plain below. In June, a limited German attack on the Meuse was beaten back, but French casualties were severe.

In September, after preparatory discussion with French and the British War Minister, Lord Kitchener, Joffre launched two simultaneous attrition offensives in Artois and Champagne, this time in the hope that perhaps a campaign-winning break-through might result following a collapse in the German cen-tre. The Artois attack opened on 25 September after four days of artillery bombardment and included a British use of gas released from cylinders. Three British armies, and d'Urbal's 10th Army, twenty divisions in all, attempted to advance on a 35-kilometre front. The French part of the attack centred on Souchez and Vimy. Joffre, however, considered the Champagne attack, due to open on the same day, as more like-ly to bring success because the terrain had fewer water obsta-cles or villages to impede an advance. Accordingly he gave Castelnau priority in the allocation of men and guns. His Centre Group of Armies, comprising the 4th Army and the 2nd Army commanded now by Pétain, totalled twenty-seven divisions, with 1,300 field guns and 650 medium or heavy pieces. They were committed on a frontage of 40 kilometres in the area of Perthes-Les-Hurlus, Tahure and La Main de Massiges, Pétain's army on the right and de Langle with seven divisions on the left. Bands, bugles and drums played in the front-line trenches as the assault began, the French breaking through the first German line and taking 14,000 prisoners. Aircraft reconnaissance and artillery spotting, with liaison practised prior to the attack, contributed to their early suc-cesses. On this occasion reserve units and formations were brought forward quickly enough, but they were unable to break the second German line and only added to the subse-quent casualty totals. Pétain wished to halt the attack but he was overruled by Castelnau. Joffre then called a temporary

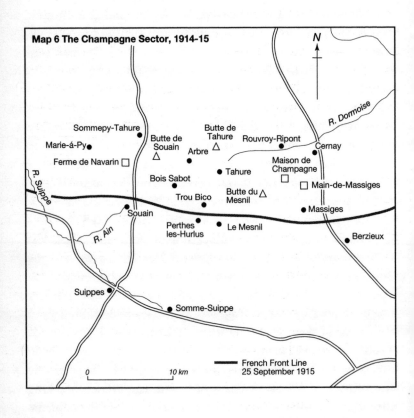

Map 6 The Champagne Sector, 1914–15

N

R. Dormoise

Sommepy-Tahure

Butte de Tahure

Rouvroy-Ripont

Cernay

Marie-á-Py

Butte de Souain

Arbre

Ferme de Navarin

Maison de Champagne

Main-de-Massiges

Bois Sabot

Tahure

R. Suippe

Trou Bico

Butte du Mesnil

Souain

Massiges

R. Ain

Perthes les-Hurlus

Le Mesnil

Berzieux

Suippes

Somme-Suippe

0   10 km

French Front Line
25 September 1915

halt, but later ordered a resumption, by which time the Germans had brought up reserves to repel it. In both phases French infantry advancing in successive waves became sky-lined on the Champagne hills and ridges behind which the Germans had constructed pillboxes and well-prepared fortifications in reverse slope positions, all within a defence system 4–5 kilometres in depth. Once again, these positions could not be neutralised by the flat trajectory of the French 75mm guns, which were fast running out of ammunition. French soldiers in their hundreds were mown down by German machine-gunners and riflemen. The same fate befell two cavalry divisions, the speed of the charge being powerless to prevent the horses and their gallant riders being massacred.

Once again Joffre's attacks served only to secure minimum territorial gains, 2–4 kilometres, positional defence mastering attack. Plans for the Artois offensive had been the subject of much prior argument between the British and French commanders and in consequence were not well co-ordinated. After only one day Joffre appreciated the strength of the German positions and ordered Foch and d'Urbal to press the attack of the 10th Army no further. In Champagne Pétain incurred criticism for his insistence on heavy preliminary artillery bombardment, which allegedly revealed his planned line of advance; more probably the Germans were already aware of it. Flaws in hurriedly manufactured 75mm shells and charges, causing numerous guns to burst and kill their crews, also weakened the effect of the artillery, at least 600 guns being lost in explosions. Haste, moreover, had led to production concentrating on the easier-to-manufacture high-explosive shells rather than airburst shrapnel now needed for harassing fire.

The cost in casualties was enormous, totally out of proportion to the minuscule gains, 190,000 French, including 30,000 killed, and 60,000 British, the German losses in comparison being 150,000 killed, wounded or missing. Severe weather conditions, exhaustion and German counter-attacks using a mixture of phosgene and chlorine gas led Joffre to order the cessation of the Champagne offensive on 6 October, and that in Artois, after a final unsuccessful attack by Foch on Vimy Ridge, on the 11th. By the end of 1915 the French army had suffered 1.2 million casualties, including 350,000 killed or missing.

The new ability to bring forward reserve units was a result of the expansion of the Service Automobile. This had possessed only 170 vehicles in August 1914, but had quickly requisitioned some 9,000 civilian lorries and omnibuses, many used in the September 1914 'race to the sea'. In 1915 six lorry groups, each capable of transporting a brigade, were initially created, the number increasing to over a dozen by the end of the year. For the ordinary line infantryman, however, preparation for these big attacks still meant long night marches carrying rifle, grenades and full equipment, two blankets, spare boots, a spade, mess-tin, water bottle, perhaps tinned rations and a gas-mask. Such marches imposed a a severe strain on the newly arrived and less well-trained soldier, particularly as they often took place in persistent rain. The aims of the attacks were generally unknown to them, although sometimes the subject of rumour. The arrival at unit level of *agents de liaison*, usually officers but sometimes sergeants from a formation headquarters, was often viewed with apprehension, since they were likely to be carrying orders for an attack.

Infantry attacks still followed the pattern of 1914, officers at the head with sword or cane disdaining a firearm. If there was initial success and the German front line was taken, almost immediately German artillery fire would descend, followed a little later by enemy counter-attack. Survivors then would retreat across a no-man's-land littered with the dead or dying bodies of their comrades. In 1915 attacking infantry began to follow the British pattern of groups of men in diamond formation rather than in line, reducing the number killed by a shell.

The costly failure of the offensives sharpened the divergence of view held by senior commanders. Junior officers, aware of their soldiers' morale, were disposed to halt attacks when it was clear that any success would be disproportionate to the casualties. At senior level, Foch, ever enthusiastic and optimistic, saw no alternative to constant attack, although he now laid stress on full preparation, in particular artillery. He remained convinced that a major breakthrough could be achieved by a momentum of repeated attacks. Pétain, cautious and pessimistic, argued that neither the French nor the British armies were sufficiently prepared for an offensive big enough to achieve a breakthrough, and that until they were ready any attacks should be for attrition only, on a limited scale to wear down the enemy. Such attacks should be on fronts broad enough to avoid destruction by immediate enemy fire and to deploy reserves, but not so broad as to dissipate strength. Against German attacks, centres of resistance in villages and deep-dug trenches with dense barbed-wire protection should be prepared. More than Joffre and Foch, Pétain was anxious both to preserve men's lives and sensitive to men's morale. Distrusted for his views, his reward was a move that proved short-lived, his 2nd Army being placed in reserve at Noailles.

Trench Warfare

Just as Falkenhayn was in practice abandoning Schlieffen so, in practice, was Joffre being forced to accept defensive measures. As early as January 1915, in a first instruction for this new *guerre des sous-lieutenants*, he laid down a pattern of active zones with fire from strongpoints covering front and flanks together with sheltered secondary positions for counter-attack troops, and heavily wired passive zones covered by the strongpoints to be held by sentinels. Two deep barbed-wire entanglements, 25 metres apart with gates to let patrols in and out, were to be laid along the entire front. A further instruction in the same month directed a second, similar strongpoint line be prepared 3 kilometres to the rear, made as far as possible shell-proof and to accommodate support companies. Later, three defensive lines became the ideal pattern, covering 3–6 kilometres with parallel lines of trenches 200–500 metres apart. The first line was to slow an enemy attack, the second to halt it and the third a reserve stop line in case of breakthrough and to provide general support. Trenches were in general 2–2.5 metres deep, with exterior protection from sandbags or bundles of wood, fencing or logs within to prevent caving-in, and duckboards to provide a floor. The trenches, laid out in zigzag or curves to avoid enfilading fire by the enemy from the flanks, were very narrow. Along the front edge was a firing step, and inside were ladders for assaults and enclosures for observation posts. Soldiers in the first line would sleep on the firing step or seated on a sandbag; if the ground was firm enough they might dig a small individual foxhole for rest. Further back, soldiers would sleep in barns, if available, or in evil-smelling, claustrophobic shacks, *gourbis*, holes scraped in the ground, lined with straw and covered with planks. In 1914–15 these were usually for one or two men. Later, better shelters were built, covered with sheet metal as well as wood, offering protection to six or seven men against German 77mm guns. Sometimes a table and benches might be provided, but more often life in the *gourbis* and shelters meant unwashed men sleeping packed together like sardines in a tin. Lighting would be limited to candles or acetylene lights. In the third line also were hollowed-out but more comfortable shelters for officers and command posts, and for rest in some areas. Companies would be rotated, often every six days, from the first to the second or reserve lines. Further back it was said that mules carrying food and munitions up to the front instinctively knew the way by following the smell of the ordure of those who had preceded them. Artillerymen dug out gun positions not visible to one another and concealed guns with camouflage nets. When issue bivouacs could be used they were not fully weatherproof.

The living conditions within this system plan varied enormously. In quiet areas or those in chalky terrain, grottoes and sizeable dugouts, sometimes furnished with furniture from abandoned villages, provided warmth and shelter. Such amenities were particularly necessary in the snow and freezing cold of a Vosges winter. But very often there were long delays before the necessary wood and sandbags even for the front line arrived, and for the soldiers of many regiments trench warfare in 1915 was life without shelter of any form. In Flanders, Picardy, Artois and Champagne conditions were particularly wretched, with mud, frequently knee- and quite often thigh- or waist-deep, seemingly endless rain and icy winds. Trenches would cave in and individual foxholes were flooded. In only a very few areas was there any provision for personal sanitation; mud became mixed with urine, excrement, sputum and tobacco, plus the body odour from soldiers who generally went unwashed for days or often several weeks on end. Trench latrines were often uncompleted and irregularly used. Corpses of horses and men could not always be taken away. Soldiers remained unshaven, hence the term *poilu* (a virile man with a beard). Rats, lice and fleas and in the summer mosquitoes abounded to add to the misery, the rats often eating the food in the men's kitbags and corpses left on the field of battle.

In terms of equipments there was slow but real improvement. From the end of 1914, *bleu horizon* uniforms, with khaki for North and Black African troops, were introduced together with puttees and képis; and a protective steel skullcap, with from February 1915 a steel helmet, the *Casque Adrian*. During the 1914–15 winter, expedients provided for infantrymen included cavalry breeches and firemen's trousers. A project to retain red trousers was abandoned when it was found that the traditional dye came from Germany. The first design of the steel helmet was over-elaborate, but more practical designs followed. *Bleu horizon* often faded to grey, and when mud-stained, provided good personal camouflage. Overalls, sheepskins, over-breeches and mufflers became available by the 1915–16 winter. The quality of boots, however, remained poor for most of the war and there were no boot repair facilities at the front. German boots taken from a captured prisoner were highly prized. Initially, improvised water-soaked face masks and goggles were issued for anti-gas protection. In May gauze pads impregnated with hyposulphite and sodium bicarbonate, to be tied round the head, began to be issued. After experiments with hoods and other pads, a thick fabric hood, soaked in soda and castor oil and a fastening of metal strips to give a closer fit to the face, was distributed. The German use of phosgene gas led to a first change in the impregnation formula, sodium thiosulphate being used; a second change following the German use of prussic acid gas was the introduction of a nickel acetate compound, used in both the 1916 M2 gas-masks and its successor, the 1918 ARS17. Systems of gas warning observation posts equipped with klaxons were organised and gas clouds dispersed with petards. Almost immediately after the Germans' first use of gas, the French army under General Curmer began to develop its own chemical weaponry. Two gases were produced in 1915–16: *vincenette,* a mixture of cyanhydric acid, arsenic chlorine and chloroform which proved ineffective, and phosgene. In 1918 a mustard gas, *yperite,* was also produced.

More than 150,000 of the old 1874 Gras rifle were rebored to fire Lebel ammunition and issued to newly formed regiments. Other rifles were purchased from Japan and the United States. The number of machine-guns per regiment was increased from six to eight in 1915; these were grouped in three, later four sections, forming one company per regiment. The unreliable Saint-Etienne machine-gun was progressively replaced by the more robust Hotchkiss 1914 gun. Earlier ammunition supply was limited to 24- or 30-round metal clips; later a 249-round belt came into service. Hand grenades, seen pre-war as defensive and unacceptable, were reissued. At first these were improvised but improved patterns appeared in 1915. The demand for them could be enormous – one army corps used 30,000 in a single twenty-four-hour period. Methods of lobbing the grenade – other than hand-throwing – were developed. Initially catapults made from branches, bicycle chains or lorry springs were used; later in 1915 rodded percussion grenades were fixed to the muzzles of infantrymen's rifles. Petards of various types were also devised to breach barbed-wire defences. Wireless and line communication equipments were developed rapidly, facilitating command and artillery fire control in defence and attack. It was realised that a lengthy bombardment served only to alert the enemy to an impending attack, while a short bombardment might prove ineffective and cost French lives. It was hoped that some form of creeping barrage might be developed to solve this dilemma.

Expansion of the artillery arm began, but only 220 new heavy guns had reached the army by the end of 1915, although old 90mm and 95mm guns were brought out and a number of 120mm siege guns converted for field work. The 75mm gun, so effective in the 1914 war of movement, was now of much less value. Trench mortars were urgently needed. Although French intelligence had warned Joffre of the German development of *minenwerfer* mortars, no action had followed. Captured German shellcases were used for an improvised mortar, the *Taupia*. The use of the obsolescent 58mm No. 1 trench mortar and its hurriedly produced successor the 58 No. 2, and an even older piece, the 1840s 150mm mortar, proved unexpectedly effective. Over 1,100 58mm mortars were in use by October 1915, together with a larger 80mm mortar converted from an 1878 mountain gun. A hastily produced 75mm mortar, capable of firing 75mm gun ammunition, was found to be defective. Crews were often artillerymen or dismounted cavalry troopers. Caudron and Farman aircraft, together with the H balloon, a copy of the German Drachen balloon, entered service for artillery and mortar observation in 1915. The balloons became frequent targets for artillery fire on the ground or air attacks with German aircraft firing incendiary bullets. Parachutes for balloon crews only became available in October 1915.

The importance of combat intelligence began, somewhat slowly, to be realised. German signals were intercepted or jammed from several posts, among them the Eiffel Tower. Direction-finding equipments and analysis of the traffic of signals often yielded valuable intelligence. The withdrawal of German divisions for use on the Eastern Front was verified and its overall strategic significance appreciated. In the field French intelligence personnel developed techniques, not always involving direct tapping but more often the use of insulated wires stretched out from a switchboard in the front line, which could pick up the currents of a German telephone line in its range. These, when amplified, enabled operators to listen in to conversations. Patrolling and prisoner questioning by skilled interrogators often provided useful front-line material. Documents, not only captured orders and marked maps but also the paybooks of ordinary soldiers recording their regiment, were often as valuable as a live prisoner. German local newspapers, freely available in Switzerland and read by French intelligence officers, occasionally indicated unit movements in accounts of the experiences of local soldiers. A small number of very brave men, trained in espionage, were transported by air to areas behind the German lines tasked to blow up bridges and collect intelligence. Aerial reconnaissance, now including the new technique of aerial photography, yielded intelligence about movements in rear areas or preparations for an attack. In the autumn of 1915 special artillery intelligence units were created in each of the front armies to furnish information for counter-bombardment purposes. The British Royal Artillery drew on French expertise in target plotting, flash-spotting and sound-ranging. The French army, however, did not engage in infantry patrolling in the same way as the British. A major combat intelligence failure in 1915, however, was the neglect of warnings given by captured German prisoners of the plans to use gas. One prisoner was actually taken with a primitive respirator among his equipment. French security in the field remained very poor, German listening of officers' conversations on French trench telephones providing them with much tactical intelligence, in particular preparations for the May Artois and September Champagne offensives.

The concept of camouflage, almost unthinkable before 1914, acquired legitimacy in 1915. A special team, formed of well-known painters, sculptors and designers, was added to the 1st Regiment of Engineers. Studios in northern France worked on canvas, painted to represent railway lines or dummy guns to confuse German observation posts. Both the French and the German armies engaged in mining and counter-mining tunnelling operations, the mines and explosive charges becoming more efficient and dangerous, releasing gas in the enemy's lines as well as simply exploding under the trenches. Sappers also established listening posts to detect German mining and were nearly always in the front line with attacking infantry to clear a pathway through barbed wire.

To provide the manpower for the trenches the draft system had to be completely restructured, for in its pre-war form densely populated areas were providing too many men, and thinly populated *départements*, or those occupied by the enemy, too few for their local units. The early months of the war had shown up the morale dangers of heavy casualties affecting people and families in particular regions. The 8th Infantry Regiment, which drew its manpower from Calais, Boulogne and Saint-Omer, for example, had lost 3,319 men by the end of March 1915. Discontented survivors of badly mauled units were split up and posted to different regiments. Officers and soldiers in cavalry regiments were transferred into the infantry – a procedure not always fortunate in cases where keen young cavalry officers were posted to battle-weary battalions. Horsed cavalry were often used to escort columns of prisoners to the rear. In 1916 six cavalry regiments were formally converted into infantry. Units of elderly reservists were frequently employed for telephone cable-digging and as carrying parties to ease the strain on the front-line soldiers. It was felt, also, that the war required an emphasis on the unity of the nation rather than a local Breton or Languedoc focus and, further, that the use of pure French, rather than patois or dialect in barracks and in action would facilitate command. For the vast mass of conscript infantrymen of peasant origin the consequent *brassage* or mixing, within which a Corsican, a Breton and a Languedoc soldier, each with his own language or patois and each unlikely to have left his home region before the draft, were thrown together in a trench, was to have mixed results; with strangers daily life, whether banter, grumbling over food distribution or the communal use of filthy latrines, became constrained. In the short term the *brassage* was useful for manning regiments. In the longer term the absence of local fellow countrymen at a time of much hardship and suffering was to have less wholesome results for the nation as a whole, creating a sense of personal isolation and contributing to the post-war divorce between the army and society.

In addition to changes in the drafting, the heavy casualties already sustained led to economies in organisation. Four regiments of reservists and two of the Foreign Legion were disbanded and all infantry companies reduced from 250 to 200 men. After these changes the distinction between active and reserve divisions was ended.

Once drafted, the soldier entered a training cycle of exercise, instruction and, for a minority, specialisation. Exercise, consisting of basic training in barracks, marching, shooting and the use of equipment in the field, was seen by officers as the opportunity to impose their authority on the men. Instruction was often very severe, field training being assigned to convalescing or partially disabled officers and NCOs. Specialisation was reserved for those with suitable education or qualifications – drivers, machine-gunners, signallers and junior NCOs – and was much sought after.

Related to the question of manpower and causing annoyance to the military was the reservation of about 500,000 men for essential industrial work, in particular railways and communications, and some 300,000 men for agricultural production. In addition, large numbers of foreign labourers were brought into France for work in munitions factories, to build the roads, bridges, railways, barracks, stores and ammunition dumps needed to supply the front armies, or again simply to help grow food. Recruitment of foreign labour began in 1915, and by the end of the war 120,000 Algerians, 50,000 Indochinese and some 100,000 of other nationalities including 82,000 Spaniards and 13,000 Chinese, together with a further 82,000 prisoners-of-war had all worked in France for the war effort, totals not including specific uniformed Black Africans and Malgache military labour, as noted in Chapter Ten. In addition, several hundred thousand French women entered into occupations in town and country previously reserved for men. The Renault factory at Billancourt, for example, employed 190 women in January 1914 a total that rose to

6,770 in the spring of 1918, working a twelve-hour shift with one free day each fortnight. Thousands more were employed in making uniforms and preparing food supplies; by the end of the war 30 per cent of the labour force consisted of women. In their work they gained an independence and earned money for themselves, so effecting significant changes in French society. After the war their dismissals and national rhetoric urging them to return to child-bearing were keenly resented. These changes were not appreciated by the men at the front, longing for a return to the pre-1914 world – a misunderstanding also to have post-war consequences.

Command and Control

Despite the reverses, the prestige earned by Joffre at the Marne secured his position. In Paris, although both President Poincaré and Prime Minister Viviani were fast losing their confidence in Joffre – a loss of confidence confirmed by their contacts with other generals and also the former War Minister, Messimy, who had been serving at the front. The threat of Joffre's resignation, however, was sufficient to bring them to heel, and he himself appointed a new Chief-of-Staff, General Pellé, to deflect criticism. He justified the autumn offensives on the grounds that they were necessary to help the Russians, and even more speciously, that they were vital for keeping the troops occupied and committed.

Internal political disputes and dissatisfaction with the conduct of the war expressed in parliamentary committees, did, nevertheless, lead to the fall of the Viviani government in October 1915. His successor, Briand, continued with the *union sacrée:* throughout the war successive French premiers were to remain republicans, anti-clerical and Dreyfusard. Also, later in the same month Galliéni replaced Millerand as War Minister. Galliéni believed that the restoration of ministerial control over the generals was essential; he was not supported by Briand, however, who continued to cover for Joffre. Briand's solution to the problem of Joffre was to promote him, on 2 December, to generalissimo, Commander-in-Chief of all French forces in all theatres, with Castelnau as Chief-of-Staff. Joffre soon marginalised Castelnau, on almost all important issues, continuing to reserve major decisions for himself.

Galliéni, in the last weeks of 1915, made a particular effort to unite politicians, officials and soldiers in working for the common good. With Joffre he established a *modus vivendi* in which Joffre conducted military operations while Galliéni concerned himself with resources. In these weeks, too, Galliéni modernised and reformed the old-fashioned War Ministry, clearing out a number of military personnel from safe, comfortable jobs – three Paris theatres, for example, were directed by army officers. He also became converted to General Mangin's project for the return of Black African troops on the Western Front, authorising an initial 50,000. Nine battalions had served there in 1914, but it had been considered that the conditions were too testing for them and they had either been returned to Morocco or sent to the Dardanelles. Mangin held that Africans had a nervous system less sensitive to pain and fear than Europeans, and that they were therefore ideal soldiers in the attack.

Galliéni personally doubted whether victory could be won on the Western Front and favoured operations in the Balkans. In this he was opposed by Joffre, and also by Kitchener, but the need to try to support or rescue the Serb army was seen to justify the continuance of the Macedonian campaign. He and Joffre agreed on the poor performance of the Macedonian front commander, Sarrail, who after his early success on the Western Front had suffered a reverse in an operation by his 3rd army in the Argonne in July, and had been intriguing against Joffre. Sarrail had been given the Macedonian command because of his known Dreyfusard radical Republican views, and a desire by Joffre to regain favour among Sarrail's political supporters while at the same time removing him from France.

The underlying differences of views between Galliéni and Joffre remained simmering only until the end of the year. Among the several issues that were to lead to a break were almost certainly Galliéni's misgivings over Joffre's plans for the coming year. At a meeting of the Allied commanders at Chantilly on 6–8 December, it was agreed to open offensives on three fronts – Western, Russian and Italian – aimed to commence in March 1916. Later that month Joffre asked Haig, who had recently replaced French as British commander to prepare plans for operations north of the Somme in April. These would be designed to wear down the Germans prior to a major offensive by the French under Foch south of the Somme. Joffre maintained that, in view of the heavy casualties already suffered by the French army, the opening attrition attacks must fall to the British. Plans and events, however, were to take very different courses in 1916.

Life in the Trenches

The military difficulties and physical miseries of mud, water and filth, the day-to-day conditions in which the French soldier had to fight, have already been outlined. They were, however, not the only causes of the very severe burden borne by the ordinary rank-and-file *fantassin* (infantryman).

Neither officers nor soldiers were prepared for the sheer violence of warfare, so much greater than anything previously experienced. Ever present in the minds of the front-line troops were four principal dreads. Of these the most insidious was the fear of German subterranean mining, betrayed by sounds below ground audible to desperately apprehensive men on the surface. The prospect of a sudden volcanic eruption of the ground in which men could, and quite often were, buried alive and against which there could be no riposte, inspired real terror.

Then there was the danger of gas, particularly when masks were either unavailable or known to be ineffective, and, from February 1915 onward, the threat from flame-throwers. Last but not least was the impact of German artillery and mortar fire, the lacerating, mutilating wounds that shrapnel could cause to men sheltering in small trenches or foxholes, and again the risk of being buried alive. The deafening, unnerving noise of sustained bombardment was liable to reduce men to tears and screams, or to bring on acute diarrhoea. German artillery shells were known as *marmites* (the British soldier's equivalent term was 'Jack Johnson'). And on a more personal level, there was the fear of the sniper lying in wait for an unwary soldier on his way to a latrine or for food, of hazardous patrols or the surprise German trench raid.

In intention, the supply of food to front-line troops – after the dislocations caused by the events of 1914 when many stores were lost – represented a praiseworthy effort. Wheat and meat were imported in very large quantities. Food reaching the troops included bread, generally but not always white and of reasonable quality, meat and fish, variable in quality (the fish often not adequately salted), cheese, but few vegetables and little or no sugar. The intention was that each soldier should have at least one solid hot meal per day served from a company mobile kitchen, but many of these were defective. In practice, too, enemy action or more mundane transport difficulties often interrupted the supply of food. Such conditions could reduce the soldier to one tepid or cold meal, perhaps at four o'clock in the morning, or quite frequently with no food or even a hot drink at all for a day or more. Very often in areas of activity the food that actually reached the soldier was a thick stew or soup brought up by brave men, the *hommes soupes*, in open containers that let in mud or earth, and had been carried along with munitions, wood and logs in packs on the back of mules, so arriving cold. Towards the end of the year

Norwegian hay boxes to keep food warm were issued to some units, but overall the lack of regular hot food added to soldiers' misfortunes. In some areas soldiers scrounged extra food or animals to kill from deserted houses and farms, or supplemented their rations by snaring rabbits or other animals. When chocolate was available it served to fortify both body and morale. But when a major attack was in progress soldiers would have to live on tins of corned beef (referred to as *singe* or monkey) or sardines and biscuits.

Each soldier carried a two-litre flask into which he could pour wine, water or, if available, coffee. Sometimes soldiers paired, one opting for wine for both, the other coffee. Wine, *'le consolateur suprême'* in the words of one private soldier, was as important as food for purposes of morale, the ration (*pinard*) being increased from a quarter to half a litre per day, a measure still considered ungenerous by most men. Delivery was quite reliable, but the quality varied, and the solidified jellied wine that had to be melted down was particularly poor. Sometimes, in exceptionally severe weather conditions or more often before an attack, a fiery eau-de-vie-type spirit, *gniole*, would be issued. Extra food and wine were generally provided on 1 January and 14 July, but not at Christmas.

An unwise attempt was made by Joffre's headquarters staff to reassure newspaper readers that troops in the front line had, in preparation for the winter of 1915–16, all that they needed in terms of wooden posts for the revetting of trenches, warm clothing and secure supplies of warm food. The information given to the press was based on the more fortunate conditions in the 5th Army area on the Aisne, but the press reports led to a mass of indignant letters from readers in less fortunate units elsewhere on the front.

Officer-soldier relationships varied greatly from unit to unit, and the consequence of the shortage of good officers and NCOs, made worse by the casualties of 1914 and 1915, were felt throughout the army. Except for those officers promoted from the ranks there was a large social gap between officers and men. Nevertheless, when officers attended to their men's welfare, bonds were excellent. They were strained if soldiers thought the officers were incompetent, not prepared to share hardships, smuggling women into their trenches, seemed principally concerned with their own careers, issued orders seen as purposeless or unreasonable, or neglected their men alive but lying wounded after an attack. Military discipline, however, was accepted in 1915, perhaps with grumbling, but because, in the last resort there was no alternative. If officers were good their men would follow them in all circumstances.

Front-line soldiers held the regimental *brancardiers* (stretcher-bearers) in the highest regard. They included men who for one reason or another were unwilling to point a gun at a fellow human being, among them priests (including the young Pierre Teilhard de Chardin). They would frequently attempt to retrieve wounded from no-man's-land under rifle or machine-gun fire, using chains, trestles and hammocks if stretchers were not available. Dogs, *chiens sanitaires*, were used to locate wounded men. Sometimes, though, the wounded might have to lie waiting for long hours or even a day or two before retrieval, their cries of pain only too audible in the trenches. Victims of flame-thrower attack suffered especial agony. Few *brancardiers* had any proper paramedical training, and the early stages of the evacuation of the wounded were often excruciatingly painful. Transport was often limited to wheelbarrows, farm carts and carriages, or pallets on the backs of mules. The army's supply of ambulances was wholly inadequate, and the ambulance in service in 1914 was a small vehicle with solid wheels and no springs, and leaving the legs of a patient exposed to the elements. The original five hospital trains of 1914 had been supplemented by thirty ordinary trains in which wounded could sit, and fifteen goods trains, consisting of wagons with neither heat nor lighting, fitted with wooden bunks. Late in 1914 more trains were adapted to provide for beds, heating, lighting and a dispensary. Nursing in the field and on the trains was not always satisfactory, some male nurses preferring safety and a quiet life.

Further behind the lines, after initial inadequacy in 1914 with overworked surgeons and crude conditions, matters slowly improved, although there were still shortages of sterilising equipment and well-lit and heated tents in the field hospitals. But for the first time the French soldier benefited from modern medicine, blood transfusions, X-rays, plastic surgery and anaesthetics. Further in the rear, schools, churches, hotels and spas were taken over for use as hospitals or convalescent centres where female company provided much-needed moral support.

Inevitably, in the insanitary conditions of trench life, sickness took its toll; in 1914–15 the over-thirties were especially vulnerable. Skin diseases were particularly common, while the numbers suffering from *commotion* or *obusite* (shell shock) and hysteria increased as the war progressed. If fit enough, injured or sick men would be returned to front-line units, the less fit to static or logistical units. Casualties were graded, priority being given to those who would make a full or a partial recovery, with less attention to those likely to die. Some units had an attached *aumonier*, or chaplain, who lived with the troops; many more had among their recalled reservists priests, curés, monks and lay brothers – 25,000 by June 1918. Some of these served as line officers and soldiers, others in non-combatant duties such as stretcher-bearers. Army chaplains had been dispensed with by pre-war anti-clerical governments, but at the outbreak of war the role was reinstated, and more than 500 were at work by 1918. Some chaplains served in the trenches and followed the lines of advancing troops during an attack, pronouncing absolution on the dead and dying, a matter of great importance for devout Catholics. Services were held for troops during rest periods, and were well attended, though the soldiers' motives were sometimes mixed, especially if the local congregation included women and girls. Only a few divine services were held in the front line.

Protective measures were successful in preventing any major outbreak of disease until the Spanish influenza epidemic of 1918. Javel water – water purified chemically by a solution of hypochloride and sodium chlorate – was used for drinking. Food was wrapped in canvas before despatch to the front. Chemical protection against insects and poison traps for rats were supplied, neither measure more than a limited success. When conditions permitted, ordure was burnt by fire. All soldiers received a leaflet advising them on health measures. Some military cemeteries were opened in the war, graves being dug by older reservists, but many men lay unburied for long periods.

Front-line units, operational conditions permitting, were entitled to a rest period after four to six days in the line, in practice often very much longer. The facilities, *cantonnements*, provided for these rest periods in 1915 and 1916 were frequently abysmal, initially barns or roadside shacks, actual buildings being limited to large, hastily erected barrack blocks, 40 metres long, intended to house a hundred men. These often had no doors at the entrances or glass for the windows. Soldiers were meant to sleep on wooden blocks; sometimes paliasses, verminous and filthy, were available. Stores were promised but often not provided, nor was lighting always available. Washing and latrine facilities were primitive or available only some distance away. Zealous officers, particularly elderly, recently commissioned NCOs, were all too frequently prone to treat battle-weary soldiers, many in their 30s and 40s, men with wives and children, as raw recruits. Officers and officious NCOs would also try to use the rest period for drills, training or parades to impress senior officers, or impose unnecessarily harsh punishments for shortcomings in hair-cuts, turn-out or saluting, *'âneries de caserne'* in the words of one soldier. Wherever possible soldiers visited local bistros to drink wine, often in excess, or enjoy female company. Soldiers from the south, however, sometimes found people in the north unwelcoming. Pipe smoking in the trenches, singing in the *cantonnements* and, conditions permitting, in the front line (a 1914 song *La Madelon* was especially popular) were features of the soldier's life. As the war progressed a few improvements were made, some *cantonnements* in villages being comfort-able, with warm rooms, gramophones and writing facilities. Sometimes, to the anger of the front-line infantrymen, these were monopolised by communications personnel. Entertainment, in the form of variety shows, came out from Paris and elsewhere.

A leave system, subject to operational conditions, was instituted in July 1915, soldiers being in theory granted seven days every four months. In practice and until 1917, permission was haphazard, some units granted leave every three months, some every six months and some at even less frequent inter-vals. At the outset travelling time had to be included within this period; given all the difficulties of travel in wartime France, including unheated trains with broken window panes, the journey could reduce the period actually spent at home by a soldier from a remote country area to a bare day or two. Ruses to extend the leave period, tales of travel difficulties or sickness, were tried by many, but punishment for claims found to be false were heavy. Leave of up to fifteen days was granted for harvesting of crops in the late summer and autumn. Compassionate leave for family deaths, marriages and births was also allowed, but abuse of this privilege and false claims were punished very severely. Soldiers with families near the front line were on occasions given one- or two-day leave passes. Galliéni introduced a system of *Foyers du Soldat* at railway stations to help and protect soldiers, but gendarmes had to be stationed later at the major Paris stations and in some other towns to ensure soldiers continued their journeys home and did not stray into bad company.

Understandably, conditions of trench life generally served to confine sexual desire to erotic dreaming, along with the telling of tales of sexual prowess and the singing of obscene songs in the fetid atmosphere of the *gourbis*. Relief came for many in the rest periods, when in the villages farm girls, waitresses, laundresses and others were often available, as anxious for a relationship as were the soldiers. Many French soldiers, particularly the unmarried and men from the midi and the south, acquired a semi-permanent consort, a *marraine de guerre*, with whom they corresponded and stayed when on leave – the scheme even being officially sponsored. Occasionally these relationships outlasted the war and became regularised. Sometimes, too, *marraines* were of additional value in urging a reluctant soldier to return to his unit. In some areas wives and girl friends appeared in base camps near the front. There exists no evidence of homosexuality and formal prostitutes were little used by ordinary soldiers unless they had private means. The daily pay of a sergeant, 4.50–5Fr, approximated to a prostitute's fee and NCOs formed the majority of their customers, sometimes over sixty per day.

Inevitably, war released passions; for many a desire to prove virility, or more sadly, a 'before I die' wish. In consequence, and equally inevitably, there was a great increase in venereal disease, especially syphilis; the venereal disease rate averaged some eighty per thousand men, taking out of service some 35,000 men each year, a rate higher than the British but lower than the German armies. The French soldier scorned any form of contraception, in any case opposed by the authorities and the chaplains. A system of anti-venereal disease was introduced in 1916, with inspections of known brothels, surveillance of clandestine ones, cafés and *estaminets* of dubious repute, and firm instructions for soldiers going on leave.

The delivery of mail from home was eagerly awaited. As the war continued a letter came to mean much more than the news it conveyed; it was a physical, tangible link with the old life, for a moment banishing the surrounding realities of war and providing incentive to struggle on. The French army correctly ensured that postal courier services were properly maintained. Food parcels from families, welfare organisations and *marraines de guerre* were especially welcomed – and generally shared with others.

From 1915 on, to eliminate profiteering traders, co-operative shops were set up in front-line and rest areas under arrangements by army divisions; soldiers could buy food, cheese, tea, corned beef and wine. The low rate of soldiers' pay, however, 50 centimes per day, even though augmented by a 'trench allowance' of one franc per day, of which 50 centimes was retained for an end of service gratuity, limited their value. Some unit officers used the shops to vary their soldiers' food. Profits from the shops went into the organisation, to families of casualties, the regimental band or the hire of halls for entertainment. Another advantage of the front line co-operative shops was that they provided the soldier with a facility to spend his money evenly, rather than waste savings in a drunken spree later.

The French soldier's view of the British army in 1915 was one of admiration and envy. The tenacity and courage of British units was (until 1918) held in the highest regard. The warm practical khaki uniform in which the BEF arrived was seen as much more sensible than French uniforms. The better conditions of British trenches, and the more reliable delivery of food, especially sweet foods such as jam, was envied. The greatly superior British army provision of medium and heavy artillery met with admiration and approval. At the same time, British officers were often thought to be amateurish, and also patronising in their manner towards their French counterparts, and language and culture differences could occasionally lead to friction among regimental soldiers. There was a general feeling, particularly in the first half of 1915 when Kitchener was still forming his army, that the British should take a greater share of the burden, and also suspicion that whereas the British fought well, they were nevertheless fighting to their own agenda of war aims, and that a unified Western Front command was necessary. In 1914–15, as a curious consequence of the work of General Henry Wilson in effecting Anglo-French co-operation, the British army was often referred to as *l'armées W, divisions d'infanterie W* etc.

The French in general treated captured German prisoners well. Hatred at this stage of the war was directed collectively against Germany, *les Boches*, rather than individual German soldiers who had been living in similar conditions of hardship. There were, however, a number of cases, recorded by the German academic August Gallinger, in which German prisoners were massacred, sometimes brutally and in cold blood as well as in the heat of battle, when small groups inflamed by passion would often kill all found in a trench captured after hand-to-hand fighting. The German record was a great deal worse, with incidents occurring of French prisoners being killed throughout the war. German treatment of French prisoners scattered in camps all over Germany was also severe, in part, but only in part, occasioned by the shortage of food at home in 1916 and 1917. Many tried to escape but only a few succeeded. A few fortunate men were sent to work on farms where they were well fed and housed. For the large majority, however, treatment was callous, men having to sleep on boards with a diet limited to beetroot soup, lacking in meat or potatoes, for many months; letters arrived infrequently, parcels even more rarely. On one occasion, learning that the French had sent German prisoners to North Africa, the Germans in reprisal sent over 2,000 prisoners to a notoriously unhealthy swamp area from which fewer than a hundred survived.

Attitudes towards the death of friends varied from fatalism to macabre fascination, or attempts to dignify the brutal end of a trench companion's life. As death became more and more an everyday event, survivors saw successive groups of friends killed or mutilated. There were long delays, even in relatively quiet situations, before notification that a soldier had been killed rather than recorded as missing was sent to next of kin. Publication of the names of men killed was forbidden. Individual soldiers sometimes sought to kill a German in an attack of personal revenge. In those stages of the war when French troops liberated areas ransacked by the Germans a new bitterness led to harshness, understandable in the context of the destruction of what was, after all, their homeland. Yet the French soldier did not kill purely for pathological gratification; the same cannot, however, be said of the North or Black African troops.

Fraternisation across the lines at Christmas time occurred in some areas in 1914 and 1915 with communal singing by both sides and, on a very few occasions, exchanges of food, chocolate and tobacco. These events were disapproved, with threats of sixty days in prison. More common were 'gentlemen's agreements' whereby artillery bombardments always occurred at the same times, so that everyone could take cover in advance. Sometimes German troops would throw stones into the French lines as a warning of a bombardment to come, and on one occasion, after a terrifying mine explosion, killing a number of soldiers, a sign saying 'Accident' appeared above the German trenches and was respected by the French.

Morale in 1915

Morale plays a very significant part in any conflict in which French soldiers are involved, and the 1914–18 struggle was to be very much a psychological war. Even though the high morale that motivated the valorous 1914 offensives had wavered when the attacks failed, the victory at the Marne and the halting of the Germans had sustained the army's spirit. But the attrition warfare of the trenches with its casualties and hardships – such a contrast to the life of cafés and female society so near but yet so distant – together with the fact that the new drafts arriving at the front did not always have the robustness of the pre-August 1914 serving soldiers, soon began to pose problems.

The front-line *poilu*'s approach to his service differed from that of his British counterpart, a difference caused by national temperament (in the case of France with its strong ingredient of *fronde* and revolution), and also methods of recruitment. The French military tradition was one of the draft, while that of the British, whether Regular, Territorial or Kitchener's army, was one of free will volunteering, a tradition that required the preservation of individual dignity. To the British observer the French soldier appeared slack and dirty, apparently lacking in any enthusiasm but nevertheless capable of bracing himself with surprising speed and fighting with tenacity and courage when necessary. He had a strong dislike of panache and unintelligent parades and training, and his general approach to warfare was more fatalistic, uninterested in anything other than immediate surroundings, than the adventurous (and in the early years still almost sporting) approach of the British.

In the trenches morale was conditioned by four factors. The first was that of immediate day-to-day life, the arrival of warm food, wine, clothing, the quality of the leadership provided by the unit's officers, the periodic arrival of post, and the regular provision of rest periods and leave. Second was the disciplined, organised peasant society from which the vast majority of front-line infantrymen came. Accustomed to the authority of an older generation, the local priest and the local authorities, a transition to a military hierarchy was not difficult. The regiment became a human community, the new village, its colour and headquarters the new village centre. A soldier must behave in such a way as not to let down his comrades in the regiment. Before the war, for many life had in any case been more about survival than enjoyment. New drafts of soldiers, encouraged by men with longer service – a very important component of a good unit – developed a measure of pride in their regiment, its citations and honours. Wounded men feared transfer to another unit. But the arrival of new drafts of young men in a unit after *brassage*, including men from different regions, could adversely affect cohesion in times of stress. Good commanding officers sought to create a family spirit in units by frequent visits to the first-line trenches, with a cheery greeting, and whenever possible organisation of additional food or wine.

Third, and still strong for most of 1915, was a belief in ultimate victory and the generals' ability, in particular *notre Joffre*, to deliver it and not risk men's lives unnecessarily. Only towards the end of 1915 did whispering and doubts begin to appear, and these were only to become serious in the following two years. The fourth component of good morale was a sense of belonging to society as a whole – more a simple consciousness or being French than any jingo patriotism. This national awareness, the product of the pre-war education curriculum, contained a belief that France best represented law, liberty, the rights of man and civilisation. For many, despite poverty, this was encapsulated in a nostalgic view of their pre-war lives, to which they wished desperately to return. Soldiers were generally not interested in political or national events, but they tended to view their defence of French soil as a defence of civilisation. Soldiers, in 1915, still believed that their hardships and sacrifices were understood and valued by the civilian world behind the front line, a belief that had been strong at mobilisation and at the Marne.

Indications that morale was under strain, however, began to appear in 1915. Delivery of mail, brief periods of home leave, the process of *brassage* in which regiments were no longer recruited on a regional basis, were starting to make the ordinary soldier feel isolated, a feeling that the artefactal measure of regimental pride could not entirely prevent. Mutual incomprehension began to show, by soldiers suspicious of the changes taking place in society, and by families unaware of the very real suffering endured by the men at the front. The gap was widened by stories of glamorous war carried in the national press and read by civilians at home, while the soldier in a waterlogged trench was experiencing *cafard* caused by monotony and the ever-present fear of death. Especially resented were journalists' propaganda representations of the Germans as cowardly, demoralised and suffering enormous losses.

In 1915, expression of resentment was limited and mostly targeted against *les embusqués*, the shirkers, and *les planqués*, those who had found a soft job. They included those who had found safe employment on the railways, in factories or the posts and telegraphs, and bureaucrats, profiteers, politicians and journalists who circulated misleading accounts of the war. Matters could become tense when a *planqué* officer reprimanded a soldier for failure to salute, or an *embusqué* signals NCO commented sourly on the filth on an infantryman's uniform and body. In 1914 the army had permitted regiments to produce their own local news-sheets which, though often short-lived, proliferated in 1915 and 1916 with titles such as *Le Poilu* (of a particular regiment), *Le Troglodyte*, *Le Crapouillot*, *La Marmite*, *L'Echo des Tranchées* or *Le*

Bochofage. These described soldiers' lives in the trenches, the monotony, rain, mud and darkness, their nostalgia for home and female company, resentments against officers and NCOs who were considered to be harassing them, and bitter criticism of *embusqués* and *planqués.* Humour tended to be macabre: 'Why scratch your head, a shell will do it for you?'

Another not insignificant danger warning was the increase in drunkenness during rest periods. Units of the gendarmerie had to be switched from their traditional military roles, such as policing of barracks, prevention of looting, subversion or sabotage, and traffic control, to supervision of the *cantonnements de repos,* staffing of military prisons and giving evidence before military courts – tasks that led to their being detested by front-line soldiers.

Inevitably, and also in some measure an indication of morale, a very small number of men were shot by their own officers or NCOs for cowardice at the height of a battle. These were, sensibly, recorded as *Mort pour la France.* The number shot *pour example,* either a summary shooting or following a court-martial sentence for cowardice, self-inflicted injury, looting or refusal to attack, is uncertain; the best estimates being 216 (or more in view of Joffre's instructions in respect of deserters) in 1914 and 442 in 1915, with an average of twenty-two to twenty-three per month to January 1917. On occasions when a unit performed badly a commanding officer would arbitrarily select one or more men from a company for a summary court-martial and execution, despite January 1915 regulations requiring all death sentence cases to be reviewed by the President of the Republic. Another disciplinary measure was the penal company, selected for particularly dangerous missions. There was also occasional evidence of *la bonne blessure,* the sought-after or self-inflicted wound – minor injuries to thumbs, fingers or toes. Senior officers were on the watch for such wounds and a few soldiers were tried and convicted. On one occasion forty men with self-inflicted hand wounds were arrested. Pétain immediately ordered twenty-five to be shot, but later directed that all be thrown into no-man's-land for a night. Others feigned illness, or deliberately made themselves ill.

The French command soon appreciated the morale dangers. In 1915 a postal control service was created in each of the armies for counter-intelligence and field security purposes. The service, developed further in 1916, received samples of soldiers' mail (a role much resented by soldiers), a minimum of 500 letters for each regiment each month. At the outset assessment of morale was only sixth in the service's priorities, below security, indiscreet talk or writing, or correspondence with foreigners. But reports on soldiers' morale were soon to become a major role. That morale was to be sorely tried for the next three years.

CHAPTER 5

1916
The Great Trial

The year 1915 had seen the transfer of the heaviest fighting from the Western Front in France and Belgium to the Eastern Front. The following year was to see its return to the Western Front where both the British and French armies were now able to field greater numbers; by January 1916 the Allies on the Western Front totalled ninety-five French, thirty-eight British and six Belgian divisions, 139 against the German total of 117. This favourable correlation of forces served to confirm the advocates of mass attacks in their views. But, in the event, as a consequence of the positional, siege nature of trench warfare and the continuing mastery of defence over attack, the only results were to be one of the most protracted battles in military history, the battle of Verdun, and one of the bloodiest, that of the Somme. Neither was to prove in any way decisive.

Allied and German Plans

The Allied plans, agreed in outline at Chantilly in December 1915, became modified in the first six weeks of the new year and were to be altered still further in response to events. In their final form before being overtaken by events, the plans envisaged a major, war-winning offensive in the early summer when full ammunition supply would be assured and, on the British side, that the new divisions of Kitchener's army would be adequately trained and strategically deployed. The British were to attack with twenty-five divisions north of the Somme in the direction of Hébuterne. The French 6th and 10th Armies, for the attack respectively under the commands of Generals Fayolle and Micheler within Foch's overall Northern Group of Armies, forty divisions in all, were to strike northward on a 35-kilometre front from Lassigny to the river. One corps of Fayolle's army was to serve north of the river so as to avoid any lack of co-ordination that might arise were the river to be an inter-army boundary. In the final planning modifications Haig agreed to make a preliminary small-scale attack in the Armentières sector in return for Joffre's abandoning his earlier project of a large British wearing-down attack. Haig also was able with his greatly reinforced strength to relieve the 10th Army, which had been holding the Arras sector with British formations on either side, for its role further south.

The preparation of these plans, however, was profoundly disturbing for the War Minister, Galliéni. His health was declining badly, pain making him less tolerant at a time when political criticism of military operations had increased following the full realisation of the failure of the autumn Artois and Champagne offensives, in particular the last badly planned assault upon Hartmannswillerkopf and its subsequent total loss. More importantly, in December 1915 a serving soldier member of parliament, Colonel Driant, had openly criticised the run-down of the guns and garrisons of Toul and Verdun, reductions made by Joffre to strengthen the line elsewhere. Galliéni agreed that these reductions were dangerous and remonstrated with Joffre who sharply rejected Galliéni's right to comment. Further friction with Joffre followed over the right to appoint generals and Joffre's practice of communication with the British without sending letters through the War Ministry. Joffre, in turn, distrusted Galliéni's contacts with generals he had replaced.

Briand tried to smooth over the rift, but in the tense atmosphere created by the German attack on Verdun, which opened on 21 February, matters reached crisis point. With a lack of foundation or reason, explicable only in terms of the aftermath of the bitter Dreyfus affair, Galliéni, now almost an invalid, was suspected by political figures of wanting to take over in a military government. On 7 March, in an address to the Council of Ministers, its passionate content barely concealed by his dry delivery, Galliéni attacked all who had in his view failed in eighteen months to understand the nature of the war by adhering to outdated doctrines, reiterating his view on the necessity of ministerial control. It will never be known whether Galliéni was here deliberately attempting to secure the removal of Joffre or simply offering the ministers present the final thoughts and experience of a popular, experienced and distinguished soldier. He then resigned, to die two months later. He was replaced by General Roques, an engineer and associate of Joffre. The whole event is significant, representing the only attempt until that in 1917 of Clemenceau, who had supported Galliéni, to assert ministerial control over commanders-in-chief.

It was, however, in the German headquarters that the plans most to affect the French army in 1916 were drawn up. Falkenhayn, at the peak of his career following the German successes on the Eastern Front, returned German attention to the west. He did so in the belief that the Russian army had been so badly mauled that it did not continue to present a serious threat to Germany and that Germany's most dangerous foe was Great Britain, but that Britain could be cut down to size, if not totally defeated, by submarine warfare and a military victory over her principal ally, France. He saw this victory being achieved by bleeding white an already weakened France in a succession of attacks on a narrow front, not primarily seeking a breakthrough, but targeted at an objective which the French could not afford to lose, thus causing ever increasing and disproportionate death totals for the French army. For these attrition attacks he selected the fortress of Verdun as the key slaughterhouse area. His ultimate goal was never fully clarified. It is just possible that in his mind was the thought that if the offensive did happen to provide a break-through and Verdun was actually taken, he could turn and attack the main French trench system from the rear and so collapse French military and political will to continue the war. But Falkenhayn's immediate priority was the killing of men, which he saw in cold calculation as attainable at little cost. Limited-size attacks by a relatively small number of divisions were to be based on the firepower of short, saturation-intensive, preliminary artillery bombardment. Surprise was to be retained by the shortness of the bombardment, infantry infil-tration tactics, and acceptance of a wide no-man's-land with-out preparation of forward assault positions for the infantry. To save the city with all its historic symbolic significance, the French army would be drawn, formation after formation, into an artillery firepower massacre delivered from three sides of the Verdun salient, dangerously exposed at the end of the 1914 fighting.

Verdun, historically an important fortress town, had formed a key part of the first frontier line of fortifications pre-pared after the defeat of 1870 to the plans of a talented engi-neer general, Séré de Rivières, the other major fortresses being Toul, Epinal and Belfort, using the heights of the Meuse and Moselle. In each of these fortress zones the main forts, in an outer and inner chain, were surrounded by a cluster of small-er forts and outpost blockhouses, generally linked by under-ground passages and with mutually supporting fire plans. In the ten years 1874 to 1884, 166 forts and forty-three outposts were built at enormous cost.

The city of Verdun was covered by twelve main forts in

two lines, eight lesser forts and forty redoubts, mostly sited on the eastern, northern and western sides, almost all on the right bank of the Meuse. In the salient were two of the strongest of the twelve forts, Douaumont, on a 1,200 foot (380 metre) high hill feature, and the smaller Fort Vaux. The stone fort of Douaumont had been reinforced by a 3.5 metre thick concrete carapace, and by 4 metres of earth – to prove effective as shells burst on the outer skin and failed to penetrate. The fort possessed retractable armoured turrets for artillery and machine-guns, and shell-proof accommodation for the garrison, but lacked secure tunnel communication to the rear for reinforcements. The blockhouse chain was reinforced by thick barbed-wire entanglements all laid out to utilise the pattern of steep hill ridges on either side of the Meuse, together providing opportunities for enfilading fire and reverse slope defence. But, as the doctrine of attack came progressively to dominate military thinking in the pre-1914 years, neglect had set in with worse to follow in 1914 despite the value, largely unrecognised, of Verdun as a rock-safe pivot for the whole French line and in particular for the defence of Champagne. The advocates of attack convinced Joffre that the rapid seizure of the massive Belgian fortresses of Liège and Namur showed that such fortifications were at best valueless, at worst like Sedan in 1870, simply collection places for eventual massacre or surrender. Accordingly, in 1915 Joffre had deliberately set about the reduction of the garrisons of all the forts, the removal of their guns and, for some, preparations for demolition – all this the subject of Colonel Driant's report and Galliéni's anxiety.

By the end of 1915 Verdun, despite the fact that the Germans were only some 15 kilometres away, had lost over fifty heavy and field gun batteries, its forts' garrisons reduced to mere handfuls of men, with equally small numbers preparing an ad hoc trench defence system. Defensive trenches were badly prepared, and the forts and strongpoints had no communication with one another. Douaumont had been reduced to one 155mm and four 75mm guns. The relative quietness of the area in 1915 had eroded efficiency and alertness, patrolling had become perfunctory, and telephone lines were not buried. Amassing against them steadily throughout January 1916 was the German 6th Army commanded by Crown Prince Wilhelm and supported by detachments from the army of General von Strantz; they comprised seventeen divisions with 1,300 heavy, medium and field guns. The artillery included thirteen 'Big Bertha' 420mm mortars whose shells weighed over a ton, a couple of 15-inch naval guns, seventeen Austrian 305mm mortars, 210mm howitzers to destroy trenches, and numbers of long-range 150mm medium guns for the harassment of supply lines and for counter-bombardment. Two and three quarter million rounds of ammunition for the guns had been brought to the sector in 1,300 trains. In addition, the Germans, recognising the value of air support, had committed over 150 aircraft, four airships and a number of captive artillery observation balloons to the Verdun sector.

The Battle of Verdun

After a local German victory at Frise in Picardy in January, the battle of Verdun opened on 21 February and was to last until the end of December. Falkenhayn had planned the assault to begin on the 13th but winter conditions had delayed the arrival of the all-important heavy artillery. The delay probably saved the French from an initial and shattering reverse. French intelligence, on this occasion, was well aware of the German plans. Movement of troops and stores had been reported as early as January. Deserters from the German army (often Alsatian or Polish) advised of the build-up of German strength in the early days of February, with indications that Douaumont would be the first German objective. In mid-February more deserters provided confirmation of the arrival of two army corps with vast quantities of heavy artillery, a confirmation corroborated by sporadic but obvious German ranging of their guns on likely targets. Other sources and deserters warned that the Germans now possessed gas shells and a large number of flame-throwers.

The Germans, however, were able to conceal the presence of the regiments of assault troops right up in the front line by the construction of *Stollen*, underground galleries into which troops were marched at night undetected. Absence of effective briefing, the February weather conditions, and German aircraft and anti-aircraft artillery had also prevented the three French air squadrons in the area from acquiring air reconnaissance reports on the artillery concentrations until the day before the German attack. Specific German deception measures had included circulation of a disinformation rumour of an attack on Belfort.

The principal difficulty facing the French Intelligence staffs, however, had been that of persuading the operations staff at GQG to listen, preoccupied as they were with plans for the Somme and unwilling to spare any troops to reinforce Verdun; and in the city itself there was prolonged complacency until General Herr, commander of the Verdun area, urgently asked for reinforcements, prompting Castelnau, President Poincaré and Joffre to visit the area. Castelnau, on 24 January, countermanded the previous orders given to Herr to concentrate on defensive works on the left bank of the Meuse, south of the city, and instead directed him to complete new works barely begun, on the right bank. No attempt was made, however, to garrison the forts for defence and the removal of their guns continued. On 12 February Herr was given two extra Territorial divisions, but even with the last-minute arrival of General Chrétien's XXX Corps and General de Bazelaire's VII Corps the French preparations remained pathetically inadequate.

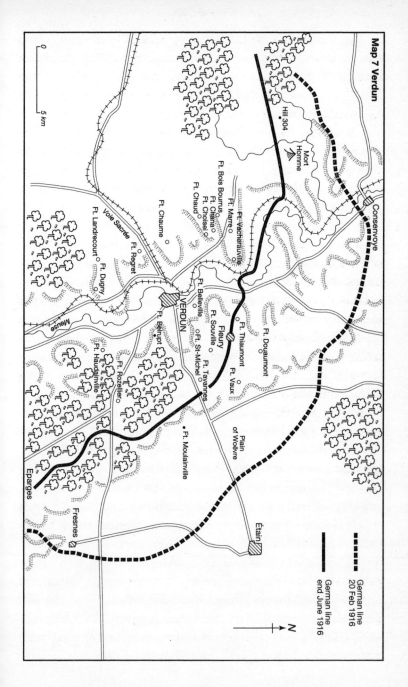

Map 7 Verdun

0
5 km

Hill 304

Mort
Homme

Consenvoye

Ft. Bois Bourrus
Ft. Marre
Ft. Chana
Ft. Choisel
Ft. Chaud
Ft. Vacherauville

Ft. Chaume

Voie Sacrée
Ft. Regret

Ft. Landrecourt
Ft. Dugny

Meuse

VERDUN
Ft. Belleville
Ft. Souville
Ft. St-Michel
Ft. Bélrupt

Fleury
Ft. Thiaumont
Ft. Tavannes

Ft. Douaumont

Ft. Vaux

Ft. Haudainville
Ft. Rozellier

Ft. Moulainville

Plain
of Woëvre

Eparges

Fresnes

Étain

German line
20 Feb 1916

German line
end June 1916

N

The German assault, Operation *Gericht* (judgement), was to be launched on a 10-kilometre-wide front on the right bank of the Meuse, attacking the salient from the north and the east. On the opening day of the battle Chrétien's XXX Corps command, including the two Territorial divisions, comprised four divisions. Two of these, the 72nd, a reserve division of men from Lorraine, and the 51st, reservists from the Lille area, were deployed forward on the right bank awaiting the German attack, together with, from VII Corps, the 14th, a regular division from Franche Comté. Bazelaire's other division, the 37th from Algeria, was in reserve. The regiments within these divisions were of very varied quality, the thirty-four battalions including two battalions of elite *chasseurs à pied*, but also many elderly Territorial reservist units, together with Zouaves and Tirailleurs Algériens. In their hurriedly prepared trench lines they were pitted against three German army corps including some of the best and most battle-hardened divisions in the German army, seventy-two battalions together with over 800 artillery pieces. A further two corps of lesser value were also in the area though not involved at the outset.

On the 21st the great assault opened at 4.00 a.m. with the biggest and most intensive artillery bombardment recorded to that day and lasting nine hours, tearing the ground to pieces, uprooting trees, and destroying the main railway lines into Verdun. The fire, when concentrated on known French positions, amounted to forty shells a minute, destroying French trench systems and concrete machine-gun posts, cutting telephone lines and inflicting heavy casualties, with men torn apart by shrapnel or buried alive. Many survivors were shell-shocked by the carnage and the terrifying noise. Unfortunately French counter-bombardment had been reduced to a few single guns; German artillery, using phosgene gas for which the French masks were inadequate protection, as well as high explosive, had been expertly targeted on the French gun sites.

After a final hour of particularly intensive fire and in fading light, the German infantry launched probing attacks, flame-throwers emitting streams of flame in the gathering darkness. To their surprise the Germans met with a spirited resistance and even small local counter-attacks in the best pre-1914 tradition from the battered French lines. Notably valorous at the point of the salient, the Bois des Caures, were the two battalions of chasseurs reservists from Lille and Epernay, the 56th and 59th battalions. As the German barrage increased in intensity several officers asked for absolution from a stretcher-bearer, Father Martimprey, who until August 1914 had been rector of Beirut University. The chasseurs commander was Colonel Driant, the Nancy deputy who had earlier incurred Joffre's anger by his criticism of Verdun's defence. His reward was now to be a hero's death.

Initial German gains were minimal, but on the following day and after a second shattering artillery bombardment they made substantial progress, encircling Samogneux and taking Beaumont after bloody house-to-house fighting. French formations and units lost cohesion, with telephone lines cut and runners killed, as well as suffering further severe casualties. By 23 February, the 72nd and 51st Divisions were almost finished and the 37th Division was moved to its support, in turn to be destroyed piecemeal. The German artillery, the bitter cold, the spectacle of dead, dying and wounded in hundreds, many horribly mutilated or burnt, proved too much for the North Africans, and the division broke. By the night of the 24th Chrétien's XXX Corps had virtually ceased to exist, and relieving troops from General Balfourier's XX Corps were arriving only slowly, the first units to arrive marching through snowstorms without food for two days and without their artillery or machine-guns. The XX Corps, however, was that which had saved Nancy in 1914, its soldiers taking pride in its title of the 'Iron Corps'. Local French commanders, fearing a breakthrough, wished to withdraw from the whole Woevre plain area to hold the inner ring of hills around Verdun, or even retreat entirely across the Meuse. In the event, the Woevre plain was evacuated following a confusion of orders.

Disaster was to follow on the 25th. The major right bank fort, Douaumont, its normal garrison of 500 reduced to some sixty elderly and weary men in the weeks prior to the battle, fell to an audacious German coup. The seizure of the fort, by only a small party of German soldiers, was a result of the neglect of elementary precautions both at staff level in Verdun and inside the fort itself. The Germans entered through an unguarded gun embrasure, having first clambered undetected up the side of the moat. The fall of the fort was a devastating prestige, moral and military blow. Evidence of panic began to appear. Only increasing German exhaustion, the difficulty of moving guns over terrain destroyed by gunfire and effective French artillery fire from the left bank of the Meuse prevented further German success. Total confusion reigned at Herr's headquarters. There then followed drama at command level. Briand directed that Verdun must be held. On the evening of the 24th Castelnau had first secured Joffre's authority to send Pétain and his 2nd Army to Verdun and a little later, daring to disturb Joffre's sleep, he secured for himself full powers of decision-making at Verdun. Rushing to the city the next day, and despite the panic and chaos, he reinvigorated the defenders and assessed that it was still possible and desirable to hold the right bank of the Meuse. On purely military argument the French would have been wiser to have conducted a withdrawal to the hill ridges on the left bank, using the ground to advantage. But the cost to prestige and the possibly fatal blow to the all-important morale of the French troops of such a withdrawal appeared insupportable; whether their morale would have stood the strain of a series of fighting withdrawals without collapse, after all that had happened since August 1914, was highly uncertain.

Pétain had been awakened on the night of 24 February in the bedroom of a Paris hotel where he was sojourning with a lady later to become his wife. His ADC, Serrigny, informed him, not altogether to his surprise, of his new command but Pétain did not set off until the morning for Verdun where, on arrival, Castelnau handed him an order to defend the right bank. From his headquarters in the cramped *mairie* of Souilly, 15 kilometres south-west of Verdun, he immediately tackled the two main issues, the fighting front and supply. The former was in practice the easier as Balfourier's Iron Corps was now fully available, and another army corps was being sent to Verdun from the Somme – to the annoyance of Haig who had to cover for both of them. Pétain directed that a new defence line, reactivating and using the forts be prepared and held, each unit being given a clearly defined sector of responsibility. He divided the front into four sectors, on the left to the river under General Bazelaire, from the river to Douaumont under Guillaumat, from Douaumont to the Woerve under Balfourier, Witz to the Meuse heights on the right Duchesne. A line of trenches called by the soldiers 'the panic line' linked the whole front. On recovery from an attack of influenza Pétain also began personally to supervise the artillery fire plans, hitherto poorly co-ordinated, to strike more effectively by flanking fire on the German positions and roads north of Douaumont. More divisions and additional artillery *groupes*, 75mm and 155mm, were requested and soon arrived. The German offensive lost momentum and by the end of the month had ground to a halt, its very real chance of success ended.

Of almost equal importance to Pétain's skill in defensive battle was the effect of his presence on his exhausted and deeply apprehensive troops. Pétain's reputation among ordinary soldiers was already that of a general who cared for their welfare and would not commit them to a battle without sound reason. He had, as already mentioned, begun the war as a front-line infantry colonel and in all subsequent operations he was frequently to be seen at the forward edge of battle with front-line soldiers. Immediately Chrétien and two divisional commanders – the unfortunate Bapst of the 72nd and de Bonneval of the 37th – were *limogé*. Herr followed a little later. A new confidence began to appear, a confidence strengthened by Pétain's man-management, in particular the regular fifteen-day rotation of units providing periods of rest, rather than keeping a regiment in the fight replacing casualties from new drafts.

Supply for the ever increasing numbers of men arriving in the Verdun area was immensely difficult, but one for which Pétain's orderly, calculating mind was well suited. In normal times the railway reached Verdun from two directions, but one had been cut by the Germans the previous September and the other was now under constant German artillery fire. Repair parties working at night were able to clear the line for a few trains to pass. Pétain was obliged to fall back on a poor-quality road, some 6 metres wide and little more than a track, that ran south-west from Verdun to Bar le Duc; a narrow-gauge light railway, the Meusien, ran parallel to it. For this road Pétain and his exceptionally able transport officers, Major Richard and Captain Doumenc of 'race to the sea' fame, developed a system of constant conveyor belt supply, which they likened to chain buckets, called *noria*. The belt was formed by some 3,500 lorries, mostly requisitioned, which drove a few metres apart with dimmed headlights. Half of them went in the right, loaded with supplies, and the rest returned on the left, packed with wounded or units being relieved. On each side of the road other troops marched in columns, either to the front or away for rest periods. Ten Territorial battalions of 10,000 men were brought up, and a number of engineer units began to lay down a broad-gauge railway on the left bank.

Keeping this vital supply line (after the war known as *la voie sacrée*) moving at its peak – 90,000 men 50,000 tons of supply each week in all weathers and mostly at night – was an astonishing achievement. Vehicles driven by exhausted drivers would collide, or in wet weather slip off the road. There was an acute shortage of men skilled in vehicle maintenance and repair. The solid tyres of the vehicles chewed up the road surface, which was maintained by a military labour division, mostly African and Indochinese, from France's colonial empire. Any vehicle that broke down was ditched and the road cleared. On occasions German artillery fire would create chaos. Horse-drawn transport was not permitted. Motor transport for war, one vehicle every ten seconds at peak periods, dramatically came of age.

Stiffening French resistance forced the Crown Prince to rethink his plans; he had originally preferred a plan for an attack on both banks of the Meuse but had given way to Falkenhayn's objections. He now returned to this plan, launching attacks on 6 March, first on the left bank against the hills of Mort Homme and Hill 304, next on the right bank against Fort Vaux, with prolonged artillery bombardments. Phosgene gas shells were also used. Pétain, however, had by now stabilised the front with the arrival of divisions of the 2nd Army, and the German assaults met determined resistance, inspired in some cases by a reiteration of the 1914 orders that units or individuals retreating would be fired upon. Despite the failure of one division, spirited French counter-attacks ensured that little ground was lost. One of the attacks by the 92nd Regiment was led in person by Lieutenant-Colonel Macker smoking a cigar and swaggering his cane, but he was later killed, with the loss of the ground originally gained. French artillery, too, scored spectacular success, notably in destroying many of the biggest German mortars and exploding a very large ammunition dump.

A fresh German six-division attack on Mort Homme and Hill 304 opened on 14 March and led to a month of bitter fighting across terrain which, after the deluge of shells from the bombardments, were no longer French linear trench lines but defended holes in the ground. The failure to achieve anything other than local small gains led the German command, on 9 April, to launch a further major attack, once again preceded by an intensive artillery bombardment, gas again being used. Violent fighting, often hand-to-hand, followed, Mort Homme changing hands several times. It was after one such temporary recapture that Pétain issued his famous if ungrammatical order, *'Courage, on les aura'* ('We will get them'). Prolonged rain converted much of the battlefield into mud in which soldiers of both armies squelched or waded, the ooze polluted by the foul-smelling corpses of men and horses. Fighting developed into combat between very small groups of men battling it out from one shellhole to another with no cover in a barren landscape. Communication was often reduced to *colombogrammes*, messages by pigeon. Teilhard de Chardin, serving as a stretcher-bearer with an Algerian Tirailleurs regiment described the scene as *'un vrai relief lunaire'*, adding that the only possible commemorative monument for so much suffering would be one of Christ on the Cross. Heavy rain constrained the German attacks which were only fully resumed, this time in sweltering heat and after another cannonade, on 3 May. By the end of the month the Germans had succeeded in taking both Mort Homme and Hill 304, so giving their artillery fields of fire across the Meuse to the right bank. They had also made an initial gain of some 7 kilometres, before being contained by effective French local counter-attacks on the right bank itself, in which the 408th and 409th Regiments distinguished themselves. The casualties incurred by both sides, however, were mounting to frightening totals. By the end of April the German figure was 120,000, the French 133,000.

The casualty figures, the manpower demands of Pétain (by 1 May fifty-two divisions to maintain his *noria* relief and supply system), and the prestige being gained by Pétain as the valiant defender of Verdun were proving increasingly irritating for Joffre, who saw his plans for the July Somme offensive being jeopardised. Accordingly, on 30 April, Joffre promoted Pétain to succeed de Langle as the commander of the Central Group of Armies, so removing him from direct command at Verdun. This now went to General Robert Nivelle, who was thought to have commanded well in the right-bank counter-attacks.

Nivelle believed in the pre-1914 all-out offensive doctrine; in this he was supported by his Chief-of-Staff Colonel d'Alenson (a soldier in a hurry being terminally ill) and the fire-eating Coloniale General Mangin, a commander of proven courage and considerable ability but indifferent to loss of life, particularly if those killed were from another continent. Soldiers labelled him *le boucher* (the butcher). Their first move, an effort in mid-May to retake Douaumont, ended in a bloody failure despite a massive 290-gun preliminary artillery preparation and French infantry briefly reaching the top of the fort. Mangin lost his command, but only temporarily.

The French reverse encouraged Falkenhayn, aware of Joffre's plans, for an offensive on the Somme, to make one further effort to take Verdun, despite the objections of the Crown Prince. A new offensive opened on 1 June and, after an epic five-day defence against gas, flame-thrower and massive artillery attacks by the French garrison of Major Raynal, the Germans forced the surrender of Fort Vaux on the 7th. This was caused primarily by the the polluted atmosphere within the fort – gas, excrement and corpses – together with the garrison's lack of water, compelling the men to lick moisture from the walls or even drink their own urine. Raynal, already wounded three times prior to this event, was accorded the honours of war by the Germans. This success was followed by an attack on the 23rd following further German use of a stronger phosgene gas in the opening bombardments, principally on the French artillery, an event that caused Pétain to wonder whether the right bank could still be held. But at this, the crisis of the whole Verdun battle, the French army managed to prevent a breakthrough, fighting every inch of the way in heat and acute thirst. Pétain even had to restrain Nivelle and Mangin who wanted to launch counter-attacks. The French, however, were to be pushed back by early July to the perimeter defence of Fort Souville and the outer defences of Fort Tavannes, forced to abandon Fort Thiaumont and suffering further heavy losses, losing the artillery duels for lack of guns and observation posts, and also with disturbing evidence appearing of cracks in morale. Again, however, Pétain as Central Group commander, had assessed that even if morale was in serious danger, any withdrawal from Verdun would be absolutely fatal to it.

On 11 July the Germans launched what was to be their final series of assaults on Verdun in the Souville area; this proved a failure thanks to a recovery by the French gunners, now wearing efficient gas-masks and able to fire their 75mm artillery over open sights at the advancing lines of Germans. The commander of the 255th Brigade, Colonel Coquelin de Lisle, was killed, gun in hand, in the defence of Fleury. There could be no follow-up as, frightened by the opening barrage of the Somme offensive, Falkenhayn had stopped further ammunition supplies to Verdun; and the vigour of French counter-attacks which continued into August – the work of Mangin, now returned to the battle – forced the exhausted Germans to turn to the defensive. German reserves had in any case been sent to the Eastern Front and in September Falkenhayn was replaced by Hindenburg, who was not interested in Verdun.

Nivelle and Mangin now turned to the attack, to be in

three waves, the first two by three divisions, the third by two; their objective was Douaumont. Nivelle, an artilleryman, with the support of Pétain arranged for the heaviest preparatory barrage yet mounted by the French Army, including fire from two 400mm railway guns and a battery of 370mm mortars, some guns using gas shells. Over 300,000 shells were fired on a 5km front. The bombardment opened on 19 October, lowering German resistance; after a feint which deceived the Germans into revealing their positions for French artillery attention, on the 24th the French infantry assault began, supported by creeping barrage mortar fire. Newly constructed underground tunnels and concentration areas provided covered approach. French air superiority denied the Germans air and balloon observation for their artillery and the German defences fell surprisingly quickly. Fort Douaumont, which had been damaged and partially evacuated by the Germans, was stormed by the elite Régiment d'Infanterie Coloniale du Maroc, at the time composed of two battalions of white Coloniale infantry, a battalion of Tirailleurs Sénégalais and two companies of Somalis from Djibouti. The regiment was commanded by Colonel Régnier. Douaumont village was taken by the 4th Régiment Mixte de Zouaves et Tirailleurs – one battalion of Zouaves and two of Tunisians. A few days later, on 2 November, Fort Vaux was recaptured and in a final eight-division-strong attack in freezing conditions on 15 December supported by 760 guns, the Germans were pushed back some 5 kilometres from Douaumont. Verdun was safe.

So ended the battle of Verdun, a battle that had long ceased to be one for Verdun or any particular piece of ground but had become an end in itself, consuming in attrition division after division of both the opposing armies and becoming the centrepiece of the French war effort. The casualties in the eleven months of fighting amounted to 330,000 Germans, of whom 143,000 were dead or missing and some 351,000 French losses,

56,000 dead, 100,000 missing or captured and 195,000 wounded. The impact of the horror of the fighting and the massive blood-letting on the French soldier is considered later. In the sense of its symbolic significance, the campaign, despite the heavier French casualties, was a French victory. The Germans were only able to reap the fruits of their effort twenty-four years later.

The Somme

Joffre's original design for forty divisions to lead the Somme offensive was rendered impractical by the needs of Verdun, in particular the number of divisions needed for Pétain's system of rotation. Joffre repeatedly asked Haig to bring forward the date of the launch of the offensive to ease the pressures on Verdun, Haig eventually agreeing on 1 July. By this time, instead of forty divisions Foch's Northern Group of Armies could only provide sixteen for the Somme offensive, of which five in Fayolle's 6th Army were to participate in the opening attack. The main burden of the offensive was now to fall on the British 4th Army, with Fayolle on the British right, and Micheler's 10th Army further south, covering the flank of the attack. The offensive duly opened on 1 July after a five-day artillery preparation, in which 1,200 of the 4,000 guns were French. As is well known, 1 July 1916 was to be one of the most disastrous days in British military history; by its end 20,000 men had been killed or were missing, and a further 40,000 were wounded.

Less familiar is the relative success of the French. Foch was able to produce a more devastating artillery preparation for a much smaller frontage and he had advantages of ground and rather weaker German defensive preparations, unable to withstand the successive rushing waves of French infantry, now attacking in small groups of men rather than in a line. Above all, he had an advantage of surprise, due both to the

German assessment that the French army was too weakened by Verdun to attack, and also to a slight delay in his assault, a delay that had lulled the Germans. North of the Somme Balfourier's XX Corps, helped by a river mist, took the German first-line positions but were unable to follow up their success as the British had not made the necessary progress. South of the Somme a Coloniale division and one from the XXV Corps had achieved even greater success, advancing well beyond the German first-line positions; on 3 July they overran the German second line, taking the high ground overlooking Péronne.

Here success stopped, the main reason being that the British offensive could only be maintained by local-level attrition attacks, in view of the casualties and ammunition shortages. Foch saw these attacks as insufficient for a further major advance which would expose his flank. The Germans took the opportunity to reinforce their positions, so containing the local attacks made by Fayolle's army. The only further French territorial gains in July were made by the left flank formations of Micheler's 10th Army.

The British continued with local attacks, costly and unrewarding, in August while plans were prepared for a big offensive in September. The reverses of July had led to friction between Haig, Joffre and Foch; in consequence the plans were not properly co-ordinated, attacks being launched piecemeal. For this offensive the British had created a new army, the 5th, moving the existing 4th to the centre. Fayolle received four new army corps north of the Somme where Foch planned his main thrust, while in early September Micheler managed a 5-kilometre advance south of the Somme towards Chaulnes. Fayolle's north of the Somme offensive opened on 12 September, securing some initial success but then stalling in the absence of ready reserves. On the 15th the French attack was resumed, coinciding with the opening of the British assault, preceded by a three-day bombardment and noteworthy for the first use of tanks. But in two weeks of heavy fighting the only gain was the capture of Combles. Autumn rains then descended on the battlefield, waterlogging guns and transport. Joffre called a halt to major attacks, but the British, at the pressing of Joffre and Foch, continued until mid-November, achieving limited local successes. As in 1915 and at Verdun, nothing had been gained commensurate with the casualty totals. Bigger armies, more extensive defensive trench systems, heavier artillery bombardments, mass attacks by thousands of men – all led only to greater destruction and bloodshed. The French total was 196,000 of which 37,000 were deaths, 29,000 missing or prisoners and 130,000 wounded. The British and Germans lost 400,000 and probably 500,000 respectively, killed, wounded, prisoners or missing; totals less than 1915 in number but much greater in their cumulative effect.

Undismayed, Joffre embarked on plans for a fresh offensive in February 1917. These, in outline, were to include an attack by three British armies north of the Somme with one French army to the south and, a little later, a French offensive in Champagne. Joffre, however, was no longer the hero of the Marne in the eyes of the political leadership. His neglect of the defences of Verdun was now known, the huge casualty lists and the failures on the Somme had led to disillusion. Covert press criticism of him increased and in November he was openly censured in the legislature. He tried to defend himself by scapegoating Foch, whose rigid adherence to the offensive doctrine throughout 1915 and 1916 was the great error of his career. The criticism grew stronger, together with malicious whispering about his health, physical and mental. He was abruptly told that he was to be replaced by Nivelle and a little later, on 12 December, Joffre was informed of his new appointment as technical adviser to the government on military matters.

Nivelle was appointed Commander-in-Chief of the Armies in the North and North-east, in other words the overall French field commander on the Western Front. Joffre retired with ill grace, his fall softened by elevation to the *maréchalat*, the first Marshal of the Third Republic, while Foch succeeded to the post of 'technical adviser'. Castelnau was also *limogé*, and Franchet d'Esperey was given the Northern Group of Armies. In a cabinet reshuffle France's second outstanding colonial general, Hubert Lyautey, was brought from Morocco to become Minister for War.

Nivelle owed his appointment to several factors. He had achieved real successes at Verdun. Franchet d'Esperey, Fayolle and Castelnau, known Catholics, were unacceptable politically. Nivelle was a Protestant and known to be anti-Catholic. From his English mother he had learned fluent English and he was – at first – well regarded by the British, including Haig. He had a pleasant, open manner, an aggressive spirit and boundless self-confidence. Above all he let it be understood that he had the formula for breaking the trench warfare deadlock and would be able to deliver success to a war-weary nation. Politicians, for whom Nivelle had contempt but an open courteous manner, felt that he was heaven-sent. Yet not for the first time nor the last in French history, the appointment of a general primarily for his political suitability was to lead to disaster.

CHAPTER 6

1916
Developments within the Army

A number of varied developments occurred within the French army while the great battles of Verdun and the Somme were raging.

Personnel and Equipment

By the end of 1916 the army, on all fronts, had expanded to a total of 114 infantry and six cavalry divisions (against the seventy-two and ten respectively of August 1914) forming thirty-three army corps, and two cavalry corps. For these there were 502 generals of division commander rank, of whom thirty-eight were commanding an army or a group of armies, ninety-five were commanding an army corps or some other grouping of divisions, and forty were serving on staffs. At regimental level the supply of officers was in part maintained by commissioning from the ranks, but the standard fell and there were shortages in many regiments, which later proved a cause of indiscipline. The main supply of rank and file for the front was maintained by the call-up of the 1917 draft on 1 January 1916, some 275,000 men, the increasing use of Armée d'Afrique North African units, and by the reappearance on the Western Front of Tirailleurs from West Africa. In respect of metropolitan France, 7.3 million men had been mobilised by January 1916, but from this total at least 900,000 were casualties – dead, captured or missing, with many thousands more wounded. The ongoing heavy casualties suffered at Verdun and on the Somme necessitated changes in organisation. The echelon of brigade in infantry divisions was discarded, an infantry division now comprised only three regiments, nine battalions instead of twelve. Battalions were scaled down to 750 men. Fifty-two regiments of which forty-five were reserve, were disbanded. In the front-line units the nucleus of old pre-1914 soldiers was often still the backbone; considered also to be of especial value were cavalrymen transferred to the infantry and the newest, youngest and keenest of the conscripts.

In the front line the Lebel rifle began to be replaced as the basic standard infantryman's weapon by the 1907 Berthier. Initially this rifle suffered from its small three-round ammunition clip, but this was soon enlarged to provide for one of five rounds. The new 50mm Vivien-Bessière grenade cup-discharger fitting provided the rifleman with a capability to fire a larger percussion grenade. Also appearing at company level were the Chauchat (Chauchat Sutter Ribeyrolles Gladiator) rifle company-level light machine-gun, useful if not entirely satisfactory being liable to jam. At its best its rate of fire was 250 rounds per minute, but with its twenty-round semi-circular magazine firing Lebel ammunition, it proved at 36 kg to be very heavy. The gun was operated by teams of two, later increased to three or four. The number of machine-guns issued to each regiment increased to twenty-four, and was to increase further to thirty-six in 1917, so providing a machine-gun company for each battalion.

Each regiment, too, was now provided with a section of three 37mm light guns, horse-drawn to the front but manhandled thereafter. The French army's first flame-thrower, the Hersent, and the first version of the Brandt pneumatic mortar both appeared late in 1916. The army's slow artillery expansion, only 590 new heavy guns in the year, was highlighted by the French artillery weakness at Verdun where at the outset there were only small numbers of 105mm and obsolete 120mm guns, but no 155mm heavy guns. At the end of May Joffre requested the urgent production of 960 medium and 440 heavy guns to prepare for infantry attacks, counter-bombardment work and the reduction of strongpoints. But for most of the year fire support for the infantry still depended too heavily on the 75mm gun, the very limited number of 240mm and larger pieces and the increased number of mortars, together with the adaptation of existing mortars to fire heavier bombs.

The first mass use of motor transport, on the *voie sacrée* to Verdun, has already been noted but perhaps more directly appreciated by the ordinary soldier, especially when injured, was the arrival of the Peugeot push chair for the recovery of wounded men and the protection provided by the efficient M2 gas-mask. Less effective was an unwieldy trench excavation machine.

The new weapons and the changes on the battlefield itself led to certain changes in tactics. The main theme, struck in new infantry regulations issued in the summer of 1916, was that of *tenir*. Ground must be held to the last man, and if lost it must immediately be recovered. Trench warfare was seen as an interim phase of a battle; if defensive, every opportunity must nevertheless be taken to harass the enemy – by artillery, mines, patrols, raids, and snipers. In practice, difficulties soon appeared. Artillery ammunition was still in short supply. Terrain was not always suitable for mining even if the special-ist troops and equipment were available. Raids could lose men while the information gained could be obtained from air reconnaissance.

In attack an assault would often be led by a line of riflemen and cup-discharger grenade throwers together with *cisailleurs* (engineers tasked to cut barbed-wire). These would be followed by a second wave of grenade-throwers and rifle grenadiers. A third wave of riflemen, some also armed with grenades, would finally clear the enemy first-line position while the first wave would continue the advance, the second acting as a reserve. The 37mm guns provided close fire support at ranges of 100 to 500 metres. Verdun, with its fort defence systems and the ground endlessly churned up, often into mud, imposed again in some areas a different local style, that of small outposts, often shellholes (*trous de loups*), supported by platoon strongholds (*grandes gardes*) with interlocking fire plans, support lines, and behind them the various wire entanglements and blockhouse chains.

Behind the front lines French industry was attempting to produce a battle tank, the result of successful argument put forward by Colonel Estienne to Joffre. Three types were under development. The Schneider factory at Creusot began the manufacture of 400 tanks of 13.5 tons, with a crew of six, an armament of a short-barrelled 75mm gun and two Hotchkiss machine-guns, armour protection between 5mm and 12mm and a maximum speed on level ground of 6 kilometres per hour, but with only a limited capability for crossing trenches and ditches. A few of these became available for service in December 1916. A further 400 tanks of a second, larger model were manufactured at the same time at Saint-Chamond by a firm of marine engineers. This vehicle's weight lay between 19 and 23 tons, with a crew of nine, a long-barrelled 75mm gun and four machine-guns, armour protection of the vital regions of 17mm and a maximum speed on level ground of 10 kilometres per hour. Its hull was too long for its chassis and its tracks too narrow, affording poor cross-country, cross-trench capability. Produced in a hurry, the tank was very unreliable, breaking down frequently. The third type was to be much smaller, foreshadowing the concept of the light tank. Initially produced by Renault in 1917–18, the tank weighed 6.4 tons, with a crew of two, an armament of a Hotchkiss machine-gun in a fully revolving turret, armour as thick as 22mm on the turret and 16mm at the front, but with a maximum speed on level ground of only 8 kilometres per hour.

The year 1916 also saw major developments in French military aviation leading to the first real 'war in the air'. In 1914 and 1915 French military aircraft had been used principally and very successfully for movement and artillery reconnaissance, but the Blériot monoplane reconnaissance machines were exceedingly vulnerable, being slow both in speed and rate of climb. The Caudron and Farman aircraft were little better as machines, being limited to dropping reports or marked maps of their reconnaissance to the ground near the French gun positions for counter-bombardment. The larger Voisin aircraft had been used as early as August 1914 in a bombing raid on German airship sheds at Metz. In November 1914 the first Groupe de Bombardement was formed from the squadrons of Voisins, its first attacks being on Freiburg railway station in daylight on 14 and 19 December. Early 1915 saw the formation of three more *groupes* which carried out attacks on the poison-gas factory at Ludwigshafen, at Pechelbronn, the Saar steel plants and other targets until September, achieving very little. The *groupes* were then broken up and given to army commanders.

In October 1914 a mechanic, Louis Quenault, firing a Hotchkiss machine-gun mounted on a Voisin piloted by Joseph Frantz, had shot down a German aircraft, the first air-to-air combat success in history. However, the French aircraft used for reconnaissance were either unarmed or equipped with a machine-gun with limited rates and arcs of fire. In general, throughout most of 1915, aircraft development was handicapped by the absence of any clear ideas on the use of aircraft in war other than, when possible, bombing or as an auxiliary to the artillery.

In late 1915 and early 1916 the Germans produced the world's first true single-seater fighter, the monoplane Fokker EIII. This machine mounted a forward firing machine-gun fitted with interrupter gear enabling it to fire through the propeller. The aircraft immediately gave the Germans air superiority, which they did not use to full advantage, limiting themselves to protecting the German observation balloons directing the artillery at the opening of the battle for Verdun and later to ineffective patrolling. At the outset, the only French success was on the evening of the opening day, the shooting down by a lorry-mounted 75mm gun of one of the four airships which were being used to bomb lines of communication. The airship, L77, was easily visible to the artillerymen in bright moonlight.

The French Air Service, however, under its head Colonel Barès, reacted with remarkable speed and efficiency in both machines and men. Barès saw clearly the need for interceptor fighter aircraft and was able to deploy small numbers of an aircraft developed in 1915, the biplane Nieuport 11 Bébé, equipped with a Lewis gun firing over the top of the wing. To fly them and other reconnaissance machines, Barès in February despatched to Verdun five fighter squadrons with specially picked pilots, the Groupe des Cigognes (Storks), together with eight reconnaissance squadrons all under the command of a former cavalry officer, the resoundingly named Commandant de Rose, Baron de Tricernot and Marquis de Rose, and after his death in an accident in May, by his successor, Commandant Le Révérend. Rose received a clear order from Pétain: 'Rose, sweep the skies clean for me, I am blind.' Members of Les Cigognes included most of the then French air 'aces' (the term *as* being given to an aviator who had shot down five enemy machines), among them Guynemer, Nungesser, Lenoir and Navarre. In May 1916 the squadron of volunteer Americans, the Escadrille Américaine, later the

Escadrille Lafayette, joined the French at Verdun, flying with notable skill and audacity. The concept of the fighter squadron now came to be accepted. The fighters operated in patrols of four or five machines flying in inverted V formations over one of the five specific sectors, shooting down the slow two-seater German reconnaissance machines and, with the new Le Prieur incendiary rockets, the Drachen observation balloons. Despite reverses and losses following the arrival of the German ace Boelcke, French successes continued with a revised tactic of flying a larger number of fighters, ten or twelve, to protect one or two reconnaissance aircraft directing artillery fire.

The German riposte, however, was the formation of specific fighter squadrons each of fourteen machines, the first becoming operational in September 1916, others following. The squadrons had been issued with the very efficient Fokker D1 in the summer when air fighting shifted from Verdun to the Somme. They regained German air superiority and inflicted losses on French and British aircraft in the autumn. German success was still further developed with the appearance, also in the autumn, of the Albatros D1 equipped with twin belt-fed Spandau machine-guns, giving a devastating rate of fire of 1,000 rounds per minute. Within this combination of aircraft and unit organisation, flying and squadron fighting tactics were now developed so effectively by the German air aces that the Allies were not able to regain effective mastery in 1916. On the Somme, however, the arrival of the improved Nieuport XVIII which mounted both a Lewis and a synchronised Vickers machine-gun together with, late in the autumn, small numbers of the excellent Spad VII with a synchronised Vickers machine-gun, did begin to pose a challenge to the Fokker D1s and the Albatros. Fortunately for the French at Verdun, the Germans moved the majority of their air squadrons to the Somme and, for no very clear reason, they only occasionally tasked their three squadrons of bombers in the Verdun area to attack the *voie sacrée*; these attacks were driven off by the French fighter squadrons. The effects of sustained air attacks on this vital communication route could well have been catastrophic. A return to French strategic bombing was made in June when Caudron G4 aircraft mounted a notable daylight raid on Karlsruhe, but the Caudron machines were slow and unsuitable for daylight work. They were therefore next used in the safer option of night bombing on German lines of communication and troop concentrations at Verdun and on the Somme. In October more effective raids were made on industrial targets in western Germany, including Essen and Munich. For these longer-range attacks British Sopwith 1 ½ Strutter aircraft were initially used, flown by French airmen, and later, the Breguet 2, 4 and 5 models. The bombers also now used the new Gros Andreau bomb, the first specifically designed for use by aircraft. Earlier missiles dropped had been limited to small steel darts or modified 75mm artillery shells. In June, a single aircraft made a leaflet raid over Berlin, that city's first experience of air war. More significant for the future, the Cigognes fighter squadron in the Somme battles demonstrated a further offensive value of fighter aircraft by attacking German infantry on the ground with small bombs and machine-gun fire, with considerable effect upon morale.

Morale after Verdun and the Somme

Three-quarters of the divisions of the French army fought at one time or another at Verdun in 1916; forty-three were committed once, twenty-three twice, and seven three times or more. On occasions twenty divisions were engaged in the fighting. Each division was meant to serve for a fifteen-day spell, and was to be withdrawn when it had lost a third of its personnel. Hundreds of thousands of Frenchmen had trudged, or if they were fortunate, been carried by lorry, along the *voie sacrée*.

On their arrival at the front they entered a world rivalling Dante's descriptions of Hell, a world of almost continuous noise, thunderous and deafening at times, of attack by either side, of phosgene gas and flame-throwers choking or burning men and horses, of a troglodyte life in shellholes, of the appalling stench from putrefying dead horses and human corpses, fragments of flesh suspended on barbed wire rusting above blood-soaked ground in the rain. Fields, woods and villages were ruined by the pulverising artillery bombardments, degraded to swamps or seas of glutinous mud, icy in February and March and again in November and December. Often, to the horror of their companions, single individuals or small groups of men would simply disappear, buried alive in the mud following a shell or mortar explosion. Above the battlefields by day there lay palls of smoke, while at ground level the light that filtered through was a dull grey. At night gun flashes and tracers illuminated the battlefields with frightening patterns of lurid fiery colours. In the summer dry weather added the torture of thirst to the existing misery caused by the non-arrival of food or relief parties, killed on their way forward. Lack of sleep and fatigue further eroded men's powers, particularly for rapid movement. There were no latrine areas, men relieved themselves as best they could at their posts. Vermin, lice and dogs, sometimes crazed by fear and sniffing out corpses, spread disease and dysentery. Finally there was fear, often stark terror, as men endured prolonged bombardments, which tore nerves to shreds, as they wondered whether the next shell would dismember them. Soldiers increasingly questioned the ability of commanders as they saw themselves entrapped in presentiment of death or a despair for which, paradoxically, an 'over the top' attack could provide temporary psychological relief. Hopelessness spread, on occasion very suddenly. Etienne Tanty, a private soldier but in civilian life a schoolmaster, vividly describes it. 'Fatigue makes the least

TOP LEFT Marshal Joseph Galliéni
(*ecpad pers 161*)

TOP RIGHT Marshal Joseph Joffre
(*ecpad pers 227*)

ABOVE Marshal Emile Fayolle
(*ecpad pers 224*)

RIGHT Marshal Louis Franchet
d'Esperey (*ecpad pers 171*)

TOP LEFT Marshal Hubert Lyautey
(*ecpad pers 279*)

ABOVE General Charles Mangin
(*ecpad pers 256*)

LEFT Marshal Philipe Pétain
(*Mary Evans Picture Library*)

ABOVE Marshal Ferdinand Foch and General Maxime Weygand (*IWM Q 66052*)

LEFT General Robert Nivelle (*Hulton Archive*)

ABOVE 75mm gun in action, Gallipoli, 1915 (*IWM Q 13251*)

RIGHT Renault light tank passing through a village in the Oise area, 1918. The tank is pulling a supply sledge and its gun turret is pointed to the rear. (*IWM Q 68001*)

BELOW Schneider 13.5-ton tank (*IWM Q 69503*)

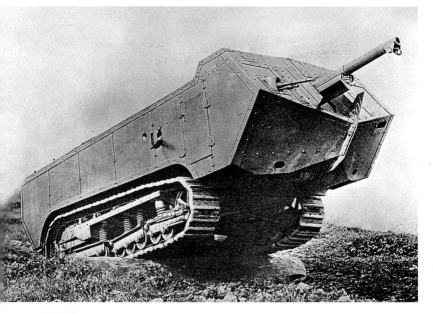

ABOVE Saint-Chamond
20-ton tank
(*IWM Q 14646*)

LEFT 58mm mortar
(*ecpad spa 13X511*)

RIGHT Assault troops training on the 60mm Brandt pneumatic mortar, 1917 (*IWM Q 93188*)

CENTRE 37mm trench gun (*ecpad spa 34X1362*)

BELOW 155mm Schneider medium gun (*ecpad spa 28X1150*)

TOP 155mm Schneider short-barrel howitzer (*ecpad spa 2EY36*)

ABOVE 155mm Rimailho howitzer (*IWM Q 69965*)

ABOVE 400mm gun being prepared for action, Somme, 1916 (*IWM Q 58322*)

BELOW An old 220mm mortar, Marne, 1915 (*IWM Q 78068*)

LEFT 75mm gun artificially
elevated for high trajectory
fire (*IWM HU 82660*)

BELOW Cavalry patrol,
Amiens (*IWM Q 10826*)

OPPOSITE TOP Spahis playing flutes in a rest period, Oise, 1916 (*IWM Q 78090*)

OPPOSITE CENTRE Tirailleurs Sénégalais on the march (*IWM Q 70084*)

OPPOSITE BELOW Infantrymen in a trench with a Chauchat light machine gun (*ecpad spa W 2021*)

LEFT Infantry soldier with machine gun, Somme, 1916 (*IWM Q 55032*)

BELOW Infantry attacking, Verdun, 1917 (*Hulton Archive*)

ABOVE Infantry soldiers
with the Hotchkiss
machine gun
(*ecpad spa 34X1364*)

RIGHT Dismounted
Spahis on exercise with
the Saint-Etienne machine
gun (*ecpad spa A 928*)

BELOW Stretcher bearers
with an improvised
stretcher
(*ecpad spa M 642*)

ABOVE Transport and
foot soldiers on the *Voie
Sacrée*, Verdun, 1916
(*ecpad spa T 1672*)

LEFT Infantry in a trench
(*ecpad aul 96*)

TOP LEFT North African
Tirailleurs in a trench, Artois,
1915 (*IWM Q 78099*)

TOP RIGHT Infantry wearing the
M2 gas mask preparing for a gas
attack (*IWM Q 79458*)

CENTRE LEFT Infantry in action,
Salonika front (*IWM Q 32215*)

CENTRE RIGHT Fort Douaumont
after its recapture (*ecpad spa J 177*)

RIGHT 'Un vrai relief lunaire'
(Teilhard de Chardin) Fort
Vaux area, Verdun, 1916
(*ecpad spa Y 1497*)

TOP Spad XIII fighter
(*IWM Q 66468*)

LEFT Nieuport Bébé
fighter (*IWM Q 66768*)

BELOW Bréguet B2
bomber (*IWM Q 66838*)

44   LES FÊTES DE LA VICTOIRE, 14 JUILLET 1919.
      Le Général Fayolle — LL.

TOP   French troops entering Monastir, 1916 (*IWM Q 32546*)

ABOVE Victory parade, Paris, 14 July 1919, General Fayolle at the head of a
cavalry contingent (*Author's collection*)

physical effort a misery, and turns men's minds to gloom and boredom. One suffers from the collapse of morale, made worse by looking back on the past. One feels beaten, in despair, with no taste for life, no hope and no confidence, depressed and indifferent. It seems as if the desire to live is extinguished and nothing matters any more.' But the only alternative to this predicament was – defeat. Would the war ever end?

The horrors of war were thus impacted on the French army at Verdun, a small geographical area, in especially concentrated form, resulting in individual and collective psychological reactions – immediate, short-term and long-term. The impact of the suffering upon Pétain himself, outwardly cold but inwardly sensitive, was profound, deepening his natural pessimism. He could never again pass a military ambulance without emotion. Also, in the opinion of Pétain and many others, Verdun had been a battle that the French had fought on their own, assisted only by their North African soldiers and not directly by any ally.

The Verdun battles provoked immediate reactions. At individual level a number of soldiers broke mentally in varying degrees of shell-shock or insanity. Others tried to desert, Spain being seen as a refuge, but those who were caught were punished very severely. The worst case of desertion occurred at Avocourt, on the west of the Verdun salient, on 20 March. Deserters gave the Germans details of the French defences and as a consequence some 2,000 men were surrounded and forced to surrender. Besides desertion, other clear evidence appeared of the collective decline in morale as a result of the fighting. The first, slight but noteworthy, was that soldiers did not sing at or on the way to Verdun; for the French soldier singing was, and is, a significant aspect of life. Gradually, too, the infantrymen came to hate the artillery, partly because of the ear-splitting noise, partly in the belief (incorrect as only a few appreciated the efficiency of German counter-bombardment) that the artillerymen had an easy life, and partly because in the absence of reliable or often broken field telephone links, French gunners would inadvertently fire on their own front line. And there was an increasing tendency for commanders to call a halt to attacks, when it was clear that otherwise only annihilation out of all proportion would result.

By May specific acts of indiscipline began to appear. A small group of fifty men who refused to return to the front line were court-martialled but received light sentences, their own officers mitigating the offence. The September 1914 system of regiment-level courts-martial, hated by the soldiers, was abolished. Protests began to be voiced in several regiments. Local attacks, when ordered, were carried out without offensive spirit and in some areas contacts were made with the Germans. In June, shortly following the German taking of Vaux and after a heavy bombardment, most of the men of one battalion surrendered. At the same time in another regiment two subaltern officers were summarily shot for ordering a withdrawal – contrary to Nivelle's strict no retreat directive – when under severe attack, a withdrawal that led to a minor rout endangering other units. Joffre ordered the disbandment in disgrace of both the regiments concerned, the 347th and the 291st Infantry, though after the war compensation was paid to the relatives of the respective officers. In December a division on its way to the final offensive bleated like sheep being led to the slaughter. Another marched to the trenches shouting '*Vive Brizon!*' (a leading pacifist) and '*A Bas La Guerre!*"

Away from the front line further evidence of the strain and morale was to be seen in the stones thrown and shouts of '*embusqué*' that greeted President Poincaré on a visit to award decorations. There was growing lassitude, indifference to the patriotic issues of the war such as the recovery of Alsace-Lorraine, and collective psychological exhaustion that affected even NCOs and soldiers with hitherto excellent records.

Rumours abounded and national press reports of the war – when they did actually reach the front line soldier – were viewed with ever-increasing distrust. The tone of many of the soldiers' news-sheets and papers became more bitterly critical of politicians, journalists who misrepresented the life of the front-line soldier, war profiteers, bureaucrats and commanders who from warmth and safety ordered troops towards danger and death. Letters from home, while always welcomed, too often showed both incomprehension and little genuine interest in the conditions of life at the front. The sense of *isolement*, living in a different world which others simply did not understand, developed; the *brassage* mixing of men from all over France seriously eroded the former mutual moral support of men from the same region. The increase in the wine ration from one-half to three-quarters of a litre per day, although welcomed was still seen as ungenerous and could not possibly on its own restore morale. Soldiers showed interest in reports of possible negotiations for a peace settlement; even those in areas relatively quiet in 1916 complained of the lack of progress. Questions began to be asked about the ability of the generals, now including Joffre, to bring about victory, although Pétain's renown was nationwide. Survivors of Verdun praised him both as the successful defender of the city and as the commander whose system of relief of units and formations showed him as genuinely concerned for the welfare of his troops.

Verdun had been an epic and in its outcome a victory. One major consequence, some reward for the suffering and sacrifice that was not foreseeable at the time, was the impression made in the United States by the French army's resolute fight, an impression that played a part in preparing American public opinion for entry into the war. But Verdun had been costly in men's lives and a traumatic experience far more profound than August 1914 for those who survived. By the end of 1916 the French army, exhausted psychologically as much as physically, was in no condition to tolerate the further bloodletting that its new Commander-in-Chief, in tragic self-delusion, was busy preparing.

CHAPTER 7

1917
Breakdown and Recovery

The year 1917 was to prove dramatic, as the entire course of the war changed. In April the United States entered the war and in November Russia collapsed. For the French army the winter of 1916–17 had been the coldest in living memory, taking further toll on morale in the trenches; April saw a major catastrophe, while during May and June there was an almost universal breakdown of morale and discipline. October, however, brought a clear military victory, limited in scale but of wide significance for morale.

The Aisne Offensive

Nivelle, the new Commander-in-Chief, discarded Joffre's plans for 1917, plans which had in any case been overtaken by events. The Germans withdrew from much of the area that Joffre had planned for the British and French attack, a withdrawal between Arras and Soissons to the powerful and well-prepared Hindenburg Line. This German straightening of their front constrained plans of attack to the flanks of the Hindenburg Line, the British to the north at Arras and the French to the south on the Aisne.

This constraint governed the strategy eventually agreed by Nivelle and Haig. The offensive would commence with a British attack in the Arras sector opening on 9 April with the aim of taking Vimy Ridge. On the 16th the major French offensive would open on the Aisne, with a smaller local attack in Champagne. Nivelle confidently expected that the methods by which he had achieved local success at Verdun could be reproduced on a grand scale on the Chemin des Dames and lead to rupture, a major breakthrough.

For the French army's role in the grand design, while Pétain was left commanding the Centre Group of Armies and Franchet d'Esperey the Northern and Castelnau the Eastern Group, a special Groupe d'Armées de Reserve, (Nivelle preferred de Rupture) under Micheler was formed for the Chemin des Dames. It comprised General Mazel's 5th Army, General Mangin's 6th Army and General Duchesne's 10th Army. Mangin's army included France's finest formations, the VII and XX Corps and the I and II Coloniale Corps. In total on the Aisne front were forty-nine infantry and five cavalry divisions and 5,300 guns. Among the infantry were Territorials and North and Black African Tirailleurs.

From his headquarters at Beauvais Nivelle exuded the confidence in victory that war-weary political leaders so desperately wanted to hear, additionally promising that the victory would be primarily French. Military leaders, both French and British, were dubious and critical; these included Haig who had been placed under Nivelle's command for the offensive and who believed Nivelle lacked experience. On being briefed on Nivelle's plans the new War Minister, General Lyautey, was horrified, remarking that the plan was that of light opera 'This is a plan for the army of the Duchess of Gerolstein' and was left wondering whether he could dismiss Nivelle. Traditional post-Dreyfus distrust of dissident senior military figures thought to have political ambitions, however, resurfaced. Lyautey's anxieties were set aside and he himself resigned as a consequence of his refusal to pass aviation secrets on to members of the legislature. He returned to his

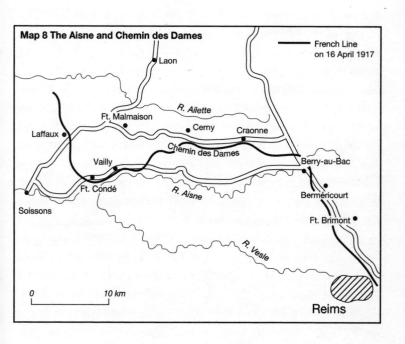

Map 8 The Aisne and Chemin des Dames

French Line on 16 April 1917

Laon

R. Ailette

Ft. Malmaison

Cerny

Craonne

Laffaux

Chemin des Dames

Berry-au-Bac

Vailly

Ft. Condé

R. Aisne

Berméricourt

Soissons

Ft. Brimont

R. Vesle

0   10 km

Reims

post as Resident General in Morocco, but his resignation led almost immediately to the fall of the Briand government. Briand was replaced as Prime Minister by the very elderly Ribot, with Painlevé, an academic mathematician, at the War Ministry. While Painlevé was not entirely reassured, President Poincaré and Ribot – and also the British Prime Minister, Lloyd George – were all confident in Nivelle's strategy. At two meetings, the second attended by Ribot, and after receiving expressions of concern from Pétain, Franchet d'Esperey and Micheler, Painlevé attempted to argue for attacks on a more limited scale. Although encouraged by the prospect of the arrival of American troops, he was profoundly worried by the course of events in Russia and was anxious not to incur risks. Nivelle's reply was simply an assertion that he would achieve a breakthrough in three days and, if he were not allowed to proceed he would resign – a threat that if carried out would have led to the fall of the Ribot government.

Nivelle's confidence in victory communicated down to the front line. Despite the misery of the cold winter, morale rose, with a belief that this time the offensive would really succeed and achieve a breakthrough. 'On les a' ('We have them') became a front-line catchword formula. The failure, when it came, was more than disillusion; it was seen as betrayal.

The sector chosen by Nivelle for his attack could hardly have been more unsuitable; he wholly ignored the warnings given him about the strength of German defences and the terrain. The Chemin des Dames ridge was over 180 metres high with a flat plateau road along the top running from Fort Malmaison to Craonne, a small village from where, at a slightly lower height, it ran on to Fort Brimont. In front of it flowed the Aisne, some 45 metres wide. The French army held a 20-kilometre bridgehead across the river opposite the Chemin des Dames; further west the right bank was held by the Germans. All along the right bank the terrain was either flat marshy ground leading to the slopes of the ridge or to the ridge itself. The ridge was a series of slopes and plateaux covered in thickets and small woods, offering concealment for defensive positions in dead ground which the French 75mm guns could not hit. To this natural defensive position the Germans had added a carefully planned defence-in-depth system. The immediate front was largely vacated, booby-trapped, with water wells poisoned. A little further behind were wire-concealed machine-gun nests, and a network of subterranean concrete machine-gun posts, their roofs only a few centimetres above ground, all forming a devastatingly effective killing ground. Much further behind lay the artillery and, concentrated beyond the range of French artillery, were massive reserves on and behind the ridge. The whole comprised a trap within which the French could advance, expending manpower and energy, then enter a reverse slope zone where artillery could not provide support, only to meet, finally and when exhausted, fresh German reserves. Furthermore, the Germans were well aware of Nivelle's plans. These had been debated in the Paris press and Nivelle himself had discussed them too freely. In addition the Germans captured orders for parts of the attack, issued too early, from which they were able to form a very clear picture. German air superiority furnished them with valuable reconnaissance reports and, finally, the directions of Nivelle's preliminary artillery bombardment completed the intelligence picture for Crown Prince Rupprecht of Bavaria, the German front commander.

The British Arras assault duly opened, in extremely difficult weather conditions, on 9 April, three British armies together with General Humbert's 3rd Army being committed. Vimy Ridge was taken in a spectacular success by the Canadian Corps, but both there and elsewhere after initial gains the Germans very rapidly brought up reserves, halting the British and French advance. Territorial gains were minimal.

Haig, however, maintained the pressure of the offensive out of loyalty to Nivelle, although Franchet d'Esperey ordered the 3rd Army to cease on the 15th. After a heavy bombardment that had begun on 8 April, the main French assault, postponed on account of very heavy rain, finally opened at 6 a.m. on the 16th. On the left, eight divisions out of the eighteen in Mangin's 6th Army led the attacks; on the right two army corps from Mazel's seventeen-division-strong 5th Army struck towards Craonne, Bermericourt and Courcy. The 10th Army was held in reserve for the breakthrough that Nivelle so confidently expected.

Nothing was to proceed according to Nivelle's plans. At Verdun he had enjoyed adequate and successful artillery support, the advantage of surprise and limited attainable local objectives; none of these featured on the Aisne. The preliminary bombardment failed to destroy the network of underground machine-gun posts. The German deep defence system first slowed down, then in the next line mowed down the French attackers as they tried to climb the slopes of the ridge. The creeping barrage of French artillery had also anticipated a rapid French advance and was of little value when the assault slowed. The German reserve units arriving from the rear added to the carnage. The French had neither a sufficient number of long-range guns to strike at these reserves nor adequate ammunition supplies for a long offensive. With great difficulty Tirailleurs Marocains of the 6th Army, including the young captain Alphonse Juin, a future Marshal of France, briefly reached their objective on the Chemin des Dames. They were one of the very few units to reach their Day 1 objective and they were later forced to withdraw. The weather continued cold and wet, so much so that one unit of Tirailleurs Sénégalais broke in its misery.

The opening day of the offensive also saw the first use of tanks by the French army, 128 Schneider tanks being used to launch an attack at Berry au Bac on the 5th Army front; their crews included a number of sailors. The tanks were referred to as *artillerie spéciale* and the crews had had three months of preliminary training. To the fury of their commander, Bossut, Mazel saw their role limited to co-operating with the infantry as close-support artillery rather than breakthrough. In the event they were to achieve nothing, the Germans having learned from the Somme in 1916 to utilise their front-line trenches as anti-tank ditches. Fifty-two were destroyed by German artillery fire directed from aircraft or observation posts, with others damaged. Bossut himself was killed. Twenty-eight tanks broke down and those that survived, not having infantry support, were either left stranded with a few gains or struggled back to their start line.

Part of Nivelle's campaign plan had included the supporting attack by General Anthoine's 4th Army in the Moronvillers hills of Champagne, to be launched on the 17th. In view of the lack of progress, on the morning of that day Nivelle ordered the 5th Army to change its axis of advance north-eastward in the hope of linking up with the 4th Army. This too proved a failure. The 5th Army were unable to take Fort Brimont and the 4th Army's attack was met by vigorous German counter-attacks, inflicting heavy casualties. In the west the 6th Army took Condé, Vailly and Cerny after which their offensive also ground to a halt.

Fighting raged for three more days, German counter-attacks recovering many of the early French gains. On the 19th Painlevé tried unsuccessfully to persuade Nivelle to halt the offensive, but the Commander-in-Chief was instead busy planning to commit the 10th Army in support of the 5th. Exhaustion and ammunition shortage, however, forced Nivelle to call a general halt on the 20th. On the 23rd, in view of the heavy casualties, inflated by rumour in Paris, and the evident slump in morale, President Poincaré forbade further attacks on the Chemin des Dames, followed shortly by orders to cease the attacks on Fort Brimont. Nivelle, hoping to resume the offensive in May, protested in vain and laid the blame for the lack of success on Mangin, who lost his command. By 25 April the French army offensives on the Aisne and in Champagne had cost over 30,000 killed, most on the opening day, 100,000 wounded, and 4,000 taken prisoner by the enemy. Many of the casualties came from the best regiments in Mangin's army. Only limited operations could follow, to prove a failure in the Soissons area, but the securing of Craonne and some clearing of a part of the Chemin des Dames were more successful and the Reims–Soissons railway line was reopened. In these May operations the Saint-Chamond tank was used, but like the Schneider it proved incapable of operating over rough and broken ground. As a result both the Schneider and the Saint-Chamond tanks were subsequently little used.

The aura around Nivelle had now totally vanished. Despite his contempt for politicians and their dislike of him, Pétain was appointed Chief-of-Staff of the French army on 29 April. Nivelle was urged to resign, which he refused to do. On 15 May Pétain was appointed to succeed him as Commander-in-Chief, with Foch as Army Chief-of-Staff. For three days Nivelle refused to go until finally on the 19th, after scenes of shouting and recrimination, he withdrew. Pétain was left with the difficult decision as to whether to abandon the few gains secured by the offensive at a further cost in morale, or to retain them, at risk to men's lives. He opted for the latter course, fortunately at little loss.

The Mutinies

Worn down by the failures of all the French offensives, that of Nivelle especially leaving a bitter sense of betrayal, the *isolement* of trench warfare and the falsehoods in wartime propaganda, the French soldier had now endured enough. One staff officer, after a visit to a division, commented on 'a sort of moral nihilism, an army without faith'. While the failure of Nivelle's offensive was the catalyst, the accumulation of suffering exploded in mass protest against command from the top down. The French soldier was now about to make his point, prepared to set his own limits on the offensives ordered by his generals, and to accept casualties and suffering only if results were thought to warrant them.

The archives relating to the French army mutinies of April–June 1917 remain closed until 2017. At the time secrecy was maintained for fear of damage to domestic morale and the impression such news might have on the British. One French military historian, Guy Pedroncini, however, was permitted to examine them fifty years after the events and publish a book on the basis of his research. The overall picture presented by his work, and that of other existing sources, is far from one of unified revolutionary mutiny, forcibly disposing of officers and turning weapons against institutions of authority, but one of scattered uncoordinated industrial actions and of that peculiar French form of political expression, the *fronde*, which sees masses of excited people rioting and rushing to barricades in a whirl of revolutionary rhetoric – all to fizzle out with surprising speed.

Pedroncini observed that the mutinies were not primarily political but rather a more human desire to save one's life. Inflammatory rhetoric, according to the evidence, was simply something to cling to, without great significance. In at least one division mutinous soldiers specifically likened their action to that of the striking textile workers, *midinettes*, in Paris, and V Corps, which contained a high proportion of soldiers from the Paris region, was particularly affected. Exceptions, perhaps, were the very few units serving near the Russian contingent on the Western Front which were directly influenced by Russian soldiers converted to the revolutionary cause, and others persuaded by the anti-war propaganda disseminated in left-wing newspapers, and in leaflets at railway stations where agitators had set up safe houses for deserters.

The vast majority of mutineers, however, were rural peasants not seeking to overturn a social order, but simply refusing to be returned to the front line to be used as cannon fodder. Many, in a paradoxical by-product of their republican education, described themselves as *'bons soldats et bons citoyens'*. Significantly, almost all the mutineers were infantrymen; the artillery was hardly affected, the cavalry not at all. Resentment against the artillery was expressed in several of the demonstrations, *'l'artillerie nous tire dans le dos.'* Infantrymen no longer believed that their enormous number of dead and wounded and their own suffering were justifiable or were serving to win the war, which seemed to stretch on without end. They longed for and demanded peace, negotiated if necessary, and a return home. Meanwhile they demanded better conditions of life, of food, of rest periods and above all regular leave, which Nivelle had curtailed. Soldiers claimed newly drafted men were granted leave before others, that leave for agricultural purposes was based on political favouritism by local municipal councils, and that officers enjoyed greater leave privileges than soldiers. They also sought measures to relieve the impoverishment of their families caused by their absence, which they contrasted with the profiteering of those who remained at home in comfort. Dark rumours were also circulating about the behaviour of non-metropolitan troops Annamite and West African, with French women-folk. The rough life and companionship of the trenches had formed the necessary social horizontal links for a measure of concerted action. The inspiration for this action, according to the Service de Renseignement aux Armées, often came from *les recuperés*, men who had been wounded earlier but posted back in the

front who arrived 'gorgés de pacifisme', and from men of the
1917 draft, not prepared for difficult conditions or the attrition
of trench warfare. But otherwise, apart from the peasant origin
of most of the infantrymen, no particular regional or occupa-
tional classification of the mutineers is evident.

Clear indication of trouble to come had appeared in the
last months of 1916, with an average monthly desertion rate of
470. This rate rose to an average of 775 in the period 1 January
to 15 April, to 618 in the second two weeks of April, to 1,291
in May, and to a peak of 1,619 in June. Figures published for
desertion in face of the enemy rose from 60 per fortnight in the
period 1 January to 15 April, to 280 in the second two weeks
of April; the actual totals are likely to have been higher, with
a number of arbitrary executions on the spot of men attempting to desert that for some reason were not notified.

The regiments and units most heavily involved were from
the armies that had been committed in the Aisne and related
offensives, the 4th, 5th, 6th and 10th Armies. West of
Soissons, where there had been no recent fighting, there were
only three minor incidents. Sixty-eight divisions were affected, some seriously, some less so. In total 129 infantry regiments, among them seven Coloniale and one Territorial,
twenty-two battalions of *chasseurs à pieds*, seven artillery regiments and one Somali battalion were involved. In all, some
40,000 men participated. Mutineers might include soldiers
with hitherto excellent battlefield records, but very rarely
NCOs. Appeals or threats by unit or formation commanders
were rejected.

The mutinies began on 17 April 1917 with peaks in late
May and early June and were to continue at diminishing levels until January 1918. Numbers of men ranging from a dozen
to as many as 2,000 would mount angry demonstrations,
sometimes leading to scuffles. Frequently the demonstrations
were staged by resting units which had been ordered to attack.

In units where soldiers feared a collective punishment men disappeared individually, as did many men on leave who failed to return. Sitting with arms folded was a frequent form of refusal to move forward. Mutiny, or any form of indiscipline in units actually in the forward line, was limited to a very few cases. Only in three divisions, at the end of May, was there any move to co-ordinate action by units together, and these moves were half-hearted. Sometimes red flags appeared and the *Internationale* was sung, in a few cases a soldiers' soviet was set up briefly. Soldiers in one unit, on being told to move to the front, paraded in good order amid rhetoric of travelling to Paris to lobby members of the Chamber of Deputies. In the event the regiment's officers regained a measure of control and the march to Paris did not take place. Occasionally there were rampages against stores or rowdy scenes at rest camps, on troop trains and at railway stations, where trains were derailed and carriages smashed. Such action might last a few hours only, or extend to a week. Some regiments mounted protests two or three times. Only on a few occasions were officers molested, as at Tardenois on the Aisne on 22 and 27 May. Soldiers were evidently very clear in their minds about officers, formation or unit commanders, whom they respected and whom they did not. In the words of soldiers of three infantry regiments who protested on 19 May, 'Too many Bazaines' (the disastrous army commander in 1870). The most serious incident was again at Tardenois on 1 June when men from two infantry regiments, the 23rd and 133rd, threatened their divisional commander, General Bulot, throwing stones at him and tearing off his star rank badges amid cries of 'Assassin, blood-sucker, death to him, long live revolution!' '*Un buveur de sang Nivelle*' was also a common cry. Rumours, possibly true, circulated among the mutinous regiments that Black and North African Tirailleurs troops were being used to surround French regiments whose mutinies were considered to be particularly serious. There were certainly some clashes between French and colonial troops.

The reaction of formation commanders varied. Some, notably Nivelle, Franchet d'Esperey, Castelnau, Fayolle and Mangin, argued predictably that the blame lay on the dissemination of pacifist, communist or anarchist ideas from Paris, Petrograd or elsewhere, perhaps in a German-organised plot, among the troops. A few, notably generals Duchesne and Fayolle, opted for drastic measures and brutal repression. It is almost certain that in a few cases regimental officers ordered men to fire on mutineers or arranged summary execution of men perceived rightly or wrongly to be ringleaders. The deaths of mutineers in these circumstances were not recorded. Other officers, in contrast and at risk to their careers, took an almost sympathetic view. In most cases, however, regimental officers played a mediating role, generally to the anger of their formation commanders. A few senior officers admitted that the youth and inexperience of junior officers, sometimes made worse by arrogance or pursuit of their own comfort, also played a part, a view strongly endorsed by the police.

Faced with this situation, Pétain, with the approval of President Poincaré and Painlevé, ordered that the mutinies be dealt with firmly, but with moderation, in his own words, 'not forgetting the fact that the mutineers were men who have been with us in the trenches for three years, our soldiers'. Of mutineers arrested and convicted by courts-martial for collective disobedience between 16 April and 31 January 1918, 499 men were sentenced to death but in the event it appears that only twenty-seven were actually shot. There may also have been other executions for offences related to the mutinies but not specifically that of collective disobedience. The remaining 471, less one escapee and one suicide, received a presidential clemency. They joined 179 who were given sentence of forced labour of varying lengths from three years to life, the 1,438 who were sentenced to communal public labour for periods between one and two years, the 515 who were placed in detention for periods between five and fifteen years, and the 742 who were sent to prison for periods between fifteen days and five years.

Pétain, however, was responsible for intiating other measures, some of reorganisation and some of reform, that enabled proper discipline to be restored. Four small-scale attacks scheduled for 10 June which Pétain had promised Haig in May were perforce cancelled. Some units were disgraced, losing their colours, others were quietly disbanded, their men distributed elsewhere. Officers, including two generals and nine lieutenant-colonels, who were considered to have been ineffective, were removed from their formation, unit or sub-unit commands. All officers were firmly reminded by Pétain of their duties in respect of the moral and physical welfare of their men. Pétain, against all French military tradition, tried to break down the excessively rigid hierarchical relationship, of unquestioning obedience between superiors and subordinates, and create instead relationships based on mutual trust, kindness, goodwill and comradeship in which problems could be discussed, with subordinates free to give opinions and comments based on their own experience. He was fully aware of the erosion of soldiers' morale that followed orders, counter-orders, apparently pointless marches and attacks ordered, prepared and then postponed.

A system of meritorious service diplomas for individual soldiers was also instituted, together with awards for regiments. In battalions, companies were given a *Fanion*, or standard, to inspire them. Senior officers were told that they had to be seen more frequently in the trenches – Pétain himself in a white-pennanted motor-car tirelessly visited ninety divisions, talking to personnel of all ranks, distributing tobacco and awarding medals, in particular the Croix de Guerre, which had been instituted in 1915. More importantly, he made it clear that the army was not going to be asked to mount any more large-scale offensives, at least until the Americans arrived. Pétain also ensured that the conditions of life of the front-line soldier were improved – refurbished barracks and rest centres, proper rest for the first four days of a rest period, the provision of fresh green vegetables and that of field kitchens with cooks chosen for their ability rather than their age and as near the front line as possible. Wine supplies, however, were to be limited to the authorised ration, and pay for the conscript remained at only 75 centimes per day. Most important of all for the front-line soldier was the regularised granting of leave with a right of appeal if leave was refused, seven to ten days every four months with proper facilities for travel home, priority for men going on leave, lorry transport to a station where a soldier could 'clean up', wash, shave and rest in privacy and comfort. Pétain also organised an appeal for money from the American Red Cross for the families of soldiers rendered destitute by the war. One soldier summarised Pétain's empathy as '*C'est le repos complet, systéme Pétain.*' In Paris the legislature passed the 'Mourier Law' to ensure more effective and fairer recruitment procedures.

The lasting effect of the mutinies, however, was that after them French commanders, formation and unit alike, had to include the morale factor as one of their most important considerations when planning all operations. In the words of one infantry commander: '*Le maniement de la troupe est devenu plus délicat.*' Costly or large-scale offensives could no longer be mounted in the conditions of 1917. Once again Pétain, *Le médecin de l'Armée*, was the nation's hero.

Operations, July–December

The failure of Nivelle's offensive and the subsequent army mutinies had a traumatising effect on the government and army command. For the latter Pétain's prescription was threefold. First, for the immediate future, was a wholly defensive strategy, for which Pétain set out detailed instructions. He was, however, prepared to sanction very carefully prepared limited attacks that could bring success proportionate to the casualties that might be incurred and wear out the enemy, together with a reiteration of his oft-stated view that 'artillery fire kills'. The limited attacks were to be launched suddenly, at different parts of the front, with one quickly following another. For a successful assault he believed that a numerical three-to-one superiority in numbers, together with massive artillery support and, if possible, tanks, would be essential. For the longer term he dismissed any idea of a breakthrough in 1917 and thought simply of the arrival of the Americans to provide the favourable correlation of forces crucial for a complete military victory. The massive British offensive in Flanders opening on 7 June engrossed German attention and gave the French army the breathing space it needed for recovery. After this necessary recuperation period the army was able to show it was undefeated in three limited offensives. The first comprised operations, opening in July and continuing to November, by General Anthoine's 1st Army, mostly men from the north unaffected by the mutinies, in support of Haig's extended and costly Ypres campaign. Supported by massed artillery, over 500 guns including 300 heavy, they crossed the Yser Canal at Ypres with minimum casualties. In the course of these, on 11 September, the French air ace Guynemer was shot down and killed at Poelkapelle, to become posthumously a symbol of patriotism, chivalry and aerial combat at a time when a national hero was much needed. The second limited offensive was that of sixteen divisions of General Guillaumat's 2nd Army at Verdun between 20 and 25 August, on a front reduced from 25 to 17 kilometres. Hill 304 and Mort Homme were retaken. In the third offensive, between 23 October and

1 November, the French retook the Chemin des Dames after a notable battle at Malmaison in which the 6th Army of General Maistre secured a very clear victory – of little strategic importance but, as will be seen later, of the greatest significance for morale.

All three operations, in particular the third, were planned meticulously with good use of intelligence, and the latter two benefited from the Germans' need to reinforce their Ypres positions. At Verdun there were two artillerymen for each infantryman, with a field gun every 24.20 metres, a medium gun every 18.60 metres and a heavy gun every 277 metres. The Chemin des Dames offensive was even more striking. A six-day-and-night artillery bombardment by some 2,000 guns preceded the attack, with a field gun every 16 metres, a medium gun every 12.20 metres and a heavy gun every 82 metres along a 14-kilometre front. At 5.15 a.m. on the 23rd three army corps launched the infantry attack, accompanied by sixty-eight tanks. The infantry advanced in serried ranks, one unit following another. The Germans were first forced back behind the Ailette River and then compelled to withdraw from the whole Chemin des Dames position. The logistics for this attack included 400 trains each of thirty wagons carrying 120,000 shells. The casualties were small, 2,241 killed, 1,602 missing and 8,162 wounded. The expansion of army artillery proceeded apace in 1917, the Schneider 155mm long and short barrelled guns, the 105mm and the new 144mm long-barrelled guns, the 220 mm mortar and over 300 very long-range heavy guns of several calibres, the heaviest being one of 370mm, all entering service in increasing numbers. The French army also acquired British 81mm Stokes mortars, ninety-six of which were used in twelve batteries to great effect at Malmaison. Other valuable weapons to enter service in late 1915 and 1916 were a new 150mm mortar, and a 140mm mortar. For purely static conditions another weapon developed at great cost was the massive 340mm mortar. This piece, on its bed with a wheeled loading tray mounted on a light railway for its 1,076lb bomb, weighed 30 tons. It had a range of some 7,500 metres with a rate of fire of one round every two minutes. Cumbersome, its use was limited, only thirty being manufactured. For the defence of forward units an anti-aircraft version of the 75mm gun was developed. Manned by former cavalry troopers, a variety of armoured-cars – Peugeot, Renault and Panhard, armed with either a Hotchkiss machine-gun or a 37mm or a 47mm cannon – all also appeared.

The most significant developments for the future, however, took place in Paris where, profoundly shocked by the failure of the Aisne offensive and the mutinies, fierce parliamentary criticism of the whole conduct of the war was being expressed in committees of both chambers of the legislature sitting in closed and often very lengthy sessions. September marked the end of the *union sacrée* when Painlevé replaced the aged Ribot as Prime Minister, retaining at the same time his post as War Minister. He was not to last long amid political scandals and a significant number of political figures arguing for a negotiated peace and expressing anti-British sentiments. President Poincaré, however, was opposed to a negotiated peace and on 16 November called on one of Briand's sternest critics, the seventy-six-year-old extreme radical, Clemenceau, to replace him both as Prime Minister and Minister for War. In the words of Winston Churchill: 'With snarls and growls the ferocious, aged, dauntless beast of prey went into action', immediately projecting his enormous vitality and combative energy into the entire government machine and silencing the defeatists. In respect of the army he began the steady, ever firmer, assertion of the government's authority over the military, and he also lowered the age limits of senior officers, thereby removing a number of both elderly and incompetent men. Divisional command generals would have to leave field commands at sixty, brigadier-generals at fifty-eight and colonels at fifty-six. Clemenceau's aggressive temperament did not match well with that of the essentially cautious Pétain. While retaining the latter as Commander-in-Chief, Clemenceau began to turn towards Foch, tending to subordinate Pétain to him. Clemenceau, however, was unsuccessful in his other main ambitions, the creation of an inter-allied strategic reserve and the appointment of an Allied Supreme Commander, in face of British and Italian opposition, one reason on the British side being the inability of Pétain and Haig to co-operate harmoniously. He paid frequent visits to the front, inspiring troops and drawing inspiration himself from his officers.

Operational Art and Manpower

As already mentioned, Pétain's post-mutiny strategy for the French army was primarily defensive, but it was also modernising. In the course of 1917 he issued a series of directives and notes setting out his strategic views and thoughts on the nature of future operations; these in sum can be said to have finally jolted the French army out of its still lingering nineteenth-century attitudes and moved it, as far as circumstances of the time permitted, into the age of new technology. They represent the nearest approach to a doctrine produced by the French army during the war, reflecting the changed military balance.

Pétain's first major directive, issued on 19 May, envisaged a series of sudden limited attacks to wear down the Germans and deny them freedom of action. No great indentation in the German line was to be made as this might form a dangerous salient. Logistic support was to be prepared with the greatest care. Although not expressed, Pétain doubtless had in mind the need to show allies and enemy that the French army, even if battered, was still in the fight. He directed that when formations were withdrawn from the line according to his rotation system, they should pass through new, specially built training camps where they could be trained in all-arms exercises for the limited offensives that he envisaged. The theme of these exercises was to be full use of and close co-ordination with artillery. This was followed by a second directive on 20 June in which senior formation commanders were to arrange studies, in special centres, where corps and divisional commanders could be updated with instruction on the lessons of recent battles and the possibilities that new weapons, in particular artillery and aircraft, could provide close co-operation both in attack and defence.

Pétain's third major directive, issued on 4 July, required that in defence infantry be organised in depth, manned by divisions in rotation. Behind the front would be created a large general reserve army group. Within this group divisions would receive new, updated training, and formation staffs were to prepare road and railway movement plans for the reserve, or any part of it to reach an area under serious threat. Taking up an idea of Nivelle's, Pétain also ordered the formation of a general artillery reserve, regiments of 75mm, together with six *groupes* of heavy artillery, drawn by tractors in place of horses, and units of super-heavy *grande puissance* guns, some to be moved by rail. Additional artillery was to be given to each front-line corps and division. Corps artillery would now include a regiment of 75mm guns, two groups of 105mm and two groups of 155mm Schneider guns. Division artillery would comprise one regiment of 75mm guns and two groups of 155mm Schneider howitzers. Heavy artillery units would receive balloon and reconnaissance aircraft units for observation.

Formation commanders were ordered to work closely in weekly meetings with their artillery commanders. A *groupe* of each existing type of tank, Schneider and Saint-Chamond, was to be given to each group of armies; the Renaults, as these were delivered, were to be kept in a special tank park. Pétain envisaged the development of air reconnaissance and observation balloons fitted with radio for contact with the ground and protecting aircraft support; a general air striking force was to also be formed. Careful study in special centres of recent German operational art was to be undertaken.

The fourth directive, issued on 20 December, set out regulations for defence in depth, to be laid out so that the main opposition to an enemy attack would be in the second position, beyond the reach (at least 2 kilometres) of the attackers' field artillery. The first line was to slow down the enemy, not necessarily to stop him. All lines were to be continuous so as to avoid outflanking. Reserves were to be located with a view to their rapid move forward by road or rail for counter-attack. Troops were to be trained in movement in and around enemy positions, and not to remain concentrated defensively in the forward line.

French combat intelligence efficiency improved notably in 1917 despite the intelligence staff's failure to convince Nivelle of the dangers he faced. Careful direction tracking of signals and traffic analysis had earlier shown up the German withdrawal to the Hindenburg line. Studies of developments in German defensive tactics noted in particular the German shift away from extended trench lines to a distribution of machine-gun posts and small strongpoints in their front, with reserve units and more substantial defence works further to the rear beyond French field artillery range. Early indications of the evolution of the German offensive tactics of 'hurricane barrage' followed by infiltration were based on reports from observers on the Eastern Front and small German attacks on the Western Front, but the full significance was not at the time fully appreciated by commanders and operations staffs. A counter-intelligence success was the December 1916 arrest, following signals interception at the Eiffel Tower of messages from the German military attaché in Spain, of the famous woman agent Mata Hari who had unwisely attempted to play a double agent role, leading to her unmasking. Her intelligence value to the Germans had been, in the event, very limited, but the publicity value of her trial and execution was a propaganda boost in 1917.

For the air war the improved Spad XIII, which had a more powerful engine than the original Spad VII and two Vickers machine-guns mounted in the fuselage, began to enter service in May. It soon proved itself superior to the German Albatros, although when well flown the Fokker DrI Triplane which appeared in the summer of 1917 was to prove a worthy adversary. Once again, though, the British Sopwith Camel and the S.E.5 fighter restored the balance for the Allies. Other French aircraft developments included the Morane-Saulnier Type P, Salmson 2 A2 and the Caudron G3 reconnaissance machines and, at the end of the year, the Bréguet XIV A2 and B2 bombers, all of which appeared in squadrons in 1917. Reconnaissance was able to take advantage of improved camera technology and developing skills of air-photograph interpreters. The excellent Bréguet B2 bombers bombed industrial targets in Lorraine at night, but the main bombing effort was concentrated by day on the German rear areas immediately behind the front line where the Bréguet squadrons commanded by leaders such as De Goys and Vuillemin struck at railway junctions, roads, bridges, ammunition dumps and other targets, often to be met with heavy anti-aircraft fire. Later in the year Italian Caproni Ca40 Triplane bombers made in France were also used. The year also saw much German airship activity, almost entirely directed against Britain. Two airships trying to return home after attacks on Britain were brought down by French arms, one at Compiègne in February 1917, shot down by anti-aircraft artillery, and one forced down by Nieuport fighters of Les Crocodiles Squadron at Bourbonneles-Bains in October.

The problem of manpower became acute in 1917, and was to worsen in the following year. In addition to the formidable casualty lists there were other drains on manpower, to the fury of Pétain, the need to release 400,000 men for agriculture and 300,000 for industry, in most cases the more elderly of recalled reservists. The expansion of artillery meant fewer men for the infantry; developments in aviation and motor transport made further inroads. Training camps for the incoming American army, with instructors, guns and ammunition, had to be provided. The class of 1918 was called up for July 1917 to help meet the shortfalls and formations were restructured to yield men. The number of independent divisions was reduced to fourteen, enabling an increase in the number of army corps of four divisions from six to fifteen, and two division army corps from twelve to seventeen. Corps of three divisions were broken up.

Morale after the Mutinies

In December 1917 General Pétain, in a letter to the newly arrived United States army commander, General Pershing, observed: 'The morale of troops and the home front are becoming essential factors in the struggle.' Events were to confirm Pétain's shrewd wisdom. The recovery of soldiers' morale after the events of the first six months of the year was not the least of achievements of this sorely tried army in the entire war.

Pétain was much aware of the wider psychological dimension of the war. Throughout 1917 he urged officers to combat defeatism among soldiers by explaining why the nation needed to continue the war, and to point out the advantages held by the Allies – the effect of the naval blockade of Germany and the entry of the United States into the war. The British 1917 offensives were to be presented as successes, and the German submarine campaign as a failure.

The mutinies had highlighted the need for the most careful

monitoring of morale. It continued to be carried out by the postal control service, which read some 180,000 letters each week. Such surveillance was resented by most soldiers, but was deliberately exploited by others to express grievances in the knowledge that their letters would be read.

The months July to December saw sharp fluctuations in morale. Throughout there remained a general longing for the end of hostilities, many soldiers at first hoping that the Paris political factions who favoured a negotiated end to the war would gain power. Others feared that the continuing war would ruin France, perhaps even leading to unrest and revolution. For them and for most, Alsace and Lorraine were completely immaterial, the concern only of the political elite. Morale received a tremendous boost after Malmaison, but sustained a slump after the news of the Italian defeat at Caporetto. Worse was the withdrawal of Russia from the war, so releasing Germany's eastern armies for battle in France. A second Verdun, or in the words of one soldier, a battle which would make Verdun seem *'un jeu d'enfant'*, was feared throughout November and early December. Numbers of men requested a transfer to the Salonika front. The onset of the fourth winter of the war brought its miseries of cold, rain and, in the Vosges, snow. The distressing condition of 'trench foot', now common, added to the general suffering. Officers noted lassitude, moral and physical fatigue, with newly arrived conscripts often breaking down in tears of revulsion at the war's brutality. Drunkenness still remained serious, needing increased control by gendarmes. At the Gare de l'Est in Paris the *permissionaire* on his way home continued to be met by women wearing red ribbons, urging soldiers to desert and distributing pacifist tracts, some even calling for sabotage. The authorities were both tardy and largely ineffective in controlling these agitators, to the anger of army commanders.

That morale was to recover by the end of the year was the

result of three factors. Verdun and Malmaison, the latter victory on the very site of the earlier drama, restored confidence in the command. Clemenceau as head of government indicated a determination that could be felt by the humblest private. And in terms of day-to-day life, Pétain's reforms restored dignity to the individual soldier, if not his sense of isolation from society. There were still issues that provoked the rage of frontline soldiers, with continuing anger against profiteers and politicians, Parliament was 'a box of thieves and liars,' wrote one soldier. Resentment was also directed against the *embusqués ouvriers* – workers who already earned several times more than soldiers striking for even higher pay packets; against incompetent or arrogant career-minded officers, especially those in staff appointments not responsive to the need for change; and against those who promised but had not yet delivered reforms such as improvements in some rest camps and delays in the increase of the trench allowance to Fr 2. Soldiers were also increasingly anxious about conditions at home with shortages of bread and coal; but there was genuine appreciation of the improved food, stronger boots and warm winter clothing, the increase in the daily wine ration to three-quarters of a litre and regular leave.

A German psychological warfare offensive deliberately targeted at French front-line troops was a failure. French-speaking lookouts were posted to the German front line with orders to play on the Italian collapse and the Russian withdrawal to disseminate revolutionary ideas, to boast of imminent massive German offensives, and to urge Frenchmen to seek peace. The effect was negated by intense French bitterness over the German scorched earth policy in areas from which they withdrew and German bombing of trenches and rest camps. Yet during November and early December there were more instances of fraternisation, the Germans providing bacon and tobacco in exchange for French bread and wine. Stern orders were issued on 20 December to stop such exchanges.

Finally, it is worth listing some further examples of the new man-management measures, mostly attributable to Pétain. A *sollicitude incessante* was demanded of officers. The greatest care was to be taken, from division level down to individual soldiers, to ensure burdens were shared equally. The presence of pacifist or defeatist papers at the front was banned; only approved papers were to be distributed. An information service for the front-line army was to be created. The spread of destabilising rumours was to be suppressed. Rest periods were to be rest periods without unnecessary spit and polish; training was to concentrate on the lessons to be drawn from recent successes. Leave for harvesting or for urgent personal affairs, marriage, deaths, etc., was to be granted if the circumstances were shown to be justified. Units were not be mixed unless absolutely necessary and special watch was to be maintained for malcontents.

By the end of the year French consciousness, though not exemplified by jingoistic patriotism, had led to a certain weary pride. As allies collapsed a common view – '*Il n y a que nous pour tenir le coup*' – emerged, a view reinforced by the success of new equipment, particularly artillery, and the arrival of the United States army which it was believed would tip the correlation of forces back heavily on to the Allied side, even if it meant that the war would drag on into 1918. One officer summed up morale as '*un fatalisme confiant*', a slightly sad resignation. Other officer views noted: '*La confiance reste intacte, un fatalisme un peu fatigué mais qui a encore le sourire*'. But perhaps the words (translated) of a soldier of the 272nd Infantry best summarised morale at the end of 1917: 'Here are my aims in this war. I fight firstly because there is a war and I am a soldier, secondly because this was inevitable, thirdly because I do not want to become a German, fourthly because they have arrived in our country and we must strive to make them leave or at least prevent them advancing further, and fifthly because they must pay for the destruction they have caused ... As for Alsace Lorraine, I could not care less.'

France was indeed to owe lasting gratitude to Clemenceau, Pétain and all who had worked to restore the morale of the army. But this morale was again to be sorely tried before the final victory of the coming year.

CHAPTER 8

1918
Limited Manoeuvre War, The Road to Victory

The last year of the war saw high drama on the Western Front. The German army once again reached the Marne and appeared poised for victory. Once again they were to be beaten back, their further offensives failures. Ensuing Allied offensives were, with other factors, to force the Germans to seek an armistice. A measure of movement resulted in both armies again resorting to a war of manoeuvre. Following the ending of operations in Russia and Romania, despite the great increase in the number of German divisions available for the Western Front, the correlation of forces was to turn decisively against Germany with the arrival of the United States army of over 300,000 fresh, fit, well-fed men by March 1918, by August over 1,250,000.

Supreme Command

Friction and dispute over and within the Allied command structure had been sharp at the end of 1917 and in early 1918 as Clemenceau sought continually to make the newly formed Allied Supreme War Council, sitting permanently at Versailles, conform to French ideas. Yet these were far from agreed. Pétain, as French Commander-in-Chief, was anxious to re-establish the authority of his office, tarnished as it had been by the failures of Joffre and Nivelle. He was in some respects well placed to do so, not being constrained by any previous plans or promises. But his concern that the arrival of very large numbers of Americans would, sooner or later, result in Anglo-Saxon domination of the Western Front led him to devise his preferred strategy for 1918, an offensive into Alsace. His thinking was interesting and significant in the light of later events. He suspected that the Germans might attack through Switzerland, but above all he doubted that any full military victory was possible. The French aim must be to ensure that France, not the Anglo-Saxons, remained the leading power – despite her worsening manpower situation – in any peace negotiations, so justifying all the sacrifices made by the French army. A descent down the Rhine, through Alsace via Mulhouse and Strasbourg and on into the Saar and beyond, would give France powerful cards to play in such negotiations. It was with these ideas, *stratégie des gages*, in the back of his mind, as well as the immediate needs of the late 1917–early 1918 situation that he had continued with Nivelle's creation of the reserve army and artillery groups, and had sought the extension of the British sector. In this design the Americans were to hold a specific area in Lorraine, so releasing French troops for Alsace, and also preventing any Anglo-Saxon collusion with the British. Curiously for so able a soldier, the great difficulties of the Alsace terrain for a war of movement did not seem to worry him.

Foch's ideas were very different. He saw the Western Front as a whole, not part-British and part-French, and believed that any planning must be for joint operations along the whole front, in which he was to foreshadow Eisenhower in 1944. He also opposed Pétain's defence-in-depth policy, adhering to the traditional *tenir*, defence of every inch of ground, yielding nothing. The arguments impeded thinking and decision-making in regard to what all knew was to come – a major, desperate German offensive which was in the event to render the entire planning controversy irrelevant. Clemenceau's support for Pétain's request for an extension of the British sector to Berry-au-Bac was seen by the British as unacceptable, but Pétain was prepared to accept an arrangement proposed by Haig, that the British extension should run to Barisis. This tasked the fifty-five British divisions with a front of 200 kilometres; the French front to be held by ninety-nine divisions was 450 kilometres. It should be noted, however, that the British divisions were slightly larger than the French, and also that while almost the entire British sector was active, some areas of the French front were generally inactive.

Operations, March–July

On the other side of no-man's-land the German commanders, Hindenburg in title and Ludendorff in practice, were acutely aware of the need to secure a decisive victory early in 1918 before they lost their superiority in numbers; in March they had 192 divisions against the Allied total of 173 on the Western Front. War weariness and unrest at home also necessitated a victory. The improved efficiency of the German railway system facilitated the rapid move of whole armies of first-class formations tried and tested in Russia. Accordingly Ludendorff planned two major offensives against the British army, the major operation *Michael* in Picardy, with a secondary operation, *St George*, later renamed *Georgette*, in Flanders. These were to be followed by a third, *Blücher*, against the French in Champagne.

For these offensives and to achieve the necessary breakthrough, the German army had developed, following experiments on the Russian front, a new operational art with an emphasis on speed and maintained momentum. The plan would be for offensives to open with an initial artillery bombardment, short by previous standards, not more than five hours, so as not to reveal too early the axis of an attack, but highly concentrated for effect. Gas would be used, the pre-ferred pattern being tear gas to delude defenders into removing their masks, followed by the deadly new mustard gas to kill or disable. These bombardments, with guns pre-registered in advance to preserve secrecy, would target both front and rear, the Germans also having the advantage of lateral railway lines for the rapid movement of guns. After this 'hurricane' bom-bardment small groups of infantry specially trained as storm-troopers and equipped with light machine-guns, grenades, flame-throwers and mortars were tasked to infiltrate their opponents' front line, breaking it into disconnected sections and pressing on to attack the defenders' artillery. Waves of conventionally organised infantry would follow, clearing and mopping-up outposts, but would sweep aside strongpoints for later waves to take, momentum being all-important. The rifle-man was now seen almost as an escort to the light machine-gunner rather than the heavy machine-gunner trying to cover the rifleman's advance. Aircraft were to be employed exten-sively in direct support of ground forces. The subsequent emu-lations of this early form of blitzkrieg by the British and French armies also saw the use of tanks on an increasing scale, with smoke shells to conceal their advance, together with motor vehicles for gun-towing. German tank development had been slow; all the German army could field in March 1918 were some 150 captured British and French tanks together with ten of their own monstrous, cumbersome A7V machines with their crew of eighteen men.

In the weeks leading to the opening of *Michael*, Allied intelligence had been confused by very tight German field and communications security, by movement of troops by night, by artillery bombardment and by fake signals traffic designed to give the impression of impending attacks. Many of the bom-bardments included mustard gas, along almost the entire Western Front. The British believed the attack was likely to

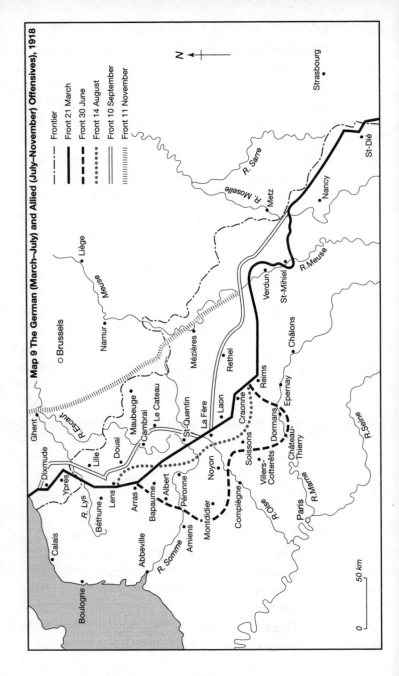

Map 9 The German (March–July) and Allied (July–November) Offensives), 1918

Frontier
Front 21 March
Front 30 June
Front 14 August
Front 10 September
Front 11 November

N

Strasbourg

St-Dié

Nancy

Metz

R. Sarre

R. Moselle

Liège

Meuse

Namur

R. Meuse

Verdun

St-Mihiel

Brussels

Mézières

Châlons

Rethel

Épernay

Reims

Dormans

Château-Thierry

Villers-Cotterêts

Soissons

Craonne

Laon

La Fère

St-Quentin

Le Cateau

Cambrai

Maubeuge

Ghent

R.Escaut

Douai

Lille

Dixmude

Ypres

R. Lys

Béthune

Lens

Arras

Bapaume

Albert

Péronne

Noyon

Compiègne

Montdidier

Amiens

Abbeville

Calais

Boulogne

R. Somme

R. Oise

Paris

R. Marne

R.Seine

0   50 km

fall on the British 3rd Army in the Albert–Arras area, the French considered the Soissons area more likely. As a consequence of the confusion reserves were wrongly placed by both armies.

Michael opened on 21 March with an attack against three British armies by three German armies – the 17th of von Below, the 2nd of von der Marwitz and the 18th of the notably able von Hutier – in total, including second echelon formations, sixty-three divisions, 6,200 guns and over 1,000 aircraft. The heaviest blow fell on the 5th Army in the St Quentin–Barisis area only recently taken over from the French and where fresh defensive positions had not been properly prepared. The weight of the attack was so great that the 5th Army was very badly mauled, suffering heavy casualties and losses of equipment. Haig's commanders lost control as their headquarters and communications were destroyed; German forces swept past Bapaume and Péronne, threatening Amiens.

More serious still was an acute danger that the British armies would be pushed back westward towards the Channel coast and be separated from the left-flank French army, the 6th, east of the Oise, also coming under attack. Pétain, now in direct command of the Northern Group of French Armies, had at the outset been critical of Haig's urgent requests for help, stating that the defence of Paris must be his priority. But late on the 21st, correctly appreciating the danger, he authorised the move of an initial three divisions, later increased by six more divisions, and eventually a further four from General Humbert's 3rd Army, and other formations from Fayolle's Groupe d'Armées de Reserve. He refused, however, to provide the twenty divisions requested by Haig, almost certainly in the belief that the severely shaken Haig might in the event simply use them to cover a retreat to the Dieppe area, abandoning Ypres, Dunkerque and Calais.

The whole crisis served to highlight the need for proper

Franco-British co-ordination and the two Prime Ministers, Lloyd George and Clemenceau, came by stages finally to accept the need for a supreme commander. Pétain had dismayed Clemenceau by his pessimism over the course of the battle, believing that the Germans were about to destroy the British and would then turn on the French; in consequence on the 26th a proposal said to have been made by Haig – principally to secure French reserves for his front – that Foch should be appointed to co-ordinate operations was generally accepted. The appointment was strengthened on 14 April to that of formal 'Commander-in-Chief of the Allied Armies in France', in charge of all major strategy but with Pétain, Haig and the American General Pershing remaining respectively in tactical command of the French, British and American formations.

On the 24th the Germans crossed the Somme, thus driving a wedge between the British and the French. On the 25th Bapaume and Noyon fell to the German advance but two days later the French were able to halt the German advance near Noyon. At one stage the Germans launched more than fifteen attacks within twenty-four hours on the French positions. Fayolle's entire Reserve Group, comprising General Duchesne's 6th Army, a cavalry corps, an additional infantry corps and the remaining units of the 3rd Army, together with the six divisions of General Debeney's 1st Army, were now all on the move to strengthen the Picardy sector, but in such haste that some divisions moved without their artillery. Fayolle was given strict instructions by Pétain not to allow himself to be separated from the rest of the French army while taking over most of the British 5th Army's sector up to the Somme. Foch, now in overall command, ordered, 'Lose not another metre of ground.' Micheler's French 5th Army was also transferred from Champagne, and four of the divisions sent to Italy in 1917 were brought back, together with their commander, General Maistre, to form a new 10th Army.

Spirited counter-attacks by the British, together with exhaustion and the difficulties of movement over the 1916 Somme battlefields, now combined to slow down and then halt the momentum of the German advance north of the Somme. British and French 3rd Army divisions covered each other's withdrawal south of the Somme, the French 1st Dismounted Cavalry Division fighting even beyond ammunition exhaustion. Although on the 27th the French lost Montdidier, by 5 April, when Ludendorff called a halt, Debeney's 1st Army, reinforced by the divisions returned from Italy together with others from a variety of sources, was on its way to restore the link with the British. At the same time Duchesne's 6th Army was attacking the Germans on the Oise. With the failure of *Michael* the Germans' best chance of success had gone. Ludendorff's error in continuing to try to break the British resistance where it was strongest, rather than reinforce Hutier's success south of the river, had been fatal. Nevertheless, the bulge created by the German advance had actually brought them to within 120 kilometres of Paris, where at Crépy-en-Laonnais they were able to install the long-range 'Big Bertha' gun. This piece, initially firing 210mm and later 235mm shells, opened a leisurely bombardment of Paris which continued until 9 August.

While, predictably, the indomitable Foch with his usual energy was planning Allied offensives on 9 April, Ludendorff in frustration launched the first of the *Georgette* offensives on the Lys, using von Quast's 6th and von Arnim's 4th Armies, thirty-six divisions supported by artillery transferred from Picardy. This offensive, sweeping aside a Portuguese formation, also gained some 15 kilometres of ground, but Quast had been checked by the British by the 18th. Arnim, after very severe fighting, was later brought to a halt by the combined efforts of the British 2nd Army and the Ypres salient five divisions of the Détachement d'Armée du Nord, but only after the loss by the French of Mt Kemmel. The German attack on the feature had been of especial ferocity, with heavy artillery bombardment, use of gas requiring French troops to wear masks for fifteen out of twenty-four hours, and extremely effective air-to-ground bombing and machine-gunning – 'un abattoir de vies humaines', in the words of one soldier. The eventual arrival of eight infantry divisions and two cavalry corps from Maistre's 10th Army, together with divisions from Fayolle's reserves, stabilised the front. The Germans had by now suffered over 300,000 casualties since 21 March, their soldiers' morale was cracking with refusals to attack in some regiments, and stores and ammunition supplies were exhausted.

Still undaunted and while Foch was anticipating him to attack north of the Somme, Ludendorff next turned to the *Blücher* plan, directed against the French in Champagne, on a 45-kilometre front on either side of the Chemin des Dames. One objective was to compel the French to withdraw the forces that had been sent to help the British, so enabling *Michael* to be resumed. The area, given one day's intelligence warning from captured prisoners of a forthcoming attack, but providing no idea of its scale, was weakly held by Duchesne's 6th Army – only four French divisions together with three exhausted British divisions that had been sent to the area to reorganise after fighting in Picardy and Flanders. Crown Prince Rupprecht's group of armies comprised the 7th Army of von Boehn and the 18th of Hutier, transferred from Picardy, in total forty-three divisions, of which many were elite formations, over 4,000 guns and a small number of tanks. Boehn attacked after an artillery preparation including gas, on 27 May, threatening Reims and with forward units crossing the Marne by means of huge ladders. This rapid advance was the result of the poor, outdated tactics of Duchesne who, contrary to Pétain's directives, massed his men in the front-line trenches where they were massacred by German artillery fire, the following infantry assault creating total confusion, during which the Aisne bridges were not blown. In the west, stiff resistance by a Breton infantry division frustrated the German advance but in the east Reims – which the army group commander, Franchet d'Esperey, had ordered to be evacuated – was saved by the rapid move back from Picardy of Micheler's four divisions, followed by twelve other divisions scraped together by Pétain. Earlier, Pétain had asked Foch for the help of British divisions, a request Foch refused, believing that a further German attack in Flanders was being prepared. Two American divisions, hurriedly deployed, counter-attacked at Château-Thierry, to immense French satisfaction. In face of his heavy casualties and supply problems Ludendorff halted Boehn's offensive on 3 June. Hutier's attack on Humbert's 3rd Army, between Noyon and Montdidier, was to follow on 9 June. Despite intelligence warnings, initially Hutier was very successful, gaining ground as Humbert, like Duchesne, attempted to hold his front line firm. One officer described the opening of the attack as 'a tornado imploding in the form of the most monstrous artillery barrage yet experienced, discharging thousands of tons of explosives and torrents of every variety of poison gas', the latter producing burning and blistering effects on bodies. Nevertheless, Hutier was forced to withdraw on the 12th following a vigorous counter-attack on the River Matz by General Mangin, brought back into a field command by Clemenceau and in charge of five divisions, some American units and forty tanks. By the 14th Rupprecht had halted his attack. Again German losses had been heavy and were compounded by the first attacks of 'Spanish influenza' afflicting the poorly fed German troops.

Ludendorff's final throw, *Marneschütze-Reims*, again in Champagne, preceded by a massive artillery and gas bombardment, opened on 16 July with an attack by three armies, Boehn's 7th, the 1st Army of von Mudra and the 9th of von

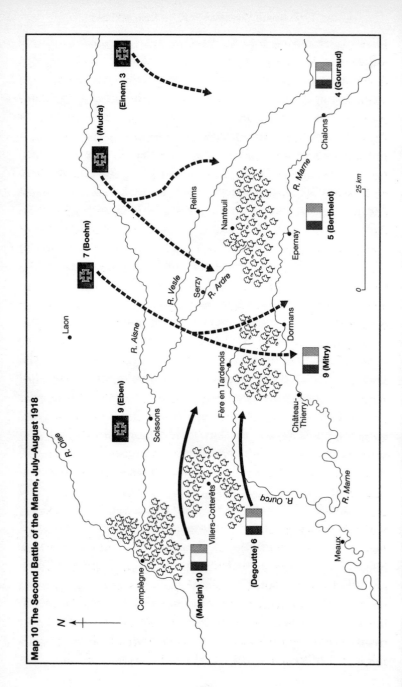

Map 10 The Second Battle of the Marne, July–August 1918

Eben, fifty-two divisions on paper but with strengths severely depleted by casualties and influenza. Intercepted signals and deserters from Alsace had warned the French of the coming attack and Maistre, now commander of the Centre Group of Armies, was determined to hold Reims. The arrival of American divisions enabled him to concentrate a strong force; in Champagne were four French armies, the 6th now commanded by Degoutte, the 5th of Berthelot, the 9th of Mitry and the 4th of Gouraud. The German attack broke through the 6th and 5th Armies as yet again too many troops had been deployed forward. Two Italian divisions yielded ground although they and the French armies were later to stop the Germans at Nanteuil-Pourcy. Gouraud stoutly held the Germans east of Reims. South-west of the city the German advance reached Dormans and again crossed the Marne, six divisions creating a bridgehead 12 kilometres long and 7 kilometres deep.

On the 18th Foch ordered his counter-offensive. The assault was led by Mangin, now in command of the 10th Army, eighteen divisions including two American in the first line and two British in the second echelon, together with 2,000 guns, 345 light tanks and 500 aircraft. Great excitement and some apprehension surrounded the preparations for the attack. After so many reverses the French army was at last about to return to a major offensive. Achieving almost complete surprise, Mangin attacked between the Aisne and the Ourcq, while Degoutte's 6th Army, nine divisions with 1,000 guns, 145 tanks and 350 aircraft, mounted a subsidiary attack between the Ourcq and the Marne. The Foreign Legion distinguished itself in the vanguard of Mangin's assault, mounted with a creeping artillery barrage but no preliminary bombardment. The Germans were forced into an orderly withdrawal made feasible by the absence of an equal attack on the eastern flank of the German salient, and also because the French were not trained or prepared for follow-up operations. French casualties had in any case been very severe, 60 to 70 per cent in many regiments, and up to 75 per cent in Mangin's 10th Army. Pétain had asked for more time to prepare a pincer attack but had been overruled by Foch in the interests of speed; Mitry and Berthelot could only offer limited support. The Germans' withdrawal was conducted with skill, gas bombardments being used to cover movements, but by now their reserves were exhausted. By late July Ludendorff had lost any capacity for a further offensive, morale had slumped further, and the Germans were reduced to preparing a strong defensive line between the Vesle and the Aisne. In Flanders, to time with Foch's offensive, a British assault recaptured Meteren.

Foch, hailed as the victor of the second battle of the Marne, was promoted by a grateful government to Marshal on 7 August. Pétain, on the same day, was awarded the Médaille Militaire. Certainly in repulsing the successive German offensives the defence-in-depth directives of Pétain, despite criticism from other generals as being too methodical and rigid, proved much less costly than Foch's passionate defence of every inch of French soil. Pétain's belief in artillery, of which four million rounds of 75mm alone were fired in the July defensive battles, was also amply justified.

Operations, August–November

Foch believed the best strategy for the Allies would now comprise a series of co-ordinated and sustained attacks with limited aims, none decisive but each preparing the way for the next, along the entire front, together with offensives in Italy and Macedonia. Although the Allies now had a numerical superiority Foch was not at this stage, August 1918, sufficiently confident of the success of any breakthrough offensive before 1919. He saw the town of Mézières, leading into the Ardennes, as the focal point for a large pincer-movement strategy for these attacks, the British forming the left and the Americans the right points of the pincer, with French armies in the centre together with other French formations supporting both the British and the Americans. Accordingly he approved Haig's plan and command for a combined British 4th and French 1st Army assault to open on 8 August, with the aim of clearing the Paris–Amiens railway line. For the assault General Rawlinson's British and Dominions contribution was a total of seventeen divisions, plus one American, and over 400 tanks. Debeney's 1st Army fielded three out of its five army corps and was supported by Humbert's 3rd Army on its right flank from 10 August. The German 2nd Army of von der Marwitz, on whom the assault was to fall, consisted of only eleven weak divisions; it broke amid scenes of panic and collapse of discipline. For Ludendorff personally it was the knock-out blow, his nerve began to collapse. But, again, neither the British nor the French were able to maintain momentum and their advance, halted on the 11th, was limited to less than a dozen kilometres.

Next to attack was Mangin, with an opening move on 17 August, developing into a full and very successful local assault between the Aisne and the Oise on the 20th. A further assault by the British 3rd Army opened on the 23rd, followed by a second combined Rawlinson and Debeney attack which in the event achieved little. Yet another British attack, by the 1st Army on the northern end of the Cambrai to the Aisne Hindenburg Line, opened on 26 August and was complemented by renewed vigorous pressure by Mangin at the southern end, forcing the Germans to withdraw from positions carefully prepared for the winter. Considerable differences of opinion arose between Foch and Pershing over the size and direction of offensives to be launched by the American 1st Army, now fully in the line opposite the German Saint-Mihiel salient which cut both the Paris–Nancy and Verdun–Nancy railway lines. Pershing aspired to a north-east breakthrough offensive towards Metz, a project initially approved by Foch. By the end of August, however, Foch and Haig had both come to believe that it might after all be possible to defeat the Germans in 1918. Foch envisaged an initial limited American assault to take out the Saint-Mihiel salient with, thereafter, a combined French-American offensive under French command to strike north-westward, as part of his pincer-strategy to be more likely to achieve success by easing the pressure on Haig. After heated argument Pershing reluctantly agreed to Foch's plan, in return the American 1st Army was to stay under American command.

The Saint-Mihiel assault by three American army corps and General Blondlat's Coloniale II Corps duly opened on 12 September preceded by a four-hour artillery bombardment in which most of the 3,000 guns were French. As it happened, however, the Germans had largely withdrawn. Pershing obeyed Foch's instructions as to the limited objectives of the offensive, and on 13 September French troops under 1st American Army command entered Saint-Mihiel. Pershing's own view remained that a breakthrough might have resulted if a larger-scale offensive had been permitted, a claim that in view of American logistic difficulties remains doubtful. His assault was again complemented in the Aisne sector by Mangin, pushing the Germans back on to the Ailette River, and a few days later, on the 18th, further British and French attacks were launched, bringing the British to within striking distance of the Hindenburg Line, so adding to the pressure on the Germans.

On the 26th, following a three-hour bombardment, a massive French–American offensive was launched in the Argonne Forest along the Meuse. French and American 75mm guns together fired 1,375,000 shells. Thirty-one French divisions of Gouraud's 4th and Hirschner's 2nd Army, and fifteen

American divisions almost twice the size of the French formations, were supported by 4,000 guns and 700 tanks. The numerically inferior German force nevertheless conducted a tough defence; the French-American advance was limited to a few kilometres and was brought to a halt by the 29th. The attack had been too hurriedly prepared, there were logistic problems and the vanguard American formations lacked experience. As part of Foch's strategy of continuous pressure, further attacks were launched by the British at Cambrai on the 27th and in the St Quentin area on the 29th, a Belgian army attack for which Degoutte had been loaned as Chief-of-Staff was mounted on the coast, and on the 30th a new French assault opened on the Aisne. At his headquarters at Spa, Ludendorff's nerve suffered a second, more serious, collapse.

More visible signs of German confusion and defeat were evident with reports of unrest in Germany, the declining morale of the underfed German troops, the armistice signed with Bulgaria and, on 3 October, the German appeal to President Wilson for an immediate armistice. The first days of October saw steady if slow Allied advances. On 8 October Haig's armies, together with Debeney's 1st Army, attacked again at Cambrai, now overrunning the Hindenburg Line and forcing a German withdrawal along the entire front. A further British and Belgian attack on the 14th forced the Germans out of Lille three days later. Despite their severe administrative problems, in particular Spanish influenza and a shortage of supply horses, the American and French forces had cleared the Argonne forest by the 10th and a few days later began a further advance up the Meuse. Mangin's 10th Army retook Laon on the 13th, while Guillaumat's 4th Army finally cleared the Chemin des Dames and were on the move in the direction of Mézières. By the 18th the Belgian coast had been liberated and on the 31st, despite the difficulties of destroyed bridges and blocked roads, British troops reached the Scheldt.

During the last ten days of fighting Foch maintained and increased the pressures. On 1 November the Americans opened a new offensive on the Meuse, reaching the Sedan area by the 6th; north of the Aisne, French troops attacked hastily prepared German defences behind the former Hindenburg Line, and continuing British advances reached the Sambre-Oise Canal. Only the exhaustion of both the British and French armies enabled the Germans to withdraw quickly and in relatively good order, covering their retreat with effective rearguard actions. Armistice negotiations opened at Compiègne on 9 November, leading to a cease-fire agreed for 11 a.m. on the 11th. The cease-fire forestalled Foch's final project, a massive offensive into Lorraine, planned to open on the 14th. This was to have been undertaken by Castelnau, brought back into the front line command of the Eastern Group of Armies, Mangin's 10th Army transferred from the Aisne and the 8th Army of Gérard leading the attack, with the 7th Army of Boissoudy and American divisions to follow. Two 520mm guns were to destroy the forts around Metz.

After over four years of continuous fighting, almost entirely on French soil, the ordeal of the French soldier, however, had ended.

CHAPTER 9

1918
Developments within the Army

The last year of the war saw three major developments within the French army. First was the successful, albeit belated, appointment of an Allied Commander-in-Chief, the second was the worsening problem of manpower only partly offset by the third development, the availability of much modern combat equipment, guns, tanks and aircraft. Morale, and its maintenance, continued to be a vital factor which neither Foch nor any of his formation commanders could afford to ignore when preparing plans.

Foch and Pétain

The figure of Foch dominated the French army from April 1918, with his pre-1914 military philosophy now once more feasible – attack the enemy wherever he may be, although the strategy was now to be one of attrition rather than outflanking. Foch's title of Commander-in-Chief, however, was more imposing than the reality. Above him he had Clemenceau, who on occasion exhibited the average French politician's paranoia that any successful general would develop into a Bonaparte, and was to criticise Foch severely either for risking men's lives or for not pressing the Americans to move more quickly. Worse treatment of Foch was to follow when the war ended. After a stormy period of recrimination during the months of Ludendorff's offensives, Foch developed a good working relationship, based on mutual respect, with Haig, but a distinctly uneven relationship with Pershing, whom Foch believed not always to understand either the military expertise gained or the suffering experienced by France in four years of war. Even within the French army it was often difficult for him to impose his authority over all levels of command from the cautious Pétain as the national army commander, to the three army group commanders, and the numerous separate army corps and divisional commanders. Some of these, notably General Debeney of the 1st Army, would place their own interpretation on Foch's orders, awaiting neighbouring formations to be the first to mount an attack, thereby weakening opposing resistance.

While Foch had the overall responsibility of the command of the largest coalition force in recorded history, he had perforce often to be one of a military broker, conciliator or co-ordinator rather than authoritative Commander-in-Chief of hundreds of thousands of men. He had now to operate by mission command, tasking subordinate commanders for broad objectives rather than tactical detail. He did, however, in a stormy interview shortly after his appointment, administer a stiff reprimand to General Gough, the hapless commander of the 5th Army.

In purely military terms his command could be characterised by a clear strategic plan but with flexibility when tactically necessary or to avoid friction, and, as with Joffre, determination in adverse situations. On the battlefield he economised strength, essential to preserve morale after the army mutinies and the German assaults of 1918, but he ensured that at the points he chose for attack he would have superiority in numbers and, more than any earlier French commander, he realised the value of intelligence, using it to ensure that the actions on the battlefield were those chosen by him and not the enemy.

His personal style, in the words of Churchill, 'vehement, passionate, persuasive but clairvoyant and above all indomitable', showed at its greatest in the desperate days of Ludendorff's offensives – expressed in his *'Cramponnez vous partout'* ('Hold on everywhere'). Later, when he was urging exhausted French generals to press their even more exhausted troops into ongoing attacks, he would meet objections by saying, 'The Germans are even more tired.' His own energy appeared inexhaustible, his command method was to visit in person the scenes of greatest danger, where he was able to extract a new maximum effort from commanders and men who believed they had reached the end of the road from exhaustion. Any assessment of his personal character must also record his strong Christian faith, facets of which included his moral courage, his almost youthful optimism even when situations were dire, his self-confidence and his immense personal charm.

To exercise his command Foch established a small headquarters at Beauvais, often communicating with Pétain's main French army headquarters, evacuated from Compiègne to Provins in March, and his forward headquarters at Chantilly by means of air couriers. Foch was also well supported by his carefully chosen staff, in particular its chief, Weygand, who was more than simply a brilliant organiser but a general whose mind was always attuned to that of Foch and was able to anticipate his reactions to events and intentions. Also important was Foch's artillery adviser, Desticker. Although major decisions were now made by Foch, Pétain's continuing work as French army commander should not be minimised. As already noted, Pétain's concepts of defence were very much more sound than those of Foch, and those generals who, like Franchet d'Esperey, Duchesne, Degoutte and Humbert who followed Foch's emotional appeals not to yield an inch of ground suffered severe reverses.

Pétain's ideas also differed from those of Foch on several other occasions, notably his reservations about the Franco-British attacks of 8 August, where he would have preferred to husband French strength for an attack in Alsace, and about the aims of the French-American offensive of September. He was not able to persuade Foch of the merits of his project for an offensive in November in Alsace, but he did suggest to Foch the alternative of an offensive in Lorraine. He also exercised a close supervision of the operations of the French army, deploying reserves and co-ordinating transport and supply with great skill. In these last months of the war he was supported by an excellent staff, successively Generals de Barescut, Dufieux and Duval for operations, and the artillery expert Buat who replaced the irascible Anthoine, scapegoated for the French reverses on the Aisne, as headquarters major-general.

Manpower

Although Pétain and Foch approached the problems of 1918 from different perspectives and offered very different solutions, both were concerned that France's diminishing manpower resources had to be used to the maximum advantage. In July 1916 the French army had totalled 2,234,000, but the casualty rate in 1917 had averaged 40,000 per month. In early 1918 Pétain estimated that the Western Front requirement would be 1,020,000 men but that he was likely only to have 836,000; in the event he had only some 750,000. The casualty attrition remained daunting, by 2 May the French army had sustained 340,000 casualties since the opening of Ludendorff's offensives. Worse, by the end of May, the German-Allied force correlation of 192 divisions against 173 of March had changed to 207 German divisions against 174 Allied. Of the German divisions only seven were committed against the Belgians, leaving 200 against the 162 French and British. Further, the

British were also experiencing grave manning difficulties, 145 battalions being broken up to strengthen the remainder. British totals were falling faster than the growing number of arriving Americans. Within the French army some 200,000 men became due for release between 1 July and 1 October. Neither the call forward of the 1919 draft to April 1918 and the recall of some reservists discharged for industrial work nor the formation of Polish and Czech units from prisoners, deserters and men from the Foreign Legion could fill the deficiencies. Some front-line units were composed almost entirely of men in their forties, some as old as forty-eight. The high casualty rates of the last months of the war, 207,300 in July, 171,000 in August, 100,900 in September and 133,000 in October, killed, missing or wounded, kept manpower as a major problem for the French army right up to the armistice. By the end of October 1918 twenty-five divisions had had to be disbanded, and the French army's total strength had fallen from the 2,234,000 of July 1916 and the 1,890,000 of October 1917 to 1,670,000. At the armistice the French army – in all theatres – had been reduced to 102 infantry and six cavalry divisions, many under strength. The arrival of the Americans filled some of the gaps – an initial four Black regiments serving as an integral part of the French army from early 1918. The American 1st Division had entered the Saint-Mihiel salient, at the time relatively quiet, in January. Agreement on the distribution of the arriving Americans was reached after much argument early in June. The Americans would deploy 170,000 men in June and a further 140,000 in July where the French required. Regiments from five American divisions, therefore, were made available from 1 June, rising to eleven by 1 July, to serve in French or British formations. But thereafter the American commander Pershing insisted that further American formations must form part of a United States army or armies in their Saint-Mihiel–Argonne sector.

Weapons and Equipment

French army firepower benefited both in quantity and quality from the appearance in the front line of several new pieces of equipment in sizeable numbers in 1918. For use by the infantry the 45mm and 60mm Brandt mortars arrived, supported by further numbers of the bigger artillery 150mm Fabry mortar from September 1918.

The great expansion of the artillery continued. In 1914 the strength of the artillery was 420,000, 20 per cent of the front-line army, by the autumn of 1918 the strength was over a million, some 38 per cent. Serman provides detail in respect of medium and heavy artillery; ninety-two regiments of which sixty-four were horsed, twenty tractor-towed, three super-heavy, five on railway lines together with five *groupes* of naval guns. These in total provided 5,700 new or reconditioned guns compared with the 300 of 1914, including 1,980 155mm howitzers, 720 155mm field guns, 576 105mm and 144 120mm guns together with a small number of super-heavy pieces. Although still very effective against bunched attackers, the role of field artillery was now of somewhat less importance; nevertheless there were 105 horse-drawn gun, thirty-five towed-gun and six-pack 75mm regiments, together with three 65mm mountain gun regiments. Many of the older 75mm guns, however, were worn out and in some formations batteries in *groupes* had to be abolished. Another complication was a shortage of hay, necessitating a reduction in rations for horses and a consequent decline in efficiency. When they became available, improved versions of the 75mm gun extended its range from 9 to 11.4 kilometres, and the ranges of the two versions of the 155mm gun were also increased. With more movement on the battlefield, the several varieties of armoured-cars proved increasingly useful, though some were to fall to German armour-piercing bullets. The cavalry divisions, reduced in number from eight to six, were reorganised with some units retaining horses, others serving as infantry and yet others providing men for the armoured-cars.

Perhaps the most effective addition for the limited mobility warfare of 1918, breaking into German infantry lines, was the Renault tank, to prove especially effective at Villers-Cotterêts in April, May and June, at Méry and Belloy also in June, and Villers-Cotterêts again in July. By this time 540 of these tanks had entered service, with a further 2,560 by November. Success, however, led to later over-estimation of its effectiveness. The tank was seen as a mobile machine-gun post and it was never appreciated that a light tank, particularly one as slow as the Renault, could represent the armoured fighting vehicle needed to break through the enemy's defences. In April eight tank regiments were formed, each comprising a *groupe* of Schneider or Saint-Chamond heavy tanks and three battalions of Renaults. But the vulnerability of the big tanks was again shown up when on 11 June thirty-seven out of forty Saint-Chamond tanks were lost in an attack at Courcelles.

Serman also provides interesting signals statistics. The fifty wireless sets in service in 1914 had increased to 30,000 in 1918, with parallel increases in field telephones from 2,000 to 350,000. By the end of the war the army had also received 98,000 lorries together with 15,000 vans imported from America or Italy, some for use as ambulances. For the bulk of the casualties there were 142 semi-permanent conversion ambulance trains, plus six fully converted and thirty-six improvised trains. Some wounded were evacuated back to hospital by river boats.

As impressive as the modernisation of the ground army was the expansion of the air arm. In April 1918 1,713 up-to-date aircraft with a further 1,092 obsolescent planes, by July 2,827 up-to-date with only 434 obsolescent. By the autumn of 1918 this strength had been progressively organised by

Colonel Duval, head of the Service Aéronautique, into twelve *groupes de combat* comprising sixty-six squadrons, which with five, eventually seven, *groupes de bombardement de jour* of nineteen squadrons were structured in a brigade and division format, the Division Aérienne. The formation of this division was opposed by the ground force commanders and Duval's own airmen who wished to keep their local aircraft under their own control, and the *five groupes de bombardement de nuit* of fourteen squadrons retained their independence.

Air warfare intensified to a degree undreamed of in 1914. At strategic level German Gotha bombers raided Paris on several occasions, and also struck at French ammunition dumps and lines of communication. French army headquarters at Compiègne, before the move to Provins, was also attacked in a series of raids at the time of the opening of the *Michael* offensive. French anti-aircraft artillery quickly learned to recognise German bomber targets from their flight paths, and so notify interception fighters, while in reply French Voisin and Caproni *groupes* maintained a night-bombing campaign on targets in Germany and at the front.

On the battlefield itself the art of air-to-ground strikes was developed by both sides, in the early part of the year particularly by the Germans. The German command organised battle flights, which as time passed grew into battle wings of several squadrons, committed to support the new offensive tactics. Deploying groups of four to six aircraft, in which the Halberstadt CLII machines, with three machine-guns and racks for small bombs, were particularly effective, the Germans had virtually an aircraft-mounted light artillery battery. The French loss of Mt Kemmel in April was in part the result of German air-to-ground bombing and machine-gunning. But, in turn, the Allied air-to-ground capacity improved. For Pétain aircraft constituted an additional full battlefield artillery. He supported the divisional concept of Duval, which in the event enabled the latter to take command of himself and to deploy aircraft in masses at critical points, with fighter squadrons escorting and protecting the bombers. On 4 June Escadre 12 of the Division commanded by Vuillemin, dropped 7,200 bombs on a German troop concentration preparing an attack near Villers-Cotterêts, leaving few survivors. In mid-July the division launched a series of mass raids (sometimes with 70–80 aircraft) against the Germans, dropping bombs from low level on the German bridges across the Marne and on advancing columns. A little later, during the fighting around Santerre, over 130 aircraft dropped 24.7 tons of bombs. The division was then moved to the Saint-Mihiel salient in support of the Americans, and then on to the fighting in Champagne where on 26 September 164 bombers dropped 36 tons of bombs on German positions. Duval's belief in mass attacks demonstrated that control of the air was now a major factor in the success of ground operations.

While in general the British and French air forces held air supremacy over the Western Front, increasing as the year passed, the Germans were able occasionally to challenge this with battle flights and wings, and with fighter wings assembled from several squadrons to give them a local superiority, usually against the British. The days of the aces and single-aircraft dogfights had now come to an end with the evolution of tactics involving two or three fighters working together. The French tendency to group the best pilots in elite fighter and bomber squadrons, however, reduced efficiency in reconnaissance and other squadrons. France also had to provide training and other staff for the Americans, fifteen out of the sixteen American fighter squadrons were flying in Spad XIII machines.

The Germans produced probably the best fighter aircraft of the war, the Fokker D VII, but it only became available in quantity during the final months, by which time the British and French aircraft totals were far greater and the Germans suffering acutely from shortages of fuel, of the linen and dope needed to cover and air-proof their machines, and of the skilled manpower needed for maintenance work.

The performance of French operational intelligence in 1918 was uneven. Hutier's arrival on the Western Front had been picked up from a report in a local German newspaper, but as already noted, there was confusion as to where the German March onslaught would fall. Despite the growing skills of French code-breakers, notably Colonel Painvin, and numerous rumours, preparations for the German Chemin des Dames attack were not recognised correctly (except by the Americans). A German signal on 3 June requesting full ammunition supply for an opening barrage, however, provided almost immediately a warning, corroborated by air reconnaissance and prisoner questioning, of Hutier's 9 June offensive. French intelligence was similarly successful in anticipating Ludendorff's final assault in July. Signals interceptions and deserter/prisoner intelligence was now supplemented by the evidence of growing German demoralisation acquired from a new, active patrolling policy. German security standards had fallen, deception ploys were easily detected and columns and depots were only perfunctorily camouflaged, so enabling the French to assess the likely weight of attack to fall on particular areas. These circumstances continued throughout the last months of the war, as skills improved in assembling and analysing the intelligence mosaic formed from patrol reports, captured prisoner and document intelligence, signals interception, code-breaking, direction-finding and traffic analysis, and air reconnaissance and photography.

In a fifth major directive, issued on 12 July, Pétain set out as doctrine the lessons learned over the previous twelve months. Attacks were to be audacious, rapidly executed and with exploitation both immediate and beyond. The greatest secrecy must be preserved before an attack which was to open with a sudden and violent artillery and air bombardment. Breakthrough was to be achieved by heavy tanks, with light tanks completing the process and repelling counter-attacks. In this new war of movement equipment – tanks, vehicles and aircraft – was to be master of the field.

Morale

On a summer's day in July 1918 French staff officers on the roads near Coulommiers and Meaux commented on the contrast between interminable columns of Americans – beardless youths of twenty closely packed in lorries, bare-headed and bare-chested, singing American songs at the top of their voices and all radiating strength and health – with French regiments trudging along in faded uniforms, men wasted by years of war, their thin, sunken eyes shining with a dull fire, bundles of nerves held together by a will to heroism and sacrifice.

Albeit slightly romanticised, these observations form a useful introduction to an overview of French soldiers' morale in 1918, a year in which fluctuations between despair and hope were extreme (the evidence again clear from letters intercepted by the postal control) and which witnessed some extraordinary examples of men, already believing that they had been pushed beyond their limit, nevertheless responding to calls for yet further efforts. More even than in 1916 and 1917, the war had become a psychological as well as a physical combat between exhausted armies, set against a backcloth of food shortages and economic hardship confronting the civilian population behind the lines – factors that added to the anxieties and stress upon morale of front-line soldiers. Bitter public disgust with the war was expressed in Henry Barbusse's very widely read *Le Feu*, published in 1916. In many areas of France agricultural productivity had fallen badly due to the absence of men. The spring and summer of 1917 had seen a wave of industrial strikes in major cities, in Paris Tirailleurs from Indochina fired on striking women workers, many of whom were the wives of soldiers; rumour compounded the injuries. The II Cavalry Corps had to be used to contain unrest in the Midi. Bread shortages led to protests, notably one at Roanne in the Massif Central, and the cost of living steadily increased. Many feared a Russian-style revolution, in the words of one civilian observer, 'The strikes are quite upsetting. Hordes of these bare-headed women with their hooligan brats are spreading revolution.' A smaller wave of industrial strikes erupted in May 1918, more obviously marked by anti-war and pacifist sentiment than the strikes of 1917. Nor was the morale of soldiers raised by the severe cold of the 1917-18 winter, followed by the sight of columns of miserable refugees, women, old people and children, once again in flight at times of German advance.

Despite earlier apprehension, morale held up well during Ludendorff's first March offensive, falling as it did mainly on the British. The German advances were attributed to the failure of the British, but a belief that the Germans were suffering such enormous casualties that the war must end in 1918 served as further encouragement. Ordinary French soldiers' opinions of their British ally ranged from fury at evidence of looting by retreating units to opinions that, deprived of his regular food, ablutions and regular relief, the British soldier became demoralised, or to a more generous assessment of '*très braves mais mal commandés*'. Criticism declined after the French loss of Mt Kemmel, but there remained the general belief in the minds of many French soldiers that they, and only they, possessed the fortitude necessary to combat the Germans. A flash of brilliance, the French Army at its vibrant best, was the Easter weekend defence of the chateau at Grivesnes, near Montdidier. Two under-strength battalions of the 350th Infantry and a handful of chasseurs held off repeated attacks by the Kaiser's Guards, a lieutenant thumping out the *Marseillaise* and the chasseurs' *Sidi Brahim* march on a piano in the ruins of the chateau.

By mid April and early May, however, morale had started to decline as a result of continued fighting, casualties, suffering and, above all, fatigue. The more open style of fighting meant, for the ordinary front-line *fantassin*, life in shellholes rather than trenches, and often two weeks or more without any change of clothing or taking-off of boots. In the rain, cold and mud, *'nous sommes sales comme les cochons,'* wrote one soldier. In the open, units suffered heavy casualties from German artillery, aircraft, machine-guns and gas, as many as 70 per cent in some battalions. For many it seemed after all that the war was never ending, no French counter-offensive could be decisive and yet another winter's misery would follow. Operational needs led to an immediate ending of all leave privileges, understood and accepted; but when these, now seen by soldiers as their right, were only restored at a trickle, discontent made matters worse. The lassitude and depression were heightened by delays in the delivery of mail. Further continuing reductions in leave permission were the more bitterly resented. 'War, every day war. And death each day more fatal and inevitable,' wrote one soldier.

Difficulties in the provision of food and water also appeared, corpses poisoning water supplies and, on account of the movable nature of the battlefield, food arriving at night, again often cold and with no *soupe*, the meat rotten and the bread mouldy. Cases of Spanish flu mounted, men described themselves as walking corpses and suicides were reported. Expression of the anguish took several forms, further exasperation against *les buveurs de sang*, politicians, war profiteers and, as a result of socialist propaganda, men loosely identified as capitalists – for whom the government was but the accomplice and soldiers were but cattle on the way to the butcher.

The will to fight, however, still flickered on. The Germans' May Aisne offensive almost destroyed that will, and the postal censors reported outbursts of extreme despair. 'We will never get the Germans, they are victorious everywhere,' wrote one artilleryman. French troops caught in the retreat across the Marne shouted, 'The war is over!', to the surprise of the newly arriving Americans. The shock of the German advance created a new defeatism, now extended to a criticism of the command for allowing a surprise attack to fall on formations supposedly resting. *'Une bande de crétins'* was the view, commonly held at this point, by one soldier. 'We are back to the first days of the war,' wrote another; and further anti-British sentiments were also voiced. Some soldiers wrote of Clemenceau as an obstinate old man who was happy to sacrifice the young. Belief in an eventual victory was lost. 'The Germans will soon be in Paris, thank God,' wrote one soldier, adding, 'I would rather live as a German than die as a Frenchman.' Others expressed similar views. Once again home leave had to be totally stopped, with the inevitable impact upon morale and renewed fear of another winter of warfare.

These *mauvais sentiments*, in the words of one postal censor, were nevertheless more a cry for help arising from anger, hardship and discouragement than the very real collapse of morale such as was affecting the German army. Spirits improved when the route to Paris was barred with the French army unbroken, and fresh anger against the Germans erupted as a reaction to the ferocity of their attacks and their killing of prisoners. Despite extreme fatigue, hunger, lice-covered bodies and uniforms, and influenza, this anger took tangible form in a tenacity in defence. In the words of an officer in a regiment resisting Hutier's 9 June attack, 'A fanatic wind for sacrifice has blown upon us all.' For the future, hopes hung upon the arrival of the Americans.

These troops were initially viewed with some scepticism, and an element of jealousy over the success that the well-paid Americans had with French women. After the first American success at Belleau Wood opinion changed to admiration, *les Sammies* being compared favourably against *les Tommys* and the apparent greater freedom of individuals and informal officer-soldier relationships making a great impression on the French soldier. Evidence of the increasing number of Americans arriving at the front was an incalculable boost for morale. By late July self-confidence had once again returned to the army, with trust in Foch and Pétain; the setbacks earlier in the year were attributed to subordinate commanders. The fighting spirit of Clemenceau, evident in his visits to the front line, was also inspirational. Hatred of the Germans increased, in the words of one infantry soldier, 'This cursed cruel and bloody people, domineering and barbarian, deserves to be crushed and annihilated totally in the interests of the universe.' Songs sung by French soldiers on the march conveyed this hatred in obscene terms. The successes in defence of Gouraud's 4th Army and in attack of Mangin's 10th and Degoutte's 6th Armies, and the vast numbers of prisoners most in poor condition taken at Villers-Cotterêts, led one soldier to comment, '*Quelle jolie page d'histoire, quelle leçon d'héroisme au monde.*' Cautious optimism that victory might actually be achieved rose after 8 August, strengthened by admiration of *les chapeaux mous* (slouch hats), the Americans, with whom at regimental level the French said that they found it easier to work than with the British.

This optimism was all the more needed in view of the stresses imposed upon the *poilu* by Foch's strategy of sustained momentum of attack, often across countryside already devastated and strewn with decomposing corpses, described as '*un veritable charnier*' by one soldier. Forced marches in heat and rain, or by night, contrasted by soldiers with the wheeled transport of the Americans and the British – 'The sweat of an Englishman must be costly,' in the words of one *poilu* – increased the exhaustion. Rats, lice, mosquitoes, clothes unchanged for three weeks or more, food supplies again not reaching extended forward units, stomach illness and diarrhoea all again took their toll upon morale. Stubborn German resistance, in particular machine-gun fire across the open country, and the use of gas still imposed a high casualty rate. Regiments could no longer be relieved for rest periods, home leave was yet again stopped, and inevitably bitterness returned.

August 1918 was one of the most trying and difficult months of the war for the front-line infantryman; and the last two months were little if at all easier, although the exhilarating vision of an end of the war before winter, as it started to appear, came to add a morale-boosting excitement, and enabled Foch to keep up the momentum. The German withdrawal, however, was orderly, and they continued to inflict decimating casualties. French army exhaustion was ever more evident in the letters examined by the postal censor, expressing a longing for rest. Phrases in letters sum up this longing: 'I have spent fourteen days of fatigue and hardship ... by day attack after attack, by night exhaustion in shell holes under the rain', 'We advance but at the cost of inexpressible wretchedness', 'Twenty days without hot food or drink, washing, shaving, changing clothes', 'Sixty days in the line without relief'. To the miseries of colder and wetter weather, absence of any shelter, and cold food ('the kingdom of fleas and lice') had to be added disappointment and criticism at the limited progress of the Americans.

Respect for the British suddenly returned following their success in Flanders, and simultaneously increasing irritation at excesses of behaviour – with a high venereal disease rate – by the Americans. Special units of the gendarmerie had to be formed for work in areas occupied by American troops. Spanish flu spread, requiring precautionary vaccinations, with a not very effective provision of permanganate mentholated Vaseline, and the disinfection of camps. Many regiments lost large numbers of men, all were worried about the effect of the flu at home. Occasionally one or two battalions refused to advance further. The news of the Bulgarian cease-fire and the German request on 4 October to President Wilson for an armistice aroused enormous interest, many hoping for an immediate end to the war, and expressing anger against *capitalistes*, governments and military leaders who wished to continue. The censors noted the number of letters expressing *pacifisme révolutionnaire*. Others doubted any sincerity on the part of the Germans and demanded punishment for their crimes. The slow progress of negotiations for peace, in the conditions of an army pushed to the limit, led to a return of lassitude. Many, foreseeing an end to the fighting, began to take especial care not to be among the last casualties, but French attacks continued to the final moment. The armistice of 11 November when it came was fêted more behind the lines than at the front, the prevailing emotion in the shellholes and trenches being one of profound relief ('*Ce cauchemar a disparu*') and reflection on the number of men killed and women weeping who would not be rejoicing. German attempts across the lines to share in celebration were rebuffed. There was also a strong feeling that final victory had been primarily the work of the French army, that the French alone had held fast in all circumstances and despite all their suffering.

This month-by-month survey of army morale in 1918 is important for two reasons. First, the cumulative effect of four years of war on the French army, the fatigue, exhaustion and torpor, were more marked than in the previous years, even in April 1917, and potentially more dangerous. Churchill's phrase, 'sorely tried and glorious', was a hard-earned and well-deserved tribute. But it was the survivors of 1918, not the dead of earlier years, who were to lead the post-war generations. The second reason is more complex, and important for any thinking about events twenty-two years later. Beneath the overt fluctuations of morale evident to the censors, the protracted war was furthering another process, the soldiers' sense of *isolement*, isolation from society in his filthy *gourbi* or shell hole. The beginnings of this alienation have already been mentioned.

For the vast mass of rural French soldiers the war was far from being one heroic; it was a common experience of suffering. They fought the war *par habitude*, resigned, little concerned with causes or war aims, only hoping that it would all end soon. The alternatives, desertion or self-inflicted wounds, were even riskier than the front line. Soldiers felt fear before attacks that were often ill-considered, they saw a technology which seemingly could not be mastered. Submission to discipline became submission to destiny and fatalism, indifference became an attitude of mind. The joy at being alive at the end of it all led to beliefs that peace counted for more than anything else – many war veterans turned to pacifism. The idea of patriotic duty, so carefully implanted before 1914, became discredited, associated with the war and its suffering. Ideology became the new area of conflict, the seed being the socialist propaganda of the last years of the war which presented the fighting as the work and desire of the capitalists, and wars themselves simply as conflicts between rival capitalists. The sense of *isolement*, of the people behind the lines never understanding, thinking of the soldier at the front as though he was at his normal daily work in field or factory, and simply enjoying or enriching themselves, served paradoxically during the war to bind the front-line soldiers together. In the words of the historian Jules Maurin, '*le ghetto de la camaraderie*'. There, too, isolation was reinforced by deaths, the vast mass war graves far from home, burials with little ceremony, corpses often laid side by side or on top of each other. The only mourners were not relatives with flowers but the elderly Territorials who dug the graves. After the war the return home was for most individuals a return to a social order much changed; civilian life seemed to have been reorganised without them. Women often appeared indifferent, even contemptuous. Where there were military hospitals the civilian population showed little interest in the wounded and convalescent. The apparently unfulfilled promises of government pensions or a better world merely led to feelings of deception and resentment, alienation from authority in a new form of *isolement*. Such feelings were played upon by anti-war pacifist and extreme socialist exponents in the years to come, finalising a divorce between the army as an institution and the society from which it drew its conscript soldiers, many of whom came to see 1939 as 'their war, not mine'. The army itself, though, saw the lesson of the war as being one in which victory could be secured by defensive strategy fortresses, and a conscript army reinforced by colonial troops, the structure of 1914–18. Its commanders were stricken, in the later phrase of Marshal Juin, by a mental sclerosis. In addition, the huge stocks of weaponry left over from the war had the effect of discouraging research and development.

In November 1939 General Sir Alan Brooke watched an Armistice Day parade of French soldiers. 'Seldom have I seen anything more slovenly and badly turned out. Men unshaven, horses ungroomed, clothes and saddlery that did not fit, vehicles dirty and complete lack of pride in themselves or their units. What shook me most, however, was the look in the men's faces, disgruntled and insubordinate looks and although ordered to give "eyes left" hardly a man bothered to do so.' While admittedly Brooke was watching a poor-quality reserve formation and most other formations were to fight very well in several stiff battles at the outset, *isolement* had taken its toll, it had been passed on to the next generation of French conscript soldiers and was to be one, and an important one, of the several causes of the 1940 collapse. Faced with German blitzkrieg, the poorly trained and commanded French soldier was not prepared to fight another protracted and possibly costly war. Verdun could not be re-enacted. The mood of *isolement* was only to be reversed by a return, in several forms, to another great French tradition – the overthrow of an oppressor, in this case an occupying power, by revolt and resistance, the tradition of *La Marseillaise*.

CHAPTER 10

1914-18
Beyond Mainland France

The Western Front was, of course, France's overriding priority in the war, but elements of the French military and navy were in action in a variety of operations outside the hexagon shape of mainland France. Some of these operations were colonial, others in Europe either to weaken the efforts of the Central Powers by operations in the Balkans or to support an ally, Italy, in need; one final operation was to stake out a claim for any post-war settlement in the Middle East.

Africans on the Western Front

Colonial troops made massive contributions to operations on the Western Front. Here and in the Middle East the troops used were entirely from the two sources of colonial man-power, the Armée d'Afrique and La Coloniale, both a legacy of the pre-1914 (and post-1919) French constitutional provision that only in exceptional circumstances, and so authorised by the legislature, should metropolitan conscripts serve outside France. As the war clouds darkened over Europe, in the first half of 1914, General Lyautey was commanding over 70,000 troops, all Armée d'Afrique or Coloniale, in extending French authority in Morocco. For the Western Front all that could be spared for pre-war France were four Armée d'Afrique Zouave battalions. At the outbreak of war the Moroccan campaign was run down – with consequences to be noted later – and in August–September 1914 an initial two Algerian-Tunisian divisions with a little later a third, together with a fourth division and two brigades drawn from Algerian personnel serving in Morocco, arrived in France. Also finally formed in September 1914 was a brigade of 5,000 Moroccans. As the war progressed and manpower needs became acute, two further Armée d'Afrique divisions were formed, and individual Tirailleurs units served at one time or another in nine metropolitan divisions. Eight *régiments de marche* were to contribute over seventy battalions of Algerian and Tunisian Tirailleurs for service on the Western Front by November 1918. A further two Moroccan *régiments de marche* provided six Moroccan Tirailleurs battalions, some serving with Tunisians and a Coloniale regiment in a new division. One Moroccan and seven Algerian Spahis regiments served on the Western Front dismounted as infantry. The Moroccans also served in Macedonia, and horsed squadrons, combined in one regiment with squadrons of the Chasseurs d'Afrique, served in Palestine and the Levant.

The North African divisions composition varied in detail but the preferred and usual pattern was that of one three-battalion regiment of Zouaves together with two to four *régiments de marche* of Tirailleurs. Elsewhere North African Tirailleurs units were grouped with one or more French units in brigades, or served in five Régiments Mixtes de Zouaves et Tirailleurs of battalions drawn from each.

Pre-war authority over La Coloniale regiments and units was divided, some being under the War Ministry for service in France, others left under the Colonies Ministry. The former included three Coloniale infantry divisions, each of two brigades of two regiments, which with a Coloniale artillery brigade formed the I Colonial Army Corps, though in August 1914 several units were still in Morocco. Recall of reservists and garrison units produced three more infantry regiments and thirty-two field batteries; these were replaced by local recruitment for further regiments among the French population in the colonies, supplemented by indigenous Sénégalais and Malgache Tirailleurs battalions. In 1915 some of these regiments, both Coloniale Blanche (white) and Tirailleurs Sénégalais, were used to form a II Colonial Army Corps of three divisions and certain additional units for service in France. As in the Armée d'Afrique, mixed regiments appeared, a main purpose being to steady hastily trained Tirailleurs. The structures varied, sometimes by battalions in a regiment sometimes by companies within a battalion. The number of Tirailleurs Sénégalais battalions on the Western Front steadily increased from thirty-seven (sixteen at Verdun and twenty-one on the Somme) in 1916, to twenty-four in 1917, with forty-five, together with six Malagasy battalions, in 1918. Most of these were front-line, others were lines of communication. It should be noted that battalions in all indigenous regiments were small, between 400–500 men.

Prior to 1914, drafting patterns varied. In Algeria a three-year conscription system, never applied universally, had been introduced despite protest and demonstrations in 1912; there were also a number of indigenous volunteers. No formal draft system was applied to Tunisia or Morocco, but pressure was brought on local authorities to produce volunteers. The Armée d'Afrique's officers and NCOs came from the metropolitan army, some for short, some for long spells. The white or very largely white Armée d'Afrique regiments, the elite Zouaves and Chasseurs d'Afrique, were in theory recruited from the white population of North Africa but were supplemented by volunteers or drafts from France. The Foreign Legion recruited generally; the numbers of men who came from enemy countries but nevertheless were prepared to serve led to its extensive use in Morocco. One Legion unit that particularly distinguished itself on the Western Front in 1914 contained a large number of Italians and was commanded by Lieutenant-Colonel Garibaldi, a grandson of the nineteenth-century Italian nationalist leader.

Coloniale Blanche was entirely volunteer, mostly from Paris, Brittany and Corsica, and French overseas territories; the few conscripts were men who applied to join for their period of service. The Tirailleurs Sénégalais were initially only recruited in West Africa among the Bambara, Tucolor, Malinke and Wolof. The Equatorial Africans were not considered martial until 1917–18; the name Tirailleurs Sénégalais was used for all African regiments irrespective of origin with the exception of units from Madagascar. Recruitment was by quota imposed upon districts and units were not formed on an individual colony basis as was the British pattern. La Coloniale officers and NCOs joined and made their entire careers in Coloniale units and formations.

In total, serving in Europe at one time or another during the war, were 150,000 Algerians, 39,000 Tunisians, 14,000 Moroccans, 135,000 Africans, 34,000 Malgaches and 43,000 Indochinese. A further 150,000 indigenous troops served in Africa and Indochina.

At their best, when well-trained, Armée d'Afrique and Coloniale units contributed a very especial élan to the battlefield. In a famous incident in 1914 a young Zouave taken by the Germans was propelled forcibly in front of an attacking German regiment on the Yser Canal; his last words were 'Tirez donc, au nom de Dieu, ce sont les Boches'. The 1st Zouaves lost twenty officers and 1,000 men in August 1914 and throughout the first two years of the war maintained their legendary reputation of fanaticism in attack. Thereafter fresh drafts were of poorer standard; the casualties, like those of Ulster on the Somme, had depleted the North African settler community. In the early offensives the Algerian

Tirailleurs charged into battle in blue tunics and white pantaloons, bugles blowing. Especially feared by the Germans were the blue djellaba-clad Moroccan Tirailleurs, whom they called the 'swallows of death'. Their fighting qualities had first become evident defending Paris in September 1914. The best Sénégalais units were those who had fought pre-war in Morocco, many using machetes to kill the enemy or even to remove the ears of dead or captured Germans – a practice their officers had to stop. As the war progressed, however, newer drafts of inadequately trained North and Black Africans proved less dependable. The Coloniale Régiment d'Infanterie Coloniale du Maroc, of Douaumont fame, and the Foreign Legion's 3rd Régiment de Marche de La Légion Etrangère, an elite shock-assault unit, commanded by the legendary Colonel Rollet, which led the attacks in July and August–September 1918, gained the highest number of awards for regimental combat valour in the French army.

There were incidents, however, that showed up the stress. A small number of white Algerian Zouaves considered the war not to be their concern and defected to the Germans. (It should be remembered that a large proportion of the *colon* population of Algeria were of Italian, Spanish or Maltese origin.) A few Algerian Tirailleurs units panicked and there were two small mutinies caused by fear and cold. One officer, an Algerian, led his men into the German lines. After defeats, particularly in September 1916 and after Nivelle's offensive, there were numerous desertions and even a few suicides. Nevertheless, at the time of the 1917 mutinies only one African unit, a badly officered Sénégalais Somali battalion, participated.

Special welfare arrangements were made for non-European troops, and in both the Armée d'Afrique and La Coloniale officers generally exercised paternal care, a concern in marked contrast to that of the civilian officials and settlers they had left behind. For the North Africans, officers sought to arrange *méchouis*, roast lamb festivals, whenever possible, together with football, dancing and athletics. Suitable food was provided in *foyers musulmanes* during rest periods. Imams officiated in temporary mosques. After a disastrous start, medical and pay facilities were greatly improved in 1915 (pay had initially been withheld from the sick and wounded), male nurses being provided from 1916. Leave home to North Africa, including extra periods for harvesting, was granted to all from 1916.

North African troops were required to remain in the field throughout the year, but Black Africans were granted winter concessions (*hivernage*), operational conditions permitting. Special hospitals, staffed by French personnel with African experience, were also opened, their main concerns being tuberculosis, venereal disease, malaria, pneumonia and psychological conditions. Sports and concerts were provided, and much private hospitality extended by ordinary French people. Mail (with help for illiterates) was arranged, soldiers received a small foreign service payment together with tax alleviation for their families, but Black troops were not granted leave home. A few North and Black Africans were granted French citizenship. Bonuses on discharge, help in securing employment on return home and pensions for dependants of those killed were all promised, to the general benefit of morale.

Amid the misery felt by North and Black African troops in the chaos, cold and carnage of the Western Front battles, there was, paradoxically, some sense of pride in this experience of suffering shared with French soldiers, of having gone up in the world. '*Ceci est une guerre de tombeau mais nous tous sommes frères*,' wrote one African soldier. There were no scruples about killing Germans and the French took care to employ as few Moslem units as possible in operations against the Turks, the Moroccans in any case looked more to their own sultan than the Ottoman caliph for spiritual guidance. On the Western Front German propaganda targeted on Algerian units was an almost complete failure.

Africa and the Middle East

The outbreak of war left France with two military commitments in Africa, that of the two German colonies in West Africa, Togoland and Cameroun, and that of Morocco. Other commitments were to follow, including one in the Middle East.

In respect of the German colonies the campaigns were conducted in partnership with slightly larger British colonial forces. Neither Britain and France nor Germany had made any serious plans for a local conflict; resources were lacking, especially (in the French case) medical staff. A British column, entering Togo from the Gold Coast, seized Lomé on 12 August, and with the assistance of three French columns, two of Sénégalais and one of irregular cavalry from Volta, ended all German resistance quickly on 26 August 1914. A French column under Colonel Maraix took the important German naval signal station at Kamina on the following day. Cameroun was much more difficult, with a stronger garrison of 2,500 German and 6,000 indigenous soldiers. Small French Coloniale and Sénégalais columns under the command of General Aymerich entered the territory from north-east and south and other small units participated in the joint British-French landing from the sea, taking Douala in September 1914. Operations, however, were to continue all through 1915. The British and French had different aims and plans were poorly co-ordinated. The Germans withdrew into the interior but continued to receive supplies via the Spanish colony of Muni despite a British naval blockade. Disease and the difficulties of conscripting and retaining porters slowed the advance of the British and French columns. German resistance was determined, the town of Garua in the north-west resisted a siege with an almost Western Front system of trenches for six

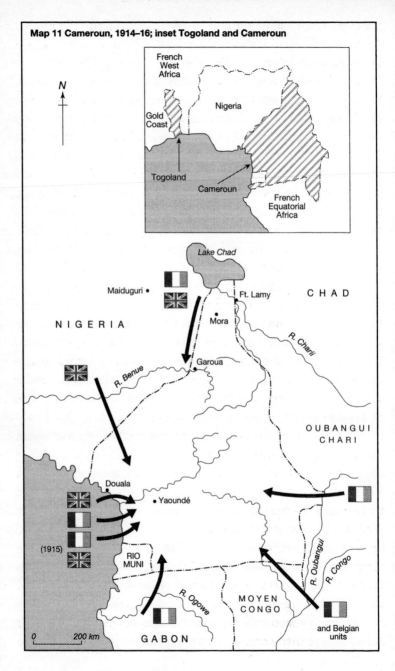

Map 11 Cameroun, 1914–16; inset Togoland and Cameroun

French West Africa

Nigeria

Gold Coast

Togoland

Cameroun

French Equatorial Africa

N

Lake Chad

Maiduguri •

Ft. Lamy

CHAD

• Mora

NIGERIA

R. Chari

Garoua

R. Benue

OUBANGUI CHARI

Douala

• Yaoundé

RIO MUNI

(1915)

R. Oubangui

R. Congo

MOYEN CONGO

R. Ogowe

and Belgian units

GABON

0   200 km

months. Fighting in several areas of the territory, notably Mora in the north, lasted until February 1916, necessitating a French contribution of over 7,000 men, mostly Sénégalais.

In Morocco, Lyautey had to yield his best regiments, forty-two battalions by mid-1915, to the needs of the Western Front, retaining only Foreign Legion units, and receiving as replacements units of elderly reservists, battalions of Tirailleurs Sénégalais and, later Tirailleurs Marocains together with Moroccan irregular *goums* of 200 men, in all some 200,000 troops. Lyautey's operations centred on attempts to hold, often under very difficult conditions, the areas already occupied in the Middle Atlas and the Rif, and to suppress particular uprisings. An attempt by a foolhardy colonel, Laverdure, in November 1914 to secure Khenifra by a punitive blow against local Zaian resistance led to a bloody reverse. Twenty-four officers, including Laverdure, and over 550 soldiers were killed, small numbers compared with the losses on the Western Front but very significant in a colonial situation. Khenifra remained virtually besieged until 1918. Of the uprisings two were especially dangerous, that of Abd al Malik in the Taza which opened in 1915 and lasted for four years, and that of al Hiba in the south, given aid by the Germans from submarines, in which an almost entire Sénégalais battalion was massacred on one occasion, and which continued until 1919. Lyautey, with great resolution and asserting that Morocco and Verdun were all part of the same war, dominated Morocco in these years. On the scene of any serious trouble, on horseback with a mounted Spahis escort, Lyautey urged his ill-assorted units to do their utmost. He was assisted by an especially able team of *généraux d'Afrique*, most notable among them being General Poeymirau who led a column across the Middle Atlas in 1917, dividing the main areas of dissidence.

While Morocco was the most serious of the French North African commitments, military manpower, usually in the form of Zouave reservists, Sénégalais, Chasseurs d'Afrique light cavalry and the Saharan camel companies, had to be deployed to meet other challenges. In 1914 the Senussi, inspired by Istanbul and proclaiming holy war rose against the Italians in Libya, seizing Ghat and Ghademes, and in March 1915 entering south-east Algeria. The revolt extended to southern Tunisia in September 1915 and all southern Algeria and the Touareg in Niger in 1916. The French were forced to abandon Djanet, and were only able to hold Fort Polignac with difficulty. It appeared that the whole French position in the northern West African colonies was in danger. Fighting on a considerable scale developed, the French deploying columns of several hundred men and camels, their opponents being assisted by Turkish and some German advisers, and equipped with captured Italian field guns. British help from north Nigeria became necessary. The events all led to the appointment by Lyautey of the dashing and experienced Laperrine to command in the Sahara. In the fighting, which extended after the war to 1920, the equivalent of a division's manpower had to be engaged in garrison or pursuit groups, the most valuable being the camel Compagnies Sahariennes, Laperrine's creation in the pre-war years, although aircraft and armoured cars were also used on a small scale.

Further calls on military manpower arose from protest uprisings against the draft. In North Africa there was minor unrest in 1915, a major revolt in the Batna area in 1915–18 requiring 14,000 troops including two regiments brought from France and artillery and aircraft in its suppression, a barrack mutiny at Bizerta in Tunisia in 1917, and cordons to restrict the number of desertions at the time of the 1918 draft. In Black Africa there was a continual series of minor revolts against the ever-increasing pressure of the draft, with ruthless corralling of teenage Africans by gendarmes seeking to prevent their escape into the bush. The most serious uprisings were in

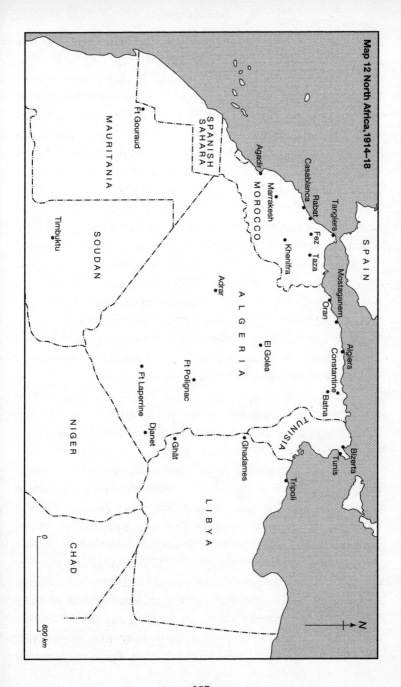

Map 12 North Africa, 1914-18

SPAIN

MAURITANIA

Ft Gouraud

SPANISH SAHARA

Agadir
MOROCCO
Marrakesh
Casablanca
Rabat
Tangiers
Fez
Taza
Khenifra

Mostaganem
Oran

Timbuktu

SOUDAN

Adrar

ALGERIA

El Goléa

Algiers
Constantine
Batna

Ft Polignac

Ft Laperrine

TUNISIA

Bizerta
Tunis

Djanet
Ghât
Ghadames

LIBYA

Tripoli

NIGER

CHAD

0

600 km

N

207

Sudan (1915), in Upper Volta (1915–16), in Dahomey (1915–18), in Niger (1916–17), all requiring small-scale military operations. One Governor-General of French West Africa, van Vollenhoven, resigned in protest against the severity of the draft, being killed in action later while serving as a captain with the Régiment d'Infanterie Coloniale du Maroc. In Indochina there was unrest in Laos (1914–16) and mutinies by several local Tirailleurs garrisons (1917–18). The severe conditions of both recruitment and transit to the battlefield were, however, alleviated in 1917–18, largely thanks to the intervention of Blaise Diagne, a Black Deputy from the pre-1789 *Quatre Communes* of Senegal which enjoyed full civic rights.

In the Middle East, to assert a French presence, two mixed regiments, one of Algerian Tirailleurs and Territorial infantry, and one of Chasseurs d'Afrique and Spahis horsed cavalry, served together with artillery and other small units under General Allenby from 1917 onward, participating in the entry to Damascus. The dash of the cavalry regiment was much admired by their Australian formation commanders.

Europe: Dardanelles, Macedonia, Italy

The sizeable French contribution to the ill-starred Dardanelles campaign is often overlooked by British writers. The first French involvement was naval under the energetic Admiral Guépratte, France losing one old battleship with two more severely damaged in the naval attempt to force the Straits. When the decision to mount a land attack had been taken, the French initially contributed a strong division, some 17,000 men, including four Sénégalais battalions in mixed regiments, under General d'Amade, to General Sir Ian Hamilton's force. On 25 April 1915 one brigade of this force landed at Kum Kaleh, on the Anatolian mainland where they held up fire from the Turkish fort while other operations were in progress. The rest landed on the Cape Helles peninsula itself, encountered

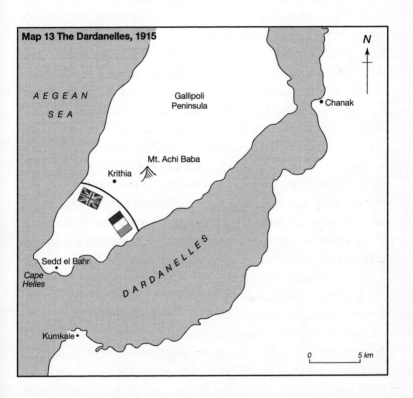

Map 13 The Dardanelles, 1915

N

AEGEAN SEA

Gallipoli Peninsula

Chanak

Mt. Achi Baba

Krithia

Sedd el Bahr

Cape Helles

DARDANELLES

Kumkale

0   5 km

fierce Turkish opposition under the German General Liman von Sanders, and in two days of fighting the French suffered 40 per cent casualties. The Kum Kaleh brigade was then withdrawn to the peninsula. A few days later a second French division, commanded by General Bailloud, arrived; but the correlation of forces in numbers, artillery and the general advantages that defence maintained over attack, halted the British and French force, unable to take Krithia or Mount Achi Baba. Many of the French units, too, were still in their uniforms of blue tunics and red trousers, which showed up only too clearly against the buff-coloured earth. D'Amade, in poor health and at odds with the British, asked to be recalled and was replaced by Gouraud who shortly after his arrival was blown over a wall and badly wounded, losing an arm, being in turn replaced in overall command by Bailloud.

Conditions for the troops in the scorching hot summer, the absence of shade, thirst, mosquitoes, flies, lice and rats, malaria, dysentery and gastric influenza added to the worsening military situation, where attacks such as those at Krithia gained only a few metres at heavy cost in lives. Morale slumped: 'Numerous cases of a wound in the left hand,' noted the army doctor Vassal. The Sénégalais units, eventually totalling seven battalions, suffered especially, and tended to become unsteady in action if their officers were killed. The failure of Hamilton's August attacks, which were supported by the French, led Bailloud to request that his forces be transferred to another theatre of operations. Withdrawal of the French forces accordingly began in October. Following the decision of the British to abandon the campaign, the last of the French forces, now under General Brulard, were evacuated in January 1916 as part of the British General Sir Charles Monro's notably skilful withdrawal. The campaign, in which some 80,000 French military personnel had participated at one time or another, cost 3,500 killed, 6,500 missing, 17,000 wounded and 25,000 sick.

The withdrawal from the Dardanelles, amid much Anglo-French friction, coincided with the opening of the very much greater and more prolonged Allied operations in the Balkans favoured by France. These were conceived defensively at the outset as an attempt to support Serbia and ease the pressure on Russia, rather later in terms of offence as a means of attacking the Ottoman and Austro-Hungarian empires. Behind these purely military considerations, however, lay wider French diplomatic and economic ambitions. The Ottoman Empire was seen to be collapsing and a strong French presence to assert French interests in the Eastern Mediterranean was regarded as necessary. But as a military strategy it could only be sound if sufficient forces were to be allotted for it; this was not to be the case until 1918. The attitude of the Greek government in these conditions was pivotal. In late 1915 Prime Minister Venizelos, following Bulgarian mobilisation in September, wished Greece to enter the war on the Allied side. He had a longer-term Greek expansionist policy in mind, greatly to embarrass the Allies later. King Constantine, however, who was the Kaiser's brother-in-law and pro-German, favoured neutrality.

Against the king's will, the French, with hesitant British concurrence, decided to send a small military force to Salonika to try to support the hard-pressed Serbs. The force, initially comprising a British division and Bailloud's division from the Dardanelles, was placed under the command of General Sarrail. The circumstances of Sarrail's selection and departure from the Western Front have already been mentioned. To keep his coalition functioning, Briand found it necessary to support a Balkans campaign for domestic political reasons. An important command for a known socialist republican general was also politically necessary even if the circumstances were from the outset ill-starred. Sarrail was seen as a suitably safe commander who would at the same time further French trading and business interests.

A Greek political crisis soon arose when Constantine dismissed Venizelos on 5 October 1915, replacing him with a minister, Skouloudis, more in accord with his own views. A few days later Sarrail arrived in Greece, to be followed over the next two months by two French and four British divisions. This force, some 150,000 strong by December, was too small and too late to prevent the Central Powers armies – German, Austro-Hungarian and Bulgarian under General von Mackensen – from invading Serbia or to give the Serb army an escape route to Salonika. The Anglo-French forces were checked in the Vardar and Cerna valleys. The Serb army was therefore pushed across the mountains to the Albanian Adriatic coast from where in late December and the early months of 1916 it was evacuated in French and Italian transports escorted by British and French warships, the French commander being Vice-Admiral Dartige du Fournet. The vast majority were taken to Corfu with a small number to Bizerta. Corfu had been arbitrarily occupied on 11 January by a battalion of *chasseurs alpins*, to the fury of the Greek government. The Anglo-French forces in northern Greece, faced with rain, mud and icy winds and without cold weather clothing, equipment, or tentage, were withdrawn to an entrenched 20-kilometre radius perimeter zone around Salonika, Sarrail forcing the surrender of Greek artillery that surrounded the port.

In Corfu the Serbs were re-equipped and reorganised into six 20,000-strong divisions by a French military mission headed by General Piarron de Mondesir. These formations were then transported to Thessalonika under the escort of a French naval squadron that had based itself at Argostoli, again to the fury of Athens. There they were included in an Allied force that by the end of 1916 was to total some 400,000 men including British divisions, an Italian division, two Russian brigades and a French army contribution that by January 1917 amounted

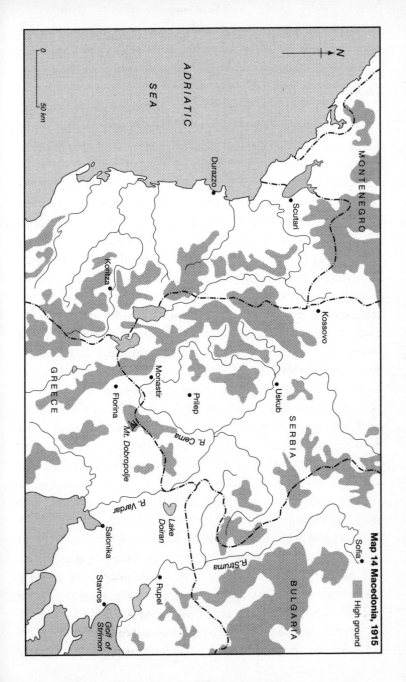

Map 14 Macedonia, 1915

High ground

to eight divisions. Included among them were fifteen Sénégalais battalions, the majority being used on lines of communication security but several committed to front-line combat.

Sarrail as Commander-in-Chief and his French force subordinate generals, Cordonnier until October 1916 and Leblois thereafter, faced a very complex situation. General Robertson in London and Joffre in France continued to press for vigorous action while at the same time insisting on priority for the Western Front, a contradiction which an unfortunate visit by Castelnau served only to worsen. Joffre's personal interest in the campaign appears to have been largely that of keeping Sarrail away from France. Relations with the British and Serb commanders were generally cordial, but the Italians created friction. King Constantine and Skoudoulis did what they could to embarrass and harass supply, this now including sabotage by Greek army reservists. Furthermore, in March they ordered the Greek army not to oppose the Austro-Hungarian and Bulgarian forces; in May the Greeks made over the fortress of Rupel on the Struma to them without a fight.

In the first months of 1916 Sarrail moved his forces forward up some 70 kilometres to form a shield for Salonika stretching from the Vardar to the Gulf of Strymon, following this up in May by extending his line towards Florina, and in June proclaiming an Allied authority over the occupied area. A competent if not outstanding general, Sarrail, however, was neither able to proceed further nor to rescue Romania, which the Germans had invaded. He lacked reserves and needed to detach a large percentage of his force to construct, and secure against attacks, roads and railway lines of communication. His forces were also seriously reduced by malaria, some units being reduced to a mere handful of men. French passenger liners were brought in to serve as hospital ships. In addition, the British divisions lacked adequate artillery, a weakness only partly offset by the arrival of some forty very useful French aircraft.

The British and French governments, threatening a military intervention in Athens, ordered Constantine to dismiss Skouloudis, which he did, and to disarm his regiments in Salonika which he refused to do. The stalemate was broken by a strong Bulgarian offensive in Macedonia, opening on 17 August. With some difficulty Sarrail checked the Bulgarian offensive and on 10 September managed to launch a vigorous counter-offensive which led to the occupation of Florina by Zouaves and the Foreign Legion on 17 September, and then Monastir on 19 November. Winter, exhaustion and the continuing advantage enjoyed by defenders over attackers then brought operations to a close for the year.

To secure his lines of communication Sarrail had had openly to support a Venizelist rebel military insurrection at Salonika at the end of August. The rebels first coerced the royalist units into joining the Allies, then installed a provisional rival Greek government under Venizelos which was able to control the area and islands. Other French forces supported Venizelists elsewhere and attempted to restore control over Epirus and south-east Albania overrun by *comitaji* bandit groups, finally leading in December to the proclamation of autonomy under a French protectorate of the province of Koritza. The end of the year, however, was to see a serious setback to Allied policies in Athens. Earlier, in September, an Allied naval force had arrived off Piraeus to make a series of demands on Constantine, the most important of which were rejected by the king. On 1 December Vice-Admiral Dartige du Fournet rashly landed 3,000 soldiers and marines, mostly French, who advanced on Athens where they were surrounded by Greek troops and hostile crowds. Warship fire secured their withdrawal after fifty-four men were killed and others wounded, but the king remained free to develop his policy of attacks on the Venizelists and Sarrail's lines of communication. Dartige du Fournet was recalled and not employed again.

To coincide with Nivelle's Aisne offensive, Sarrail launched a general attack on 22 April, which lasted until 23 May. The British sought to advance towards Lake Doiran, the French, now under General Grossetti, to advance north from Monastir. Both efforts failed disastrously, the soldiers suffering from sickness, the climate, mountain marches and inadequate food supplies, now of necessity often supplemented by scrounging, for which severe penalties were imposed if discovered. The men had gone without leave for a year, those who had been at the Dardanelles for over twenty months. Friction between the different national and colonial forces broke out. Morale slumped, suicides rose. Paradoxically the taking of Monastir, after an initial rise in morale, had the reverse effect when it became evident that the only result was a return to the *cafard* of trench warfare. Lassitude and a desire for peace with a measure of 'forgotten army' dejection increased and mutinies broke out. In contrast to the events in France, NCOs figured prominently among the mutineers. Sarrail and Grossetti suppressed the disorders, but since these were more in the nature of industrial strikes than revolutionary uprisings, they acted with restraint; there were no executions although forced labour and prison sentences were imposed. Leave privileges were granted as a concession.

The political crisis was to last until May 1917 when the Allied governments authorised Jonnart, the French High Commissioner in Greece, to force the abdication of Constantine. A powerful squadron commanded by Vice-Admiral de Gueydon and including 13,000 men, arrived in the bay of Salamis on 11 June while at the same time Sarrail despatched a division into Thessalonika. Constantine abdicated in favour of his son, Venizelos arrived to form a new government and at the end of the month formally declared war on the Central Powers.

After the restoration of order and discipline, Sarrail mounted a second offensive to the west of Lake Ochrida in the direction of Albania, opening on 27 August and lasting until 25 October. The Italians, however, had their own agenda for this region; they refused their support and requested Paris to halt the offensive. In September Grossetti was replaced by General Regnault as commander of the French forces, in turn to be succeeded by General Henrys at the end of the year. Sarrail himself, again involved in intrigues with accusations of satrap ambitions, was replaced by General Guillaumat as Commander-in-Chief earlier in the same month.

Guillaumat followed the Pétain strategy of attacks of limited scale until sufficient strength for a real breakthrough was available; the most important of these saw the 16th Coloniale Infantry Division and a Greek army corps take the Bulgarian position of Skra di Legen, west of Lake Doiran, after stiff mountain fighting. The build-up of forces continued throughout the first six months of 1918 totalling 650,000 men, against the Central Powers' 450,000. Included in the French contribution were now three Coloniale divisions, the carbine cavalry Spahis Marocains and some 180 aircraft. The Allied strength was more impressive on paper than in fact due to very heavy losses from malaria and scurvy, and a little later some British forces were withdrawn.

Supply was a major problem for the armies. Stores could be sent by land to Taranto, but thereafter were at grave risk from submarine attack. It was for this problem that Guillaumat had immediately sent for Henrys, a general with extensive Moroccan experience. An ambitious agricultural programme was set in hand by Henrys, to produce by mid-1918 ten tons of vegetables per day, with in addition large quantities of hay and straw. The army became known as the 'gardeners of Salonika'. A water supply system of reservoirs, wells, horse ponds and pipelines both for the military and the local civilian population was laid out. French military engineers built 900 kilometres of roads and improved a further 300 kilometres of existing tracks, 13,000 military labour personnel being involved together with 12,000 local labourers, lorries, ox wagons and steam-engine rollers.

In June Guillaumat was replaced by Franchet d'Esperey whose reputation on the Western Front had been damaged by the German May–June Aisne offensive advances and was no longer considered fit for a command there. His aggressive energies were undiminished but had to remain frustrated, the collapse of Russia seeming again to emphasise priority for the Western Front. On 15 September 1918 he was at last able to open a powerful and meticulously planned combined French and Serb offensive against the Bulgarians in the Moglena area, using flame-throwers for the first time in Macedonia, and taking Mt Dobropolje; General Jouinot-Gambetta's cavalry brigade, frequently dismounted, in epic mountain marches followed this up with the capture of Prilep on 23 September and Uskab on the 29th. The Bulgarians, faced with mutinies, signed a cease-fire, King Ferdinand of Bulgaria abdicated, and on 16 October a French regiment entered Sofia. Franchet d'Esperey wished to advance further to invade Austria–Hungary and take Vienna but he was restrained by Paris. His army was broken up, part sent on to the Turkish front, part directed towards the Adriatic to menace the Austrians in Albania in order to prevent the Serbs from entering Bulgaria. Units left to him entered Kosovo, a spirited cavalry charge taking Mitrovitza on 9 October. The Turks signed an armistice with the British on 30 October. Sickness remained a constant problem throughout the whole Salonika–Macedonia campaign and was to continue with fever-stricken soldiers suffering recurrent bouts of malaria long after the war was over.

The second European commitment of French forces but

outside France was in Italy. On 24 October 1917 the Italian army suffered a shattering defeat at the hands of the Austro-Hungarian forces at Caporetto. Total collapse threatened. To reinforce and stiffen the routed army, a force of five British and six French divisions were sent to Italy, the French contingent being under the command, successively, of Generals Duchesne, Fayolle and Maistre. It was thought that the subtraction of these eleven divisions from the Western Front would be compensated by the arrival of American formations. Initially, at the insistence of Foch, the French and British divisions were held in reserve in case of an Austrian breakthrough, but they were committed to the front line in December, the French formations in the key area between the Piave and the Brenta rivers. On 30 December the chasseurs of the 47th Division conducted a splendid assault, clearing the Austrians from Monte Tomba. Four of the French divisions and General Maistre himself had to be withdrawn and hurriedly returned to France to form the new 10th Army in the critically dangerous situation of late March 1918. The two remaining French divisions continued to serve on the Piave front, containing Austrian attacks and contributing to the Italian General Diaz's decisive victory at Vittorio Veneto in October. French aircraft were also notably effective in harrying the Austrian retreat from the Piave to the Tagliamento. An armistice was signed on 3 November.

Mention should also be made of the despatch, in the context of the collapse of Russia, of a 1,000-strong Coloniale force to Vladivostok, later joined by an American contingent. Their purpose was to cover and provide for the return to the war of the Czech Legion, formerly prisoners of the Russians, who had travelled right across Russia in their quest for freedom.

CHAPTER 11

Aftermath

The Allied armies had won the Western Front war. The support of the British for the French had been vital throughout the war, and the arrival of the Americans in 1918 served to shorten it by forcing the Germans into unsuccessful and costly offensives and participating themselves in the final operations. Through the four years, however, the French army had led the way, with the greatest number of troops deployed, and suffering the heaviest casualties. Although none of the great French offensives of the first three years had enabled France to impose her will on the Germans – at the Marne, in 1915, at Verdun or in the 1918 battles – French soldiers had prevented German victory on the most important land front of the war.

With the end of the fighting, the Germans were given two weeks to evacuate French territory and Alsace-Lorraine, in the event of their withdrawal taking a little longer. A triumphal entry into Alsace and Lorraine began on 17 November; on the 19th Pétain, promoted to Marshal of France and accompanied by Fayolle, entered Metz. Foch followed on the 26th. Gouraud was the first commander to enter Strasbourg, with Pétain and Foch following. The band of the 4th Zouaves, in traditional baggy red trousers and small red skull-caps, with the regimental drum-major throwing his mace high into the air to the delight of the crowds, led the triumphal entry into the city.

Allied troops entered Germany on 1 December but could only cross the Rhine in the three strategically important bridgehead areas, Mainz, Coblenz and Cologne on the 13th. The French entry into Germany was commanded by Fayolle, the 8th and 10th Armies providing the troops. The people of Alsace and Lorraine welcomed the French with rapture, but when French troops entered the area of Germany earmarked for French occupation, the mutual animosity was strong.

Many French generals, among them Pétain, considered the armistice terms too lenient. Pétain urged a complete surrender of all German army tanks and guns and an Allied occupation of areas on the east bank of the Rhine as well as the west bank lands. After initially reaching the Rhine frontier, Foch was content with the surrender of a large proportion of the German army's artillery and machine-guns together with control of the three Rhine bridgehead areas. These he saw as sufficient security and he needed a speedy armistice before American power became overwhelming.

For some formations military operations were not over. Three divisions, later reduced to one, were sent to Romania and the Ukraine to support White Russian forces initially under the command of General Berthelot, then Franchet d'Esperey, in the belief that the Bolsheviks could be contained and defeated. Stubborn Bolshevik opposition that had not been expected led to withdrawal from Kherson, Nikolaiev and Odessa in late March and early April 1919. Following serious mutinies in the French navy's major units in the Black Sea, French forces were finally withdrawn from Sevastopol on 29 April. A small contingent serving in North Russia was also withdrawn.

In the Middle East a small French detachment occupied Latakia in Lebanon from early 1919, a presence leading to the first of ongoing French military pacification operations in Lebanon and Syria in the years to follow.

Demobilisation of the army began rapidly. The call-up classes of 1889–91 were released in December, 1892–96, in January 1919, 1897–1901 in February, 1902–5 in March, 1906–9 in April, 1910–14 in August, 1915 in September, 1916–17 in November, 1918 in June 1920, and 1919 in March 1921. Certain special cases were advanced or retarded according to circumstances.

Casualties and Costs

Between August 1914 and November 1918 France had mobilised 8,700,000 men, a figure not including the totals of indigenous colonial personnel noted in Chapter Ten. Different figures of casualties according to varying methods of calculation and estimation have appeared. The most reliable indicate a death roll of at least 1,350,000. Of these some 36,000 were Algerian, 10,000 were Tunisian and an unknown number Moroccan, with also 29,000 Africans, 4,000 Malgaches and 2,000 Indochinese, all mostly killed in France. The Germans took few African prisoners.

More than 3,200,000 were wounded in varying degrees of gravity, of these, 1,100,000 remained disabled, 390,000 mutilated (many thousands with hideous facial injuries) and 200,000 gassed. Uncounted thousands of men returned home psychologically scarred, many brutalised. It is estimated that the dead and those who died later as a result of war injuries left some 700,000 widows, and the number of orphaned children beyond any estimation. France mourned, and was to mourn for long. The 600,000 prisoners-of-war held by the Germans who survived their captivity returned to France debilitated physically and psychologically. The Germans made efficient arrangements for their return home, but in France there was little welcome and poor reception arrangements. The highest percentage of fatal casualties was in the infantry, 22.6 per cent, with 7.9 per cent in the cavalry, 6 per cent in the artillery, 6.4

per cent in the engineers and 3.6 per cent in logistic units. In the infantry itself, the heaviest losses were taken by the elite Coloniale infantry, the Zouaves and *chasseurs à pieds*. These regiments had continuously been used to mount attacks after the failures of line infantry battalions.

Three appallingly mutilated men pushed in wheelchairs followed by a large contingent of other *mutilés*, blind, armless, bandaged men, led the triumphal 14 July 1919 victory parade in Paris. In the months after the war groups of relatives visited the battlefields in organised parties hoping that excavations might yield the identities of their relatives among the corpses. Streets were filled with the crippled and mutilated, hospitals both physical and mental remained crowded for many years.

Many thousands, however, had come to bless the name of the indefatigable president of the National Association of War Wounded and later Minister of Pensions, André Maginot.

The exhaustion of the French army created a major problem in the provision of troops for the occupation of Germany, recourse being made to the Armée d'Afrique and La Coloniale, which led to subsequent German allegations of the deliberate use of Black troops to humiliate the population. In the first eighteen months, some 35,000 (a figure including non-metropolitan Frenchmen serving in Coloniale regiments) were not native Frenchmen. The main component of the occupying army were a Moroccan division, some thirty-three Algerian and Tunisian Tirailleurs battalions, about 3,000 Tirailleurs Malgaches, a Spahis brigade and a Zouave regiment with, on rotation, a Coloniale Blanche regiment. To June 1920 there was one Tirailleurs Sénégalais regiment, but thereafter the only Black personnel in the occupation force were French *citoyens* from the pre-1789 colonies in the Caribbean or Senegal, serving, as was their right in Coloniale Blanche regiments. In 1921 the Malgaches were withdrawn, followed in 1925 by the North Africans.

The behaviour of the non-French forces was generally of a very high standard despite German propaganda, at its most vocal in areas not occupied by the French and at times of reparations payment. The non-French personnel did not harbour passionate emotions towards the Germans; many of the Malgache were devout Roman Catholics. The units were kept under very strict discipline with heavy punishments, collective or individual (including death sentences) for murder or rape. Where shooting occurred it was usually in self-defence following German provocation. From January 1919 to June 1920, the period of the largest concentration of indigenous troops, there were only sixty-six sexual assault cases, of which twenty-eight were convicted. Fuel for German propaganda, however, was provided by the North African troops' preference for German prostitutes, as being cheaper than those provided by the French military brothels.

The war left France exhausted financially as well as socially. State expenditure rose to Fr 38 milliards in the war years, compared with Fr 5 milliards before the war. Money was raised by indirect taxation, from 1916 a tax on incomes, taxes on industries profiting from the war, advances from the Bank of France, interest-bearing national defence bonds issued by the Treasury, the printing of notes and four large National Defence Loans, in 1915, 1916, 1917 and 1918, launched by means of flag days. Other loans were raised from Britain and the United States. The national debt rose from Fr 32,800 million to Fr 114,200 million in 1918 and Fr 171,353 million by 1 January 1919. The state contracted with many hundreds of private enterprises for the manufacture of war materials ranging from pickaxes to tanks and aircraft engines, co-ordinating their programmes by advances and subventions. The loss of coal mines and steel plants at the start of the war stimulated the sizeable growth of replacement industries elsewhere. The expenditure, debt repayment and vast war damage costs in the northern provinces led to the popular demand for reparations from Germany; the armistice conditions required in particular the immediate hand-over of German railway wagons.

1940

The measure to which the misery, hardship and exhaustion of France after the 1914–18 war, and the belief that France could not survive another Verdun-scale bloodletting, contributed to the disaster of 1940 will always be a matter of debate, most of which must remain outside the scope of this work. That it was an important cause none can doubt. The contributions of the First World War to the pacifism, anti-militarism and socialism of the 1920s and 1930s; the absence of men of the lost generation and the leadership of the country falling into the hands of men scarred by the experience of the war and especially Verdun; men often of indifferent political ability and honesty reducing France to a state of undeclared civil war; the disturbing effect of the excesses of the Republicans in the Spanish Civil War and the ghosts of the 1871 Paris Commune on political leaders and senior officers; the limited capabilities both of French industry and the French economy to provide for fully effective rearmament in the 1930s – all of these factors are evident. The pre-1914 culture of military patriotism was reversed; disobedience, self-mutilation and fear were represented as the true virtues. 'Never again' messages were conveyed in oils and stone, by Jean Galtier-Boissier's famous painting of the mutilated at the 14 July 1919 parade and by the huge Ossuary Memorial at Verdun. The same message was repeated in Louis-Ferdinand Céline's *Voyage au bout de la nuit*, published in 1932 and very widely read. In addition, propaganda on the theme that the British were only making a token contribution to the war was widespread both in the army and society as a whole. By 1940 all these factors combined to present a clear case study for students of 'mentality history'. Was the war, the effort, the inevitably French sacrifice, really worth it? At the same time, however, there were other positive factors which make historical evaluation complex. The French economy had recovered from the devastation and costs of the war more successfully than anyone had expected. France by 1939 was producing good tanks, the Char B 1 being one of the best in service anywhere at the time; the French navy of 1939 was one of the best in the nation's history, with a number of fine modern ships. There were within the military some notably able men, in particular Colonel de Gaulle and, for all his later faults, Admiral Darlan.

In respect of the army, earlier chapters set out the two principal issues at soldier level. The first was low morale and divorce from society which left recalled reservists, in the words of one observer, *désoeuvré*; the second was the sclerosis of the higher command, where in 1939 there was still an unshaken belief that the triumphs of 1918 could be repeated. In 1940 the former issue was exacerbated by the debilitating effects of the period September 1939–May 1940 with no great stimulus from military action, the lulled sense of security provided by the Maginot Line, and a very severe winter. The latter was further compounded by disastrous complacency, faulty strategic planning and poor communications, with branches of the staff scattered, together with failure to appreciate lessons that should have been learned from the German onslaught on Poland – lessons, nevertheless, that had been well assessed by intelligence staffs.

Two less-known consequences of the 1914–18 war also merit mention here. The French army was acutely aware of the effect of the lost generation on the numbers of conscripts who would be available by the middle and late 1930s. In 1914 France possessed one and a quarter million men aged between twenty and twenty-five, in 1940 there were only 600,000. Anticipating this shortfall, a major military priority had been to ensure that the final pacification operations, involving very large numbers of troops, in Morocco would be complete by mid-1934. Indigenous troops were then available to fill the gap on the mainland. In comparison with 1914, when no indigenous colonial units were stationed in France, in July 1939 there were four entire North African divisions present; these, together with other independent North African units, totalled eight regiments of Algerian, two regiments of Tunisian and four regiments of Moroccan Tirailleurs, together with a regiment each of Moroccan and Algerian Spahis. In addition, in the south of France, located to assist in repelling any Italian invasion, were six regiments of Tirailleurs Sénégalais. In both North and West Africa were further formations ready for transport to the mainland, three more North African divisions arriving in late 1939 and early 1940. Valiantly as many of these had fought in the 1914–18 war and although a number of them were again to try their best in 1940, they were neither trained nor equipped to resist a German 1940 blitzkrieg.

The second, curious but less familiar consequence of the 1914–18 war was the lesson perceived to be drawn from the Macedonian campaign, although this time the enemy likely to be attacked on a southern front would be Italy and any Italian aggression in the Balkans. A force of approximately the size of two divisions, again mostly North African but with a Sénégalais regiment as well, was stationed in Syria and Lebanon; in late 1939 General Weygand was despatched to command it. (The force was also considered for a second possible role, an attack on Baku, as a consequence of the August 1914 Soviet–German agreement.)

It is arguable, in conclusion, that the tragedy of 1940 was not entirely an inevitable consequence of the First World War. There did exist both the men (witness the virility later expressed in resistance and by an army in exile) and the resources that, properly led, above all with an imaginative use of armour might have prepared France to withstand the German onslaught. A total British commitment, particularly in the air where there was a real major French weakness, would of course again have been necessary. But if a Joffre and a Plan XVII had existed earlier, in September 1939, while the Germans were attacking Poland, subsequent events might well have been very different. France's need after the First World War was a psychological *renouvellement*. This, however, was only to come after a succession of further divisive and debilitating disasters – 1940, Indochina and Algeria. Yet when it came, *renouvellement* was to be the achievement of a veteran of the Great War trenches, Charles de Gaulle.

French Army Organisation at the Outbreak of War

1. Order of Battle

The order of battle of the French army on mobilisation was as follows:

North-east Army Group, General Joseph Joffre, Vitry-le-François.

1st Army, General Augustin Dubail, Epinal Sector:
VII Corps (14th and 41st Divisions)
VIII Corps (15th and 16th Divisions)
XIII Corps (25th and 26th Divisions)
XIV Corps (27th and 28th Divisions)
XXI Corps (13th and 43rd Divisions)
with, also, the 6th and 8th Cavalry Divisions, and the 1st Reserve Group (58th, 63rd and 66th Divisions) at Vesoul.

2nd Army, General Edouard de Curières de Castelnau, Nancy Sector:
IX Corps (17th and 18th Divisions)
XV Corps (29th and 30th Divisions)
XVI Corps (31st and 32nd Divisions)
XVIII Corps (35th and 36th Divisions)
XX Corps (11th and 39th Divisions)
with, also, the 2nd and 10th Cavalry Divisions and the 2nd

Reserve Group (59th, 68th and 70th Divisions).

3rd Army, General Pierre Ruffey, Verdun Sector:
IV Corps (7th and 8th Divisions)
V Corps (9th and 10th Divisions)
VI Corps (12th, 40th and 42nd Divisions)
with, also, the 7th Cavalry Division and the 3rd Reserve
Group (54th, 55th and 56th Divisions).

4th Army, General Fernand de Langle de Cary, Sainte-
Menehould–Commercy area:
XII Corps (23rd and 24th Divisions)
XVII Corps (33rd and 34th Divisions)
Colonial Corps (1st, 2nd and 3rd Colonial Divisions)
with, also, the 9th Cavalry Division.

5th Army, General Charles Lanrezac, Rethel Sector:
I Corps (1st and 2nd Divisions)
II Corps (3rd and 4th Divisions)
III Corps (5th and 6th Divisions)
X Corps (19th and 20th Divisions)
XI Corps (12th and 21st Divisions)
with, also, the 4th Cavalry Division, the 38th, 52nd and 60th
Divisions, and the 4th Reserve Group (51st, 53rd and 69th
Divisions) in the Hirson area.

GHQ Reserve
Cavalry Corps (1st, 3rd and 5th Cavalry Divisions).

General Staff Reserve
61st, 62nd and 67th Divisions.
North-east France Mobile Defence Force (51st, 71st, 72nd
and 73rd Divisions)
XIV (Lyon) and XV (Marseille) Region Reserves (64th, 65th,
74th and 75th Divisions).

2. Organisation

No fixed structure existed for an army. Heavy artillery was to be allotted according to an army's role.

An army corps comprised usually two, occasionally three, infantry divisions, a cavalry regiment, a field artillery regiment, usually a heavy artillery *groupe*, an engineers company and a reserve brigade.

An infantry division comprised two brigades, a cavalry squadron, a regiment of three field artillery *groupes*, an engineers company, logistic, medical and administrative sub-units and, on mobilisation, two reserve regiments for duties in the rear. A few divisions also possessed a *chasseurs groupe* of one, sometimes two, battalions. The full war establishment of an infantry division was 400 officers and 15,470 men.

Each brigade comprised three regiments, on war establishment 145 officers and 6,500 men with, if the division possessed them, *chasseurs* units.

A four-year manoeuvre cycle was designed to co-ordinate. In the first two years exercises were at divisional level, in the third at army corps level, while in the fourth year *grandes manoeuvres* armies participated.

The 173 metropolitan infantry regiments generally comprised three battalions with, on mobilisation, two battalions of its reserve regiment; eight of these, fortress regiments (the 157th, 158th, 159th, 164th, 165th, 166th, 170th and 173rd), however, possessed four battalions. The war strength of a battalion was a little over 1,000, organised into four companies plus one machine-gun section, each company on full establishment, three officers and 250 men. Companies comprised two platoons, themselves divided into two sections. In addition thirty-one *chasseurs à pieds* battalions had six companies. Each of these also possessed a reserve battalion. There were also 350-strong *chasseurs à pieds* detachments known as *groupes cyclistes*, attached to sixteen cavalry divisions.

The 1st, 2nd, 3rd and 4th Reserve Groups or Divisions were seen as having roles as flank and rear protection of their respective armies.

In North Africa there were units of XIX Corps, Algiers, commonly referred to as the Armée d'Afrique. These included four elite Zouave regiments, together on paper comprising twenty-four battalions and nine regiments of Algerian and Tunisian Tirailleurs, *les Turcos*, with a local strength of forty battalions. Of these units four Zouave battalions were the only representatives in France on 1 August 1914. The battalions of these regiments, Zouave and Tirailleurs, in the early months of the war generally pooled their resources to produce one fully effective *régiment de marche* of three battalions. The same came to apply to the two Foreign Legion infantry regiments and the five semi-penal battalions of African Light Infantry, petty offenders sentenced by French metropolitan courts and known as *les Joyaux*, the joyous ones.

The best infantry regiments of all, however, were the *marsouins* (dolphins) of the Troupes Coloniales, long-service regulars with a few selected conscripts, raised originally for the defence of naval bases at home and overseas, transferred from the navy to the army in 1900, and still retaining a semi-autonomous status protected by the legislature. Twelve of these regiments, each of three battalions, were in France, a further fifteen battalions were overseas. Among their duties were the sponsoring of indigenous African, Malagasy and Indochinese Tirailleurs regiments, none of which were in France at the start of the war.

Each cavalry division consisted of three brigades of two regiments, a *groupe* of two or three 75 mm horse artillery batteries, the 350-strong *groupe cycliste* and, in theory, an aircraft reconnaissance squadron. Regiments comprised four squadrons (expanded to six in army corps units on mobilisation), and on war establishment totalled thirty-five officers and 734 troopers. There were twelve cuirassiers, thirty-two dragoons, twenty-one *chasseurs à cheval*, fourteen hussars and six *chasseurs d'Afrique* regiments, the latter producing one *régiment de marche* in 1914. The horses purchased for the cavalry were not the most suitable, selection being made according to budgetary and agricultural considerations, an economy to prove false in 1914 when large numbers of horses died.

The artillery was organised into nine regiments of coast and fortress artillery, sixty-eight batteries; five differently composed *groupes* of heavy artillery, provisionally one for each of the five armies, drawn from fifty-eight batteries; two regiments of mountain artillery, fourteen batteries; and sixty-two regiments of field artillery, 618 field and thirty horse artillery batteries. Regiments forming part of an infantry division possessed three *groupes* of three batteries each of four guns, regiments allotted to an army corps possessed four *groupes*. Batteries in the Coloniale Divisions were part of the semi-autonomous La Coloniale, their personnel being known as *bigors* (seashells).

In France in 1914 were seventy-one field engineers companies, with fifteen fortress, sixteen railway, twelve telegraph, two wireless and twenty-one searchlight engineers companies. Of the twenty-one *train*, logistic squadrons, one was attached to each army corps. A small Service Automobile had been created in 1914, also recently formed was the Aviation Militaire with air squadrons (some balloon, some aircraft, one airship) and approximately 160 combat aircraft had been produced for training. The combat aircraft were formed into *escadrilles* of either six two-seater or four single-seat machines. Aerial reconnaissance had proved useful in Morocco, but military aviation was still at an early stage.

Fortresses had suffered from neglect in the years prior to 1914. Plans had been drawn up for a modernised fortress protection of a number of key areas, including the Grand Couronné, the Trouée de Charmes and along the Meuse, but work had begun only on the Grand Couronné by the outbreak of war. No thought was given to the fortifications of Maubeuge or Lille.

3. Conscription, Reserves and Mobilisation

Under the 'Three Years Law' of 1913 all fit nineteen-year-old Frenchmen were liable for twenty-eight years of military service – in the active army for three years, in the active army reserve for eleven years and in the Territorial army for seven years and the Territorial army reserve for a final seven years. The conscript was paid 50 centimes, about ½d, per day when in service.

The younger classes of the active army reserve brought units up to war strength. Older classes generally formed reserve units and formations meant to support first-line formations in the field. The Territorial units were envisaged as interior garrison troops, and in consequence the *groupes* of Territorial divisions possessed no heavy artillery. In the reserve and Territorial units many highly qualified and professional men were called upon to serve as ordinary soldiers.

Active army reservists attended two training periods, the first of twenty-three and the second of seventeen days during their eleven years. Territorial army personnel had one nine-day training period; the Territorial reservists, referred to as '*les pépéres*' (grandpas) by younger soldiers, mustered for one day.

Conscription had evolved on a regional basis, under the auspices of the general commanding the eighteen joint military regions and army corps headquarters of metropolitan France and the nineteenth in Algeria. The corps areas were divided into subdivisions for the drafting system, in some of the more heavily populated areas there were also division headquarters, usually infantry but with a few cavalry. The corps headquarters were as follows: I Corps, Lille; II Corps, Amiens; III Corps, Rouen; IV Corps, Le Mans; V Corps, Melun; VI Corps, Châlons sur Marne; VII Corps, Besançon; VIII Corps, Dijon; IX Corps, Tours; X Corps, Rennes; XI Corps, Nantes; XII Corps, Limoges; XIII Corps, Clermont-Ferrand; XIV Corps, Lyon; XV Corps, Marseille; XVI Corps, Montpellier; XVII Corps, Toulouse; XVIII Corps, Bordeaux. A military governor held command in Paris. Junior employees of the railways, public works, shipyards and telecommunications services were drafted to the engineers and artillery. For the cavalry, *chasseurs* and hussars there were 1.6m height and 65kg weight limitations. The great majority of the conscripts went to the infantry. Infantry regiments were linked to each military region, the number of regiments varying according to the local population. Within the region, divided into the subdivisions each supervised by a brigadier-general, recruits might be posted to a regiment inside or outside their own home subdivision according to the need to bring the region's regiments up to strength. Regiments from the thinly populated frontier regions were strengthened by drafts from Paris and Lyon. In practice this system as a whole often created not only regiments but also brigades and divisions recruited from particular geographical areas of France. At one level this made the soldier's life more acceptable as he was among men from his own region. There was, however, a downside both in peace and war. In 1907 there had been considerable industrial unrest among Languedoc wine growers, troops had to be called out and at Narbonne five people were killed and many more injured by the local garrison. The following day the local Béziers regiment, the 17th Infantry, mutinied in sympathy with the wine growers and 550 soldiers were sent to a penal posting in Tunisia as punishment. In 1914–15, when a formation suffered heavy casualties, these bore heavily on the region of origin.

Each of the 173 infantry regiments possessed a linked

reserve regiment, its number being that of the parent regiment plus 200. The thirty-one *chasseurs à pied* battalions, elite light infantry intended for fast-moving skirmishing tasks, had similarly a linked reserve battalion, its number being that of its parent plus forty. On transferring to the reserve soldiers would, wherever possible, be posted to the unit nearest their homes. Stores distributed all over the country equipped the reservist on recall. The state of training of the reserve units, however, was often very poor; funds and training ranges had not been provided and there was an acute shortage of officers.

The Territorial army totalled 145 regiments of three or more battalions linked to the subdivisions within the military regions, thirty-six squadrons of cavalry, forty brigades of field artillery with fourteen battalions of foot artillery (coast and fortress) and twenty-one engineers battalions.

4. Equipment

The basic infantry weapon in 1914 was the 8mm Lebel rifle designed in 1886 and modified in 1893. The rifle suffered from the serious defect that its magazine was a longitudinal hole bored in the fore-end, its eight cartridges being pushed to the rear by a spring. As the magazine emptied, the centre of gravity of the weapon changed, affecting the aim. With a bayonet 1ft 6in long fixed the rifle's length was a conspicuous 5ft 8in. The machine-gun in infantry regiments was the 1907 St-Etienne water-cooled gas-operated gun, also an unsatisfactory weapon liable to jam and with a complicated mechanism. Because of its unreliability and to save wear on barrels, regulations ordained that except in cases of urgency only one of the two guns in a machine-gun section should fire at the same time. It was quickly replaced by the Hotchkiss 1914 gun.

The cavalry regiments were all armed with slightly better small arms, the 1892 Lebel 8mm carbine. The cuirassiers and dragoons had a sabre, hussars and *chasseurs à cheval*, a light curved sword. Except for cuirassiers, most regiments were issued with lances, but these do not appear to have been used often.

The artillery possessed six main types of mobile gun. The field artillery's 3,840 75mm guns fired a high explosive shell or a shrapnel shell over a range of 8,000 metres, the horse artillery's 3-inch gun fired a 14.33lb shell. The heavy artillery's new 1913 model 105mm quick-firing gun had a range of 11,000 metres; its shell weighed 35.27lbs. Only a very few were in service in 1914. The excellent 155mm Rimailho 1904 howitzer fired a 90lb shrapnel or an 88lb high-explosive shell to a range of 6,000 metres. Of less value were the 1890 short-barrelled Bange 120mm gun (in present day terms a howitzer) and the even older 1878 90mm gun. Both were due to be replaced by the new 105mm gun. There were also a considerable number of guns in fortresses and specialist siege units. Among these were old 90mm guns, 155mm and 280mm howitzers, 120mm siege guns and 150mm and 220mm mortars. Many of these were obsolescent, some even having only cast-iron ammunition. Ammunition supply soon became a major concern. French industry in 1914 could only manufacture at most 14,000 shells per day, and existing stocks provided for only some 1,400 rounds for each 75mm gun. Wartime production was facilitated by the use of cast iron turning lathes rather than compressed steel.

The army's artillery and other transport was almost entirely horse-drawn. In peacetime the army was using between 140,000 and 150,000 horses. The British General Staff's *Handbook of the French Army* estimated that a further 454,000 would be needed on mobilisation.

A French soldier was supposed to receive a daily ration of 700g of biscuit or 750g of bread, 500g of fresh or tinned meat, 30g of lard or 50g of salt pork, 100g of vegetables, 20g of salt, 24g of coffee, 32g of sugar and a quarter of a litre of wine, together with a weekly issue of 100g of tobacco. Each battalion had, or was supposed to have, a bakery.

5. Officers

The French army recruited its officers from a variety of sources. The cavalry, infantry and La Coloniale drew about one half of their officers from the Ecole Spéciale Militaire at St Cyr, the remainder being commissioned senior non-commissioned officers, or in a few cases young men from major technical colleges or from reserve subalterns. The course at St Cyr lasted two years; boys from the age of eighteen were admitted. While the tone was set by equestrian society in northern France it was possible for Alphonse Juin, a future Marshal of France, the son of a humble gendarme living in Algeria, to pass out first in 1912.

Future career artillery and engineer officers attended a more rigorous academic course at the prestigious Paris Ecole Polytechnique, whose students also included naval officers and future state civil servants. Each arm of the army – infantry, cavalry, engineers and medical services – maintained its own specialist school providing courses for officers and non-commissioned officers.

The Ecole Supérieure de Guerre, the Staff College, took selected captains and subalterns under the age of thirty-seven for a two-year staff training course at the Ecole Militaire building in Paris. The college from 1910 also provided a higher level course, for majors and lieutenant-colonels, lasting ten months, training officers in the operations of armies and groups of armies.

Career progress was slow. All the army commanders in August 1914 were aged between sixty-one and sixty-four. A curious anomaly in the senior rank structure was the absence of the ranks of full general or lieutenant general. A *général de brigade* could be promoted to a *général de division*; if he then commanded an army corps this was only an appointment although it carried distinctive insignia. Above *général de division* the only formal rank was that of Marshal of France, for which no one had been appointed by the Third Republic. Pay levels at all ranks were poor. As a consequence the army was short of some 400 officers at the outbreak of war. An even more serious shortage of well-trained sergeants and corporals had its effect on the level of training of the rank-and-file soldier.

6. General

By the Constitution, the President of the Republic was the supreme commander of the French armed forces. Under him, the Minister for War, an appointee of the Prime Minister of the day, was responsible for the army and as such answerable to the legislature. In 1906 the Conseil Supérieur de la Défense Nationale was formed to co-ordinate the work of all departments of government concerned with defence. Its members included the Prime Minister and the Ministers for Foreign Affairs, the Interior, Finance, War, the Navy and the Colonies. The Conseil normally met twice a year, its work assisted by specialist consultative committees of officials. Under the Minister for War there also existed the Conseil Supérieur de la Guerre, headed by the minister himself and including the Chief of the General Staff, and ten senior generals who either were or had been army corps commanders. The Conseil had to be consulted on virtually all issues concerned with the army, its training, mobilisation, weaponry, and fortifications and it was supposed to meet at least once a month. In July 1911 the Conseil was reorganised to strengthen the position of Joffre as designate Commander-in-Chief. Individual membership was limited to one year, renewable. The office of vice-president of the Conseil was abolished, the Chief of the General Staff fulfilling the role. The Chief of the Army Staff would act as deputy in time of war, remaining in the ministry. A further change followed in January 1912 when the post of Army Chief of Staff was abolished. The Chief of the General Staff was now to be assisted by two deputies, one to serve at his headquarters, the other in the ministry. For the former, as noted earlier, Joffre chose Castelnau, partly to assist the priority of professional ability and partly because of Castelnau's special knowledge of mobilisation arrangements. In 1914 a new Conseil Supérieur de l'Aéronautique was formed to consider the development of aviation for both the army and the navy.

In August 1914 the President of the Republic was Raymond Poincaré, the Prime Minister was René Viviani, and the Minister for War Adolphe Messimy.

Commanders and Headquarters Staff

Commanders

The French army has always produced a great variety of personality in its commanders, never more so than in the First World War. The British field commanders were all gentry or upper middle class, all (with the exception of French who had been a naval cadet but came from the same social background), products of expensive private schooling, sharing common sets of values, patterns of social behaviour and working relationships. Further, all were reared in the tradition of commanding regiments of volunteer soldiers with a squirearchy obligation of concern for the 'other ranks'. The British army was so small that everyone knew everyone else. In the very much larger French army these factors were not the case; commanders' backgrounds could range from the village peasant society of Pétain, to the uncouth Guadaloupe settler colonialism of Lanrezac but also to the aristocratic castle upbringing of de Castelnau. Perhaps from the necessity imposed by these very different backgrounds the style of command, whether among equals or top-down to subordinates or to soldiers, was much more acerbic, often with Gallic explosions of temper which would not have been admissible in British headquarters. Almost all were in their early or mid-sixties, a few even older. French commanders, too, even more than Haig, had to keep an eye on their political masters and the domestic political situation to add to the tensions of their command. Many on their way up the promotion ladder had had experience of political intervention, Sarrail to his advantage, de Mitry and Anthoine, both deeply religious Catholics, to their disadvantage. They were, too, fighting to defend their own country, towns and countryside they knew. There is an element of high drama, of passion at critical moments, the tension between volatile Latin temperament and a profession requiring order and discipline – Galliéni's order for the defence of Paris, Joffre's order to Castelnau to defend Nancy and his order of the day before the Marne, in the indefatigable spirit of Foch and Franchet d'Esperey. The notes that follow summarise the careers of the war's major military commanders prior to 1914, the eight who became Marshals together with Castelnau, Mangin, Nivelle and Weygand.

Edouard, Vicomte de Curières de Castelnau, an aristocrat from the Pyrenees, was born in 1851 at his family's ancestral castle, Saint-Come near Saint-Affrique. Educated at a Jesuit school, he held very strong devout religious beliefs which led to his being distrusted by anti-clerical political figures. Castelnau entered St Cyr in 1869, and in the Franco-Prussian War fought as a subaltern in the Army of the Loire and against the Paris Communards. He then followed the largely garrison duties career of an infantry officer, but in his spare time read extensively in history and philosophy. He entered the Ecole de Guerre in 1878 and served on the General Staff in 1893. After regimental command he returned to the General Staff for work in connection with mobilisation plans. He became a brigadier-general in 1907 and a major-general commanding a division in 1910. In 1911 he attended the newly formed Centre des Hautes Etudes Militaires, and from 1913 was a member of the Conseil Supérieur de la Guerre. Joffre, after his appointment as commander-in-chief designate, selected Castelnau as his deputy but on the outbreak of war he was given an army command. He had twelve children, four daughters and eight sons, three of whom were killed in the war. Short in stature, Castelnau had a charm of personality in addition to quick wit and exceptional ability. His tenaciously held religious beliefs – his 1918 Groupe des Armées de l'Est was often referred to as the Groupe des Amis de l'Eglise – appear to have been the reason why he was never made a Marshal. He died in 1944.

Emile Fayolle. Fayolle was born at Puy in 1852 and after studies at the Ecole Polytechnique and the artillery school he became an artillery officer. He served initially in artillery regiments in France and in the 1881 Tunisian campaign. On his return to France he served in a succession of artillery regimental and staff appointments and attended the Ecole de Guerre. He became assistant professor and later professor of artillery tactics at the Ecole, after which he was promoted successively lieutenant-colonel, colonel and brigadier-general in 1902, 1907 and 1910 respectively. He was placed on the reserve list in 1913 but selected for a brigade command in the event of mobilisation. Throughout his career he was noted and well reported upon for his abilities, but his strong Catholic faith and views appear to have affected his pre-1914 career. His wartime career was furthered by Pétain who valued his artillery expertise, but after the end of the war and his command of the French occupation forces in Germany, he was still in the substantive rank of brigadier-general. A vehement campaign in the press corrected this manifest injustice and in 1921 Fayolle was created a Marshal. He died in 1928.

Ferdinand Foch. Foch was born at Tarbes in the Pyrenees in 1851 into a family of Napoleonic military tradition, although his father was a minor civil servant. The family were very devout Catholics, as was Foch himself to be throughout his life – the main source of his energy and self-confidence. He enlisted in the infantry in 1870 but saw no fighting. His academic ability made him a Polytechnician and thereafter an artilleryman. He served in regiments in France until 1885 when he entered the Ecole de Guerre, after which followed a staff appointment. In 1890 he was selected to join the elite Third Bureau of the General Staff where he served for two years, with a further year in 1894. He then in 1895 became an instructor at the Ecole de Guerre, promoted there in 1896 to the professorship of military history, strategy and tactics. His teaching centred on the moral power of commanders, to some neglect of equipment. While he advocated an offensive strategy he was also concerned with the importance of intelligence and secure movement in attack – issues he dealt with in his two books, *Principes de la Guerre*, a monograph on a Prussian advance guard operation in 1866, and *La Conduite de la Guerre*, a study of operations in 1870. Foch's career then suffered a check on account of his and his family's religious convictions. Posted to an artillery regiment in 1901 he was denied promotion until in 1903 he became a colonel and commander of an artillery regiment. In 1907 he became a brigadier-general but very shortly afterwards, in 1908, he was appointed commandant of the Ecole de Guerre, having with difficulty managed to convince Clemenceau, then Prime Minister, that he was loyal to the Republic. At the Ecole Foch instilled his views in the other instructors, added a new preface to *La Conduite* including his own observations on the Russo-Japanese war, and developed a friendship of enormous importance for the future with his British opposite number, Henry Wilson. He also brought to fruition a project, already under consideration, of a Centre des Hautes Etudes Militaires, in its first form an extension of the Ecole course for a further year but later changed to be a course for more experienced officers, the most promising among lieutenant-colonels. However, Foch's thinking still failed to appreciate the power of machine-guns and barbed wire in defence or the possibilities of new technology such as aircraft for reconnaissance, despite their effective use by Lyautey in Morocco. In 1911 Foch was given successively command of a division and then an army corps, the latter at Bourges. In 1913 he was transferred from Bourges to command of the XX Corps at Nancy, an elite corps in a key strategic area. Foch believed France should have secured a Rhine frontier in 1919, and remained sceptical over German adherence to the Versailles Treaty and the efficacy of the League of Nations. He died in 1929.

Louis Felix Marie Francois Franchet d'Esperey was born at Mostaganem in Algeria in 1856. After a notable career at St Cyr Franchet d'Esperey served with the Tirailleurs Algériens in Algeria and Tunisia from 1876 to 1881, when he entered the Ecole de Guerre. After a brief staff appointment in Algiers, Franchet d'Esperey served in the Indochina fighting against the Black Flag nationalists from 1885 to 1887. There followed staff and infantry regimental appointments in France until 1899 when he was chosen to be Deputy Commandant and Director of Studies at St Cyr. Within a few months, however, he was in action again, this time in northern China as a staff officer of the forces fighting the Boxer uprising. On his return he was given successively regimental (1903) brigade (1908) and division (1912) commands, all in France but later in 1912 he was appointed commander of French forces in Western Morocco. There he led a number of successful operations in the Oued Zem, Mogador and Tadla areas. On his return he was selected to command the I Corps of General Lanrezac's 5th Army. Franchet d'Esperey's indefatigable energy and offensive spirit led to his nickname in the British Army 'Desperate Frankie'. He was made a Marshal in 1921 and died in 1942.

Joseph Simon Galliéni was born in 1849 in Saint-Béat, a town in the central Pyrenees. His family were originally Italian but his father had risen from the ranks to be a captain in the French army before retiring. Destined for the army, Galliéni went to a pre-military school and then on to St Cyr. As a subaltern he was taken prisoner at Bazeilles, the scene of the epic stand of the Infanterie de Marine, in 1870. After his release he served as a junior officer in Réunion and West Africa. He first displayed his outstanding abilities in colonial penetration and occupation without open warfare in West Africa in 1880 and then again in 1886–8. From 1892 to 1896 as a colonel he played a leading role in the pacification of Tonkin. In 1896 he was posted as a general, to Madagascar where a French army largely composed of ill-prepared metropolitan soldiers had just suffered a disastrous reverse, 4,613 soldiers dying of disease. With one brief interruption Galliéni was to remain in Madagascar until 1905, initially conducting a series of successful military operations firmly suppressing primary resistance in the different regions of the island and then creating a new colonial administration. In this government the military, almost entirely Coloniale officers, played a rewarding social and developmental role providing roads, a railway, markets, some medical services and in some towns a school. This policy Galliéni called *tache d'huile*, (the 'oil stain'), the spreading of pacification by benevolent colonial paternalism; it was to prove very successful. In 1906 Galliéni became Military Governor of Lyon and commandant of the Army of the Alps. From the same year he also became a member of the Conseil Supérieur de la Guerre until his formal retirement in April 1914. In this period he expressed reservations over the limited offensive strategy, advising instead fortification of the northern frontier, the development of artillery and, interestingly, aviation for reconnaissance, together with the study of intelligence reports, comments seen as out of place coming from a colonial soldier. A dry, precise man, Galliéni tried to avoid politics, his personal beliefs being secular and republican and these were reflected in his colonial policy. He died in 1916 and was made a Marshal posthumously in 1921. Galliéni will always be regarded as France's most distinguished colonial soldier in addition to being the defender of Paris in 1914.

Joseph Césaire Joffre. Joffre was born at Riversaltes in the Pyrenees in 1852. His father was a cooper. Through his own abilities Joffre became a Polytechnician; during the siege of Paris he commanded a battery. Opting to become an engineer officer, most of his early service was abroad, first in Indochina, then in 1894 in West Africa leading a column entering Timbuktu, and then under Galliéni in Madagascar. In these operations he gained a reputation as an efficient organiser. After his return from Africa Joffre was given command of an artillery *groupe*, he was then made director of engineers in the War Ministry. In 1907 he was appointed to the command of an infantry division, in 1908 to the command of an army corps; he was thought to have shown especial ability in the 1908 army exercises. In 1911 at the time of the Agadir crisis he was appointed Chief of the General Staff with its linked designate Commander-in-Chief in the event of war. He was also made a member of the Conseil Supérieur de la Guerre. From 1912 he was also Vice President of the Conseil, giving him still further powers. His advance was rapid, especially since he had not attended the Ecole de Guerre and his experiences as an infantry formation commander were brief. He received backing from well-placed radical political figures such as Doumergue and Sarraut as he was seen as politically 'safe', unconnected with the Church or any particular military faction. His plebeian rural background and his engineering training both combined to give him a slow, down-to-earth approach to problems and to the judgement of characters. Joffre died in 1931.

Louis Hubert Lyautey was born in 1854 at Nancy; his father was an engineer but the family had a strong monarchist, Catholic and military tradition. Lyautey's early years were much affected by the results of spinal injury. After schooling in Nancy and cadetship at St Cyr he served in the cavalry in Algeria and in France, his personal beliefs changing from monarchist to a concept of social duty, a form of paternal conservatism expressed in an important journal article, 'On the Social Functions of the Officer under Universal Military Service'. In 1894 he arrived in Indochina in a senior staff posting; there this traditional Catholic aristocrat met and served under the secular republican Galliéni. Despite their different backgrounds and beliefs they shared a common view on the role of the military in colonies, military pacification had to be followed by development – roads, railways, telegraphs, crops and markets. With Galliéni he put these ideas into practice in Indochina and later Madagascar. Returning to France in 1902 he was given command of a cavalry regiment but in the following year was despatched to South-western Algeria and promoted to brigadier-general. In addition to his local frontier command duties Lyautey was also involved with his country's wider ambition, the acquisition of Morocco; he extended his pacification into eastern Morocco.

Returning to France in 1910, Lyautey was given command of an army corps but in 1912 he was appointed Resident-General in Morocco, to complete the pacification campaigns and establish the French Protectorate. The military operations were extensive and complex, far from complete by August 1914. Wherever possible Lyautey preferred to display rather than use force, but when he did resort to force his action was thorough and firm. More important for Morocco's future, the post of Resident-General provided Lyautey with the opportunity to put into practice, on a viceregal scale, his views on military involvement in post-pacification development. Zones of pacification (the Galliéni 'oil stain' policy) received military aid in administration, in road building and the opening of markets. Commanders were told not to treat the Moroccans as a conquered people but to respect traditional authorities, customs and the Moslem religion. In the history of French imperial rule Lyautey was the greatest French proconsul and administrator and in 1921 he was made a Marshal. Except for the brief 1916–17 period as Minister for War, Lyautey remained in Morocco until 1925 when he resigned. His almost royal gubernatorial style and criticism of his handling of the Rif rebellion had aroused opposition, much of it political malice, in Paris. The malice extended to his return home for which no official reception was arranged; the only mark of respect being that provided by two destroyers of the Royal Navy. Lyautey died in 1934.

Charles Mangin was born in 1866, the son of a conservator of rivers and forests in Lorraine. Following the defeat of 1870 his father received an equivalent appointment in Algeria. The expulsion from Lorraine and an African boyhood were formative influences on Mangin. After St Cyr he joined the Infanterie de Marine (Coloniale after 1900), serving in a series of West African campaigns including Marchand's expedition to Fashoda. In the course of these operations Mangin was wounded three times. In 1901 he was posted to a battalion command in Indochina, to last until 1904 and to be followed by further regimental service in France. During this time his reputation, which had at the outset been notorious, steadily grew and in 1907 he became Chief-of-Staff of French forces in West Africa, taking the field as commander of a pacification operation in Oubangui-Chari. Later, while at Dakar, Mangin published his *La Force Noire* in which he advocated the expansion of the existing Tirailleurs Sénégalais into a massive reserve of Black manpower eventually to total 70,000, a project not immediately well received. The developing operations in Morocco, however, were to give Mangin his chance. Arriving in 1912 in command of a brigade of Tirailleurs he proved himself as an outstanding field commander. Tirailleurs expansion became accepted despite opposition from the Treasury, colonial administrations and the political left. Returning to France in 1914, Mangin was given command of an infantry brigade which he led well, resulting in his appointment to command of the 5th Infantry Division, an appointment to take him to Verdun in 1916.

Of a headstrong and ruthless temperament, Mangin remained a controversial figure throughout his career. He died in 1925.

Michel-Joseph Maunoury, born in 1847, was a Polytechnician artilleryman. His pre-war career had included the Ecole de Guerre and a period as an instructor at St Cyr before becoming a full colonel. He commanded an artillery brigade and then from 1905 became successively commander of the III and later the XX Army Corps. He was a member of the Conseil Supérieur de la Guerre and finally Military Governor of Paris, being earmarked for command of an army in the event of war. He was a keen advocate of the offensive. In 1912, reaching the age-limit, he was retired but was recalled by Joffre in 1914. He was badly wounded in the eyes in 1915. Maunoury died in 1923, being created a Marshal posthumously.

Robert Nivelle was born at Tulle in 1856, his father's family was part Italian, his mother was English, the daughter of one of Wellington's officers. The family tradition was military and Nivelle entered the army as a Polytechnician, becoming an artilleryman. His career development was assisted by the fact that he was a Protestant and known to be anti-Catholic, and also that he was an excellent horseman; he in fact passed through the cavalry school at Saumur. At the outbreak of war Nivelle was commanding an artillery regiment. At the battle of the Marne Nivelle led his regiment through a French infantry formation on the verge of collapse to open fire on the Germans over open sights at point-blank range. The Germans were routed and Nivelle received the command of a brigade in October 1914. Divisional command followed early in 1915, with corps command at the end of the year. After the failure of the Aisne offensive Nivelle was exonerated from any serious misconduct and given sinecure military appointments. Although he was a disastrous army commander his personal bravery was undoubted. He died in 1924.

Henri Philippe Benomi Pétain was born in 1856 into a peasant family in a small village in the Pas de Calais. He was educated by Jesuits and later by Dominicans before entering St Cyr in 1876. He served first in the *chasseurs alpins*, to which he returned after graduating at the Ecole de Guerre and being appointed a staff officer. From 1893 to 1899 he served on the staff of the military governor of Paris before returning as a major to the Chasseurs. After a brief spell as an instructor at the musketry school at Châlons where he fell out with the commandant, he served with an infantry regiment for two years, then returning to the Ecole de Guerre as a tactics instructor. There, again, his views were unorthodox, being critical of the offensive doctrine, realising its dangers in face of the firepower of artillery and machine-guns. As a result he was returned to infantry soldiering, by 1911 a full colonel commanding a regiment. In 1912 he was sent with General Durand on a confidential mission to Belgium to study the defence implications for France of a violation of Belgian neutrality, a study that can only have confirmed his reservations over the limited offensive strategy. In 1914, prior to the outbreak of war, he was given command of a brigade. Pétain's career to this point had not been distinguished, he had not achieved fame in any colonial campaign, he had expressed unfashionable military beliefs and in normal circumstances he would have very shortly been retired. His very successful exercise of his command in the retreat from Belgium and at Arras immediately brought him to the attention of Joffre and the start of his rapid wartime career. Features of his character that were later to become prominent were, however, already in evidence by 1914, a natural pessimism with defensive rather than offensive thinking, a narrow-minded dislike of politicians, a simplistic tendency to authoritarianism, and a distrust of the British. The experience of Verdun was to sharpen all of these and, further, in the inter-war years when his influence remained considerable, to play an important role in the ossification of French military policy, with all its subsequent catastrophic results. On 14 July 1919 Pétain mounted on a splendid white horse was cheered to the echo by the Paris victory parade crowds, his great moment of glory. His tragedy was that such glory was later to be so tarnished.

Maxime Weygand. The early life and background of Weygand is obscure and extraordinary. He was probably born in Brussels, but the birth certificate was later deliberately removed and the infant taken to France by foster parents. The probability is that he was the son of a member of a European royal house and a Mexican Aztec, he himself was never told. The first name he was given was not Weygand; at St Cyr he was Maxime de Nimal, a Belgian. To enter the French army he was adopted by an elderly widower, thereby gaining the name Weygand and French nationality. He entered the cavalry serving in different regiments and instructing at the Saumur cavalry school. He chose not to serve in the colonies as he wished to identify more closely with France, and not to enter the Ecole de Guerre which he thought too abstruse and academic.

In 1912, however, he was selected for entry to the new Centre des Hautes Etudes Militaires. The outbreak of war found Weygand commanding a cavalry regiment until, unexpectedly, he was ordered to report to Foch. The partnership of Foch and Weygand was to last the entire war, a common identity of personalities and minds. Often when some problem or issue was presented to Foch, he would simply say, 'Ask Weygand, it is the same thing.'

Criticism and controversy justifiably surround Weygand's decisions in June 1940. It should, however, always be remembered that two post-1945 enquiries into his actions both found that he had never collaborated with the Axis, and second that in 1940–1 he was to perform his greatest service to France, the preservation and covert expansion of the Armée d'Afrique. This expansion provided the backbone of General Juin's French Corps in the 1943–4 Italian campaign and General de Lattre de Tassigny's 1st Army that landed in the south of France in August 1944. Some evidence suggests that Weygand's personal uncertainty over his identity and even nationality affected his judgement in 1940; there is no evidence of any such confusion in the 1914–18 war.

The Headquarters Staff

At the Grand Quartier Général staff work was organised to provide for the Personal Staffs of the Army Commander and Chief-of-Staff with thereafter three bureaux each headed by a general. The First Bureau was concerned with men and munitions, the Second with intelligence and relations with Allies, conducted usually through their respective missions, and the elite Third Bureau with Operations. A Direction de l'Arrière was responsible for lines of communication. Over four hundred officers were at work at GQG, where day-to-day administration of the headquarters was the responsibility of a major general as a director of staff duties. In 1916 a Theâtre des

Opérations Extérieures was established to deal with theatres of the war other than the Western Front, including its own First, Second and Third Bureaux; it was, however, transferred to the War Office in 1917. Interestingly, as an early example of recognition by the military of the importance of the press, GQG's staff included an Information Section, attached to the Third Bureau. It was initially tasked with the production of the daily communiqué but its duties soon extended to relations with the press and the preparation of articles. The Information Section, however, was not popular in political circles, being seen as providing the military with a voice which it might use to secure more and more power.

The quality of staff work varied. There was frequent friction between strong personalities and the different bureaux, especially between the Second and Third. Factions, known as *chapelles*, furthered controversies. As a result of a very rigid training staff officers were often inflexible, lacking in imagination, slow to adapt to the possibilities of new weapons and equipments. Security was often poor. A number of officers were concerned with their career development and a few with a preference for *la vie du château* rather than the trenches. In theory all GQG officers were meant to serve for periods with front-line units. In practice a number were exempted for one reason or another, in many cases previous experience and wounds. Amid the changing fortunes of the war waves of ill-humour, against the British or the Americans, would sometimes sweep over headquarters.

Staff work was perhaps at its best with movement. The logistics for a mass mobilisation army were daunting. In 1914, for example, to maintain 500,000 men at the front, twenty-three train loads per day were necessary, ten for foodstuffs, five for artillery ammunition, two for engineer stores and equipment, one for other stores, two for stones for road maintenance and three for troop reinforcements. As ammunition became more available and used more lavishly, additional ammunition trains were needed. The movement of an army corps from one section of the front to another could involve over one hundred trains of different types. Road transport, as it developed during the war, came also to require the most precise co-ordination. Columns of vehicles and guns could be as long as 90 kilometres, crossings of columns had to be foreseen, and necessary halts provided for. Convoys were routed by colour codes, each convoy being given a colour and boards of that colour set out along the route.

In sum, the largely mathematical training of French officers was proved to be justified for the handling of vast quantities of material and men required for the fighting. But as noted in earlier chapters, while intelligence staff work developed in efficiency, on too many occasions intelligence officers were unable to convince operations staffs, with costly results.

A French Infantry Regiment
1914–20

The war record of a representative French infantry regiment is interesting as an illustration of the services of, and changes in, regimental life during the war. The three battalions of the 8th Regiment of Infantry, drawn from Boulogne, Calais and Saint-Omer, were mobilised and entrained for the front on 5 August 1914. The regiment was part of the 2nd Infantry Division in General Franchet d'Esperey's I Corps, itself in General Lanrezac's 5th Army. The regiment went into action first on 15 August at Dinant and then participated in the retreat to the Marne. After the Marne battle the regiment was moved to the Champagne sector where, by March 1915 its casualties, killed, missing or wounded, since the outbreak of the war amounted to 3,319, including four colonels, more than the strength at mobilisation.

The regiment was then re-formed, command passing to Colonel Jacques Roubert, a St-Cyrien whose earlier service had been in the Infanterie de Marine under Galliéni in Madagascar. Roubert remained in command until June 1917. In April 1915 the regiment was involved in the heavy fighting around Europe, February 1916 found the regiment at Verdun and September 1916 on the Somme. From April 1915 to December 1916 a further 3,376 members of the regiment had been lost, by April 1917 the total, augmented by a severe winter in Champagne, had reached 8,035 since the outbreak of war; of these 3,010 were killed or missing.

It was, therefore, already a war-weary regiment that was to be committed to Nivelle's April 1917 offensive, where largely on account of insufficient local artillery support the regiment suffered a further 982 casualties in four days, this total including twenty-three officers, and 272 dead or missing. The regiment, withdrawn from the front line after the fighting, was badly affected by the wave of mutinies, two members being sentenced to death, a sentence apparently not carried out.

Discipline was restored during an eleven-week period at Mailly and at a rest camp at Provins. Roubert left on promotion, his successor Gaston Duffour was staff-trained and set in hand the modernised combat training of Pétain's directives. The regiment was brought up to strength with men from the Classe 17 and a number of young officers; its firepower was increased by the machine-gun company for each battalion, the deliveries of the Chauchat light machine-gun, and small teams of grenadiers from each battalion.

So renewed, the 8th and its reserve unit, the 208th, both part of the 2nd Infantry Division, were despatched to Flanders to participate in the great British July 1917 offensive. The regiment joined in the fighting on 16 August and remained committed until mid-October, an experience in which food was limited to *singe*, morale was raised by *gniole* and regimental life became that of two men in shell craters. After Flanders there followed action in Pétain's limited offensives of Verdun and Malmaison. Casualties were very much lighter than in the earlier battles, and the regiment benefited from the ordered system of rest periods. At the end of October Duffour was replaced by Lieutenant-Colonel Gégonne who commanded the regiment for the rest of the war. At first Gégonne could enjoy the relative calm of the 1917–18 winter period. In the successive 1918 battles, however, two of the regiment's three battalions were involved in the heavy early June fighting around Villers-Cotterêts and, in the next month, the 2nd Division having been transferred to the 6th Army, with further fierce fighting, at times hand-to-hand, in defence of Reims. During the last German major offensive of mid-July the 8th were involved in the heavy fighting along the Ourcq, after which followed a rest period to last until the end of August. The 8th was then included in one of General Mangin's attacks near Pont Saint-Mard. The regiment's immediate adversaries were the Prussian Guards, though these at the time were weakened by fatigue and food shortages.

In mid-September the 8th was transported by rail to Alsace, in the hills west of Mulhouse, where fighting was limited to patrolling and the taking of prisoners. In late October the regiment was moved to the Nancy area to participate in Foch's proposed Lorraine offensive, in the event not to take place.

After the armistice, the 8th, band and regimental colour at its head, paraded through the villages of Lorraine enjoying the welcome of the inhabitants, especially girls in local traditional dress. The 8th then lodged briefly at Sarrelouis before making a triumphal entry into Mainz, from there moving on for a ceremony at Wiesbaden and preparation there for the arrival of Pétain.

The reserve 208th Regiment was disbanded in February 1919 and the first elements of the 8th Regiment returned, with due ceremony, to Calais in March. There, although most of the soldiers now no longer came from the Pas-de-Calais, six months' work in clearing the war-damaged areas of stores, munitions, debris, ruins and corpses human and animal, awaited them before release.

From 1916 the French army awarded collective decorations to its regiments (and occasionally also to British regiments). These included citations in regimental, brigade, division, army corps and army orders and after specified numbers of citations the award of *fourragères*, embellishment cords with medals attached to a regiment's colour and a loop of coloured braid to soldiers' uniforms. These were in ascending order of merit, the green and red cord of the Croix de Guerre, the yellow and red cord of the Médaille Militaire and the red cord of the Legion of Honour. In 1918 double *fourragères* were authorised.

By the end of 1916 the 8th had been twice cited for merit and carried the *fourragère* of the Croix de Guerre on its colour. By the end of 1917 the regiment had been awarded further citations and the yellow *fourragère* of the Médaille Militaire. Three further citations followed in 1917 and 1918, and on 20 September 1920 President Poincaré conferred the Legion of Honour on the regiment with the following citation: 'A magnificent regiment whose soldiers converted into heroism their anguish at knowing their families were enslaved and their homes destroyed. Participating in all the major actions of the war, on no occasion did the regiment withdraw in face of an enemy attack (Verdun 1916–Aisne 1918), and on no occasion were the enemy able to resist the impetus of their attacks (Somme 1916–Flanders and Aisne 1917).'

Bibliographical Essay

Any student of the history of the French army in the First World War, unless he is going to make it the work of his entire lifespan, must necessarily make some selection of the documents and published works available, and some drawing on the quotations and references included in works within that selection for particular detail. This essay presents a selection which, it is hoped, is both useful and sufficiently comprehensive.

First, more for recourse for detail than to read as a whole work, must be the French General Staff's *Les Armées Françaises dans la Grande Guerre* (Paris, 1922–1939), in 102 volumes, and the massive holding of cartons at the Service Historique de l'Armée de Terre at Vincennes.

Several general histories of the war contain valuable information on the French army, and a number of these offer rewarding material on the 1914–18 period. In this latter category William Serman's and Jean-Paul Bertaud's *Nouvelle Histoire Militaire de la France 1789–1919*, (Paris, 1998) is preeminent, both as a guide to the complex series of events and in its provision of much detail relating to personnel and equipments. Also especially useful are the two volumes of General Jean Valluy, *La Premier Guerre Mondiale* (Paris, 1963), Pierre Miquel, *La Grande Guerre* (Paris, 1983) and the older Henry

Bidou, *Histoire de la Grande Guerre* (Paris, 1939).

Although generally dated in their approach, there is much interesting detail in Colonel J. Revol's *Histoire de l'Armée Française* (Paris, 1929) the sixteen volumes of Gabriel Hanotaux, *Histoire Illustrée de la Guerre de 1914* (Paris, 1915–23), and the work of Section Photographique of the Ministère de la Guerre, *La Guerre* (Paris, 1916), two volumes. A detailed study of the impact of military service and the war on soldiers from Languedoc, but which also contains more general context material of great value, is the work of Jules Maurin, *Armée, Guerre, Societé, Soldat, Languedociens* (Paris, 1982). The total effect of the war on France is superbly set out in Stéphane Audouin Rouzeau and Annette Becker, *14–18 Retrouver la Guerre* (Paris, 2000) and in Frédéric Rousseau, *La Guerre Censurée, une histoire des combattants européens de 14–18*, (Paris, 1989).

English-language texts of course include Correlli Barnett, *The Swordbearers* (London, 1963), Niall Ferguson, *The Pity of War* (London, 1998), John Keegan, *The First World War* (London, 1998) and B. H. Liddell Hart, *History of the First World War* (London, 1970). Also very valuable is a chapter, 'French Strategy on the Western Front' by David Stevenson in Roger Chickering and Stig Forster (eds) *Great War, Total War* (Cambridge, 2000). Jean de Pierrefeu (translated by Major C. J. Street), *French Headquarters 1915–1918* (London, n.d.) provides a fascinating perspective on the work and personalities at the Grand Quartier Général throughout most of the war.

A very valuable study of French society in the war appears in Jean-Jacques Becker (translated by Arnold Pomerays), *The Great War and the French People* (Oxford, 1985). Two other general studies throwing light on morale and therefore instructive are Stéphane Audouin Rouzeau (translated by Helen McPhais), *Men at War 1914–1918 National Sentiment and Trench Journalism in France during the First World War*

(Oxford, 1992) and Leonard V. Smith, *Between Mutiny and Obedience, The case of the French Fifth Infantry Division during World War I* (Princeton, 1994).

Works that include material on the years 1871 to 1914, the first eighteen months of the war and other periods and topics, are covered in sections of this essay that follow. For the period 1871 to December 1915 specifically the important French texts include Charles-Armand Klein, *Galliéni Portraits Varois* (Barbentane, 2001), Marc Michel, *Gallieni* (Paris, 1989), Commandant Muller, *Joffre et la Marne* (Paris, 1931) and Jean Ratinaud, *La Course à la Mer, de la Somme aux Flandres* (Paris, 1967). An article, '*Du Recruitment régional au Recruitment national pendant la Grande Guerre*', by Philippe Boulanger in the *Revue Historique des Armées*, 3, (1988) sets out the important changes in the drafting system made in 1915.

In English, Hew Strachan's *The First World War Volume 1. To Arms*, (Oxford 2001) is in a class of its own in the provision of detail and analysis of events prior to the outbreak of war and during the early months of the conflict.

The state of the French army at the outbreak of war can be assessed by three works, the British army's General Staff, *Handbook of the French Army 1914* (reprinted London, 1995), Douglas Porch, *The March to the Marne, the French Army 1871–1914* (Cambridge, 1981) and the slim but useful Ian Sumner and Gerry Embleton, *The French Army 1914–18* (London, 1995). For the first months of the war, of especial help are Robert E. Asprey, *The First Battle of the Marne* (London, 1962), Joseph Joffrey (translated by Colonel T. Bentley Mott), *The Memoirs of Marshal Joffre* (London, 1932), John Keegan, *Opening Moves, August 1914* (London, 1973), B. H. Liddell Hart, *Foch, The Man of Orleans* (London, 1931) and Barbara Tuchman, *The Guns of August* (New York, 1962). Three personal accounts of front-line soldiering in 1914 and

1915 appear in Henri Desagneaux, (translated by Godfrey J. Adams), *A French Soldier's War Diary 1914-1918* (Morley, 1975) and Roy E. Sandstrom (ed), *Comrades in Arms, The World War I Memoir of Captain Henri de Lecluse, Comte de Trevoedal* (Kent, Ohio, 1998), and in French and of especial value, Etienne Tanty, *Les Violettes des Tranchées, Lettres d'un Poilu qui n'aimait pas la Guerre* (Paris, 2002).

For the year of Verdun and the Somme, Guy Pedroncini, *Pétain le soldat et la gloire* (Paris, 1989) is essential; also useful is Louis-Eugène Mangin's *Le Général Mangin* (privately published, 1993).

In English, in a class of its own is Alistair Horne, *The Price of Glory* (London, 1963). Also of very great value are Georges Blond (translated by Frances Frenaye), *Verdun* (London, 1965), A. H. Farrar-Hockley, *The Somme* (London, 1954) and Henri Philippe Pétain (translated by Margaret MacVeagh), *Verdun* (London, 1930).

A concise but well-researched English-language biography of Pétain is that of Nicholas Atkin, *Pétain* (London, 1992); also useful is Richard Griffith, *Marshal Pétain* (London, 1970).

For the troubled year 1917, four French works are indispensable, Pedroncini's *Pétain*, also his *Les Mutineries de 1917* (Paris, 1967), Mangins *Le Général Mangin*, and for any study of morale, Jean Nicot, *Les Poilus Ont La Parole, Lettres du Front: 1917–1918* (Vincennes, 1998). A very useful guide to the Aisne Chemin des Dames battlefields, not only for 1917 but also for previous and subsequent battles, is set out with several clear maps in a Michelin battlefield guide, *Le Chemin des Dames* (Clermont-Ferrand, 1920).

My chapter, 'Robert Nivelle and the French Spring Offensive 1917', in Brian Bond (ed), *Fallen Stars* (London, 1991) considers the disastrous Aisne offensive.

Gregor Dallas, *At the Heart of a Tiger, Clemenceau and his World 1841–1929* (London, 1993) offers a biography of this key figure who appeared at the end of the year.

For the final year of the war, the biographies noted earlier of Foch, Pétain and Clemenceau are essential; also useful are the chapters on Foch and Clemenceau in Winston Churchill, *Great Contemporaries* (London, 1941). For morale study Nicot's *Les Poilus ont la Parole* is indispensable. Some interesting detail appears in Bernard Destrumeau, *Weygand* (Paris, 1989). English texts include C. N. Barclay, *Armistice 1918* (London, 1968), the slim but very useful Randal Gray, *Kaiserschlacht 1918, The Final German Offensive* (London, 1991) and Barrie Pitt, *1918, The Last Act* (London, 1962). Lyn Macdonald, *To The Last Man, Spring 1918* (London, 1988) provides a graphic account of the defence of Grivesnes.

Certain special subjects are best noted separately. Mortars and other trench artillery are set out in two articles by Jean-Pierre Verney, '*Artillerie de tranche, le crapouillot*' and '*Du 58 au mortier Fabry*' in *14–18 le magazine de la Grande Guerre* issues 1 (April–May 2001) and 2 (June–July 2001) respectively. Another fascinating study of trench warfare weapons, mostly British but with a number of French devices well illustrated, appears in Anthony Saunders, *Weapons of the Trench War 1914–1918* (Stroud, 1999).

The subject of intelligence is well covered in Douglas Porch, *The French Secret Services* (Oxford, 1997). The air war and details of aircraft are set out briefly in Alan Clark, *Aces High* (London, 1973); in greater detail Aaron Norman, *The Great Air War* (New York, 1968); in two works edited by E. F. Cheesman, *Fighter Aircraft of the 1914–1918 War* and *Reconnaissance and Bomber Aircraft of the 1914–18 War*, published at Letchworth in 1960 and 1962 respectively; Walter Raleigh, *The War in the Air, I* (Oxford, 1922); Douglas H. Robinson, *The Zeppelin in Combat, A History of the German Naval Airship Division, 1912–1918* (London, 1962) and the issues of *Jane's All The World's Aircraft* of 1918 and 1919. The formation and actions of the Air Division are described by Patrick Facon in an article *'La Division aerienne on l'emploi en masse de l'aviation en 1918'* in *14–18 le magazine de la Grande Guerre*, 3 (August–September 2000).

Gas warfare is the subject of a general survey by Olivier Lepick, *'Une guerre dans la Guerre, les armes chimiques 1914–1918'* in the *Revue Historique* 2 (1996). French 1914–18 tank development is well described in Christopher Chant, *World Encyclopaedia of the Tank* (London, 1994). In respect of artillery a useful survey appears in Général Gascouin, *L'Evolution de l'Artillerie pendant la Guerre* (Paris, 1920). In English texts artillery is briefly summarised in the relevant sections of Joseph Jobe, *Guns, An Illustrated History of Artillery* (London, 1971), John Batchelor and Ian Hogg, *Artillery* (London, 1972) and Curt Johnson, *Artillery* (London 1975).

An article, *'Pourquoi les "crapouillots" de l'artillerie de tranchée de 1914–1918 ne soient pas oubliés'*, by Pierre Waline in the *Revue Historique*, 3 (1977), is also interesting.

Readers should bear in mind that the term (and specific concept of) medium artillery was not in use in the 1914–18 war when anything larger than a field gun was seen as heavy artillery. Also when French texts refer, for example, to the 155mm *court* (short) gun, in present-day terminology this would be described as a howitzer.

The organisation, recruitment and uses made of French colonial soldiers in the *Armée d'Afrique* and *La Coloniale* are covered generally in General R. Huré and others (eds), *L'Armée d'Afrique 1830–1962* (Paris, 1977) and *Les Troupes de Marine 1622–1984* (Paris, 1986). An excellent special study of Black African troops appears in Marc Michel, *L'Appel à l'Afrique* (Paris, 1982). English-speaking readers may find that the relevant chapters in my *France, Soldiers and Africa* (London, 1988) covers the field.

In respect of the Dardanelles campaign, two articles *'L'Expedition des Dardanelles'* and *'Les Dardanelles, opération amphibie'* by Philippe Masson appear in *14–18 le magazine de la Grande Guerre*, issues 1 and 2 respectively.

For Macedonia, Captain F. J. Deygas, *L'Armée d'Orient dans la Guerre Mondiale* (Paris, 1931) and an article, *'La Victoire de 1918 en Orient'*, by Pierre François in the *Revue Historique*, 2, (1969) are useful. The specific morale crisis is the subject of *'La Crise du Moral en 1917 à l'Armée Française d'Orient'* in the *Revue Historique*, 4, (1977), and disciplinary and control of civilians by the gendarmerie in Jean Michel Nowak, *'La Gendarmerie prévôtale à Salonique'* (1915–1917) in the *Revue Historique*, 1, (1999). For English-speaking readers Nigel Steel and Peter Hart, *Defeat at Gallipoli* (London, 1994), Charles Packer, *Return to Salonika* (London, 1964); G. Ward Price, *The Story of the Salonika Army* (London, 1918) and an article by David J. Dutton, *'The Balkan Campaign and French War Aims in the Great War'* in the *English Historical Review*, 370, (1979) are of especial value. An article *'Le 8e R. I de Saint-Omer'* by Romain Durand in *Carnet de la Sabretache*, (September 2000), provides a history of the 8th Infantry Regiment.

In considering the military dimension of causal connections between the events of 1914–18 and those of 1939–40 a reader can make no better start than with Alistair Horne, *To Lose a Battle* (London, 1962).

It should be noted that different texts give varying total figures for men killed, missing or wounded. These can, in any case, never have been assessed precisely. This work has selected those totals that appear the most reliable.

Index

Jutland 1916
Peter Hart
0 304 36648 X ☐
£7.99

Fatal Silence
Robert Katz
0 304 36681 1 ☐
£8.99

Weapons of Mass Destruction
Robert Hutchinson
0 304 36653 6 ☐
£7.99

Acts of War
Richard Holmes
0 304 36700 1 ☐
£8.99

Eisenhower
Carlo D'Este
0 304 36658 7 ☐
£9.99

Blood in the Sea
Stuart Gill
0 304 36691 9 ☐
£7.99

Enigma
Hugh Sebag-Montefiore
0 304 36662 5 ☐
£8.99

The War of the Running Dogs
Noel Barber
0 304 36671 4 ☐
£7.99

Fire from the Forest
Roger Ford
0 304 36336 7 ☐
£7.99

Swordfish
David Wragg
0 304 36682 X ☐
£7.99

A Storm in Flanders
Winston Groom
0 304 36656 0 ☐
£7.99

The Siege of Leningrad
David Glantz
0 304 36672 2 ☐
£8.99

Churchill's Folly
Anthony Rogers
0 304 36655 2 ☐
£7.99

Dare to be Free
W.B. 'Sandy' Thomas
0 304 36639 0 ☐
£7.99

Rising Sun and Tumbling Bear
Richard Connaughton
0 304 36657 9 ☐
£7.99

For Valour
Bryan Perrett
0 304 36698 6 ☐
£8.99

Mud, Blood and Poppycock
Gordon Corrigan
0 304 36659 5 ☐
£8.99

Operation Barras
William Fowler
0 304 36699 4 ☐
£7.99

Pursuit
Ludovic Kennedy
0 304 35526 7 ☐
£7.99

The Last Valley
Martin Windrow
0 304 36692 7 ☐
£9.99

All Orion/Phoenix titles are available at your local bookshop or from the following address:

> Mail Order Department
> Littlehampton Book Services
> FREEPOST BR535
> Worthing, West Sussex, BNI3 3BR
> *telephone* 01903 828503, *facsimile* 01903 828802
> *e-mail* MailOrders@lbsltd.co.uk
> (Please ensure that you include full postal address details)

Payment can be made either by credit/debit card (Visa, Mastercard, Access and Switch accepted) or by sending a £ Sterling cheque or postal order made payable to *Littlehampton Book Services*.
DO NOT SEND CASH OR CURRENCY.

Please add the following to cover postage and packing

UK and BFPO:
£1.50 for the first book, and 50p for each additional book to a maximum of £3.50

Overseas and Eire:
£2.50 for the first book plus £1.00 for the second book and 50p for each additional book ordered

BLOCK CAPITALS PLEASE

name of cardholder ....

address of cardholder ....

delivery address
(if different from cardholder)

....

....

....

postcode ....

....

....

....

postcode ....

[ ] I enclose my remittance for £..

[ ] please debit my Mastercard/Visa/Access/Switch (delete as appropriate)

card number [ ][ ][ ][ ][ ][ ][ ][ ][ ][ ][ ][ ][ ][ ][ ][ ]

expiry date [ ][ ][ ][ ]   Switch issue no. [ ][ ]

signature ....

prices and availability are subject to change without notice